ISLANDS

ISLANDS

A
NEW ZEALAND
JOURNEY

BRUCE ANSLEY AND **JANE USSHER**

GODWIT

Contents

Introduction

Love of islands lies deep inside us, sustained by romance, myth, even geography, although rarely by experience. Most of us know the North Island, and the South Island. Some have been to Stewart Island/ Rakiura. That's where familiarity ends and imagination takes over.

We dream of escape, difference, freedom, a reordering of things thought important such as houses and cars, simplicity, self-reliance, purity of purpose and of life. We have common heroes, Robinson Crusoe, the Swiss Family Robinson, Ralph and Piggy in *Lord of the Flies*, King Kong on Skull Island. We take holidays on Castaway, Thursday, Aitutaki, Bora Bora.

Refuge, sanctuary, mystical properties attach to small bodies of land surrounded by water, and there's always a boat or a plane home.

How does reality fit? Perfectly, sometimes. Awkwardly, inconveniently, perhaps. People who love islands, love islands. People who love dreams . . . well, sometimes they work out, sometimes they don't.

New Zealand has many hundreds of islands. We faced the problem of narrowing them down for this book. We chose near-shore islands, plus some in harbours, lakes, rivers. That reduced the number to around 600. So we decided that every island should have a human touch: people had to live there, or have left their mark. We had to see where they'd been.

The islands we selected then ranged from the wild Great Barrier to an islet, hardly more than a rock, in Port Levy on Banks Peninsula once inhabited by three generations of a single family.

We immediately encountered the basic problem of islands, or their essential appeal, depending on your thinking: they were difficult to get to. For some the problem wasn't much: a ferry queue for Waiheke, the most accessible island of all. For others, well.

The most common trouble lay in the definition of an island: they are surrounded by sea. We learned to pray for good weather. The power of prayer being what it is, we often bounced, banged, rocked and thrashed our way over turbulent seas in craft ranging from a tiny aluminium dinghy to a huge old workboat.

Just getting to the islands made us skilled negotiators.

It took six months of parleying to get onto Hauturu/Little Barrier Island. The place was a conservation and cultural vault locked so tightly Atlantis would have been easier. The Titi Islands in the far south were a tale of their own.

The Roaring Forties knocked our boat around but were a mere breeze

Previous Bay of Islands, from the Marsden Cross lookout

compared with the islands themselves. They were only inhabited, by mutton-birders, for two months a year, and you had to be born into their exclusive circles to land there.

Some islands were so accessible they'd almost disappeared. The Rangitata River in South Canterbury surrounded a large island, but State Highway One crossed it so effortlessly many did not know it existed. A woman whose family farmed on the island told me that a country boy had once accused them of thinking they were smart, because they owned an island. The girls were puzzled. They used to rumble across the river in a Land Rover to get home. How could it be an island? It was joined underneath.

There were islands we might have included but did not, some not for want of trying. We tried to reach Moutoa Island in the Whanganui River, scene of the Hauhau defeat in the early 1860s. We scrambled, climbed, slithered through flood debris and along crumbling banks from both directions for most of a day. We could see only its tips, low shingle scarcely rising above the water, covered in beaten-up scrub. How the island survived I could not say. We gave it up.

All sorts of people lived on islands but we discovered one thing about them: they were invariably kind.

Islanders were not misanthropists as some thought. They liked company. We were made welcome by people proud of their islands.

Even the rich, with their legendary attraction to islands, loved their places. Only one or two were fiefdoms, whose owners repelled all boarders.

I heard the expression 'master of my own domain' several times. But I never heard 'mistress of my own domain', not once.

Most islanders were people of a certain age. Few young people lived on islands, except the biggest and most populated. They could not. There were no schools on most of them, and few jobs on all of them.

Islanders shared qualities such as self-reliance and that essential of self-preservation, caring for others. Most of all, they had a real need of beauty, the rawness of it, the all-encompassing beauty of islands that changed with sun, wind and rain.

Islands are slightly out of control, still wild even in the absence of wildness. They have a strange effect on you, as if your life has shifted somewhere else.

I have not seen a New Zealand book like this one. It was so difficult to do that I may not see another.

But what an adventure it was.

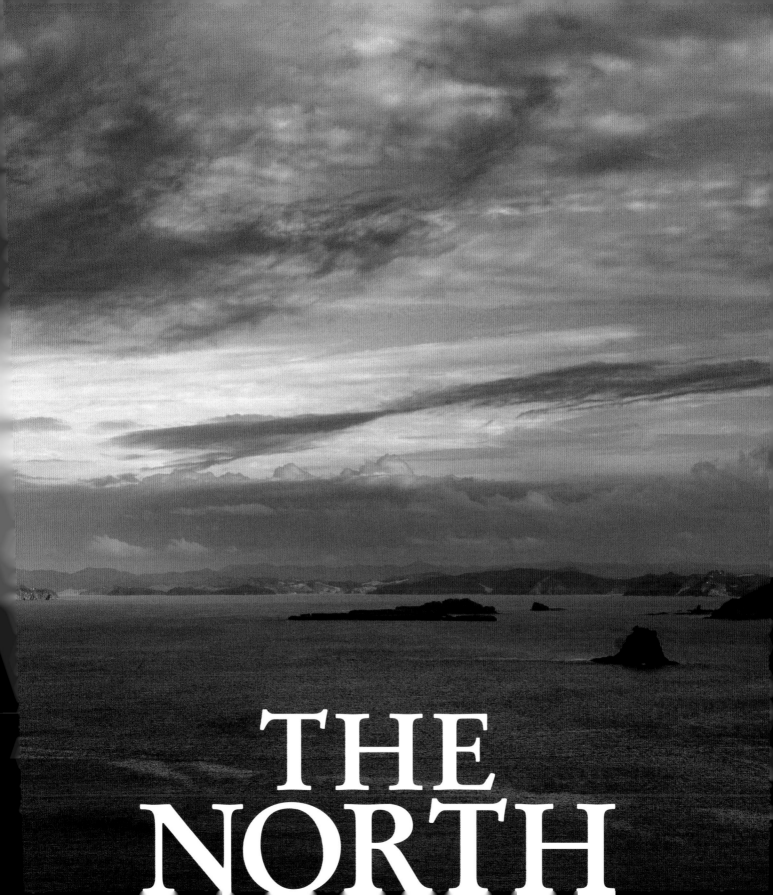

THE
NORTH

THE CAVALLIS

'This was the beginning, the place where the old met the new, where Aotearoa became New Zealand.'

A great scatter of islands lay across the sea in this place, where the last of the North Island gathered before running out to North Cape.

Humps, lumps, stacks, pipes, reefs rose from the sea and formed the Cavalli Islands. They were dazzling, and foaming, not like the diamonds or hazelnuts in the northern vernacular of early explorers, but in the New Zealand way, enticing and forbidding at the same time, blue and black and green and grey and always, always wild.

This was the beginning, the place where the old met the new, where Aotearoa became New Zealand.

———

Hohepa Epiha looked out of place in the carpark of the Doves Bay marina in the Bay of Islands. He was unobtrusive, self-effacing, and seemed remote from white plastic and tinkling masts. He was wearing a blue T-shirt and fuzzy grey trousers, and he had my immediate attention for his people had lived on the Cavalli Islands for 350 years and he remembered all of them, weighted with the knowledge of centuries.

So we climbed aboard our craft, a former Team New Zealand chase boat, and set off, down the Kerikeri Inlet, up the Bay of Islands, around Cape Wiwiki then northwards to where the Cavallis lurked behind the darkening doors of an unwelcoming weather forecast. The boat belonged to Richard and Vanessa Owen. They were taking us there for the same reason people up and down New Zealand wanted to show us their islands: they loved them and they wanted to tell their stories.

Their boat seemed impervious to weather forecasts, bounding from swell to

Pages 8–9 Bay of Islands

Previous The Cavallis, with Matauri Bay in the foreground

swell, the growl of the big outboard pushing us through the sea six times faster than the huge waka which once swept across this sea.

The waka *Mataatua* arrived here centuries before, its captain Toroa navigating from Hawaiki with his brother Puhi and sister Muriwai on a path that took them down this coast, past Aotea/Great Barrier Island, along the Coromandel coast and southwards, and giving birth to Ngapuhi, Ngati Awa, Tuhoe, Ngaiterangi and others. *Mataatua* was said to have landed at Whakatane where the brothers quarrelled and separated, Puhi heading northwards.

The crew spotted the estuary lying inside the bar at the Takou River entrance near the Cavallis. A big surf was running. A woman, Tawhiu Rau, was arguing with her husband. She and her children were thrown overboard to appease the gods and settle the sea. They turned to stone and the rock, Kohakoha, still stood at the entrance. The waka sailed into the lagoon and safety and Puhi settled at Takou.

Today surfers rode easily over the waves beside the rock, full of grace and beauty and kinship with the sea, and the woman and children were forgotten by everyone except the people who'd made this place their home.

Takou became the final resting place of the mighty *Mataatua* waka.

Hohepa's account differed slightly, but was the same in essence. You might not like the story, he said, but that was the trouble with history. It happened.

Everything meant something to Hohepa. He took me later to a pohutukawa tree just up the coast from Matauri Bay at Te Ngaere which lay close to the Cavallis.

Here chiefs had gathered in 1807 to make laws regarding the land, sea and the air (papatuanuku, tangaroa and ranginui) when they saw the white wave of Pakeha coming.

They used the tree as their marae, first to congregate and eventually to live under until the laws were agreed upon and pronounced at Waitangi in 1835.

The tree was called *Te Kahi Paihau*, The Bearded One. Now its huge limbs spread along the bank of a stream, relaxing on the ground like a tired old man who'd laid down to rest.

———

Dark clouds rolled over us as we sat on the bay in the place where Captain James Cook first stopped in New Zealand in 1769 and found himself becalmed for two hours.

We were lying off Motukawanui, the biggest Cavalli island, near the great sheltered bay Papatara which had been harbour and home to Maori and the European settlers who followed them. A pa squatted on a long headland beside the bay, shaped like a club with what must have been a strong fortress on the blade at its end, with another pa on the tiny island Te Karo all but joined to it.

Just across the water on the mainland lay Matauri Bay, where four waka sat

Left Cavalli Islands
seascape: humps, lumps,
stacks, pipes

on the beach as Cook arrived. We imagined Tapua, the chief, his sons Waka Nene and Patuone running towards them leading hundreds of warriors who packed the canoes and paddled out to the ship.

The *Endeavour*'s sails hung loose. The waka reached the ship in minutes.

Patuone later described that first meeting: '. . . the canoes were paddled to the vessel, the chiefs went on board and my father received presents of garments.'

'The history in my family's book,' Hohepa said, 'recorded that four war canoes championed by Tapua, the father of Waka Nene, his brother Patuone and 776 warriors paddled out to intercept the *Endeavour* and showered it with cavelle fish, raumarire.'

Cook named the islands the Cavelles, which became the Cavallis. But these fish were known to smell, pong, after a few minutes out of the water. 'So I don't know whether they were showered with hospitality or hostility.'

As it happened, hospitality *did* turn to hostility.

All was well until people in the waka began throwing stones at the ship and Cook's crew fired muskets in response.

Only a few years later, in 1793, the Lieutenant-Governor of Norfolk Island, Philip Gidley King, was wondering how he could produce cordage for the British Navy from flax. He devised a plan. New Zealanders were good with flax. Ergo, why not import a couple of them to show the locals how to do it?

That is why the ship *Daedelus* under Captain James Hanson arrived at the Cavallis early in 1793 with orders to 'procure' a couple of Maori. Two of them, Tuki and Huru, were lured on board, kidnapped and packed off to Norfolk to train convicts in the ways of flax. But the two were high-born, and treating flax was women's work. They were grief-stricken and shocked in a community that was in many ways far more barbaric than their own. The plan collapsed under a fatal misunderstanding: they knew very little about dressing flax.

The two, according to Anne Salmond in her book *Between Worlds*, were the first Maori to spend time in a European community. They were, as much as they could be, good-natured and pleasant, and won King's sympathy. They were returned to their people later the same year they'd been taken, an episode whose historical grandeur almost, but not quite, erased its shame.

They drew a map of their home coast for Governor King, which at first sight seemed little more than a child's sketch. But as you looked more closely it told you much about the coast and their islands and their history and significance. A spirit road led to Cape Reinga, where souls of the dead left for the underworld.

Motukawanui was described in an unknown hand, which belonged to neither of the two young men, as inhabited by 100 people, the size of Norfolk Island (in fact, it was only a tenth the size of Norfolk) with few trees but much flax.

Today, autumn and humid, the swell sliding ominously, almost a quarter-millennium after the *Endeavour* sat on this spot, a faint current pulsed through our high-powered waka.

Vanessa, whose boat we were on, its huge outboard motor carrying us in an hour over distances it had sometimes taken Cook a day to sail, felt a murmuring connection.

She was born and raised at Langbaugh Hall, the estate which owned the cottage where James Cook grew up. As a child she played on Captain Cook's monument, a strange obelisk on Roseberry Topping, on a hill behind the village of Great Ayton in Yorkshire. James and Grace, Cook's parents, left their initials over their doorway. The cottage was dismantled in 1933 and shipped in 253 packing cases to Melbourne where it now stood in Fitzroy Gardens.

In the end, his house travelled almost as far as Cook did and so for that matter did Vanessa.

————

The archipelago became the Cavalli Islands in that all-encompassing, bland way of European names, covering some 36 islands.

Their Maori names were more poetic. The islands were a family. The biggest, the father figure, was Motukawanui. The next biggest was Motukawaiti, the mother figure.

Around them lay the children, 34 islets ranging from islands to rocks, and their names rang like bells, Whatupuke, Kahangaro, Motutapere, Haraweka, Motumuka, Nukutaunga.

Four mokopuna, grandchildren, were yet to be born, lying under the sea. All of those names, stories, fables, wrapped up in a single word which was not even the original: Cavallis.

Earlier we'd driven along the high ridge road above Matauri Bay. Hohepa bade me stop the car, get out and follow him with my eyes closed. He led me to the edge. 'Open your eyes.' Far below me the archipelago covered the sea, a huge reef, father, mother, tamariki, the mokopuna sometimes peeking from the water, sometimes throwing a tantrum and splashing foam, like children in a bath. All of the mystery and history was coming and going in shafts of light.

Hohepa believed his people lived mainly on Motukawanui. Their big waka had trouble with the heavy surf and backwash on the mainland beaches of Matauri Bay. Motukawanui offered a sheltered anchorage.

The most important archaeological work on the big island had been done in the late 1970s, the investigation recording 70 sites, pa, middens, pits and terraces, traces of extensive cultivation and a thriving people.

The archaeologists concluded that the Cavallis were extensively cultivated and had supported a 'fairly large' population. Historians believe they left the islands in the early nineteenth century when the introduction of European muskets made them vulnerable.

Following Korowai, the magic cloak

Maori lost the big island in 1912 when the Maori Land Court declared Motukawanui freehold and available for European farming. Forest was cleared, the land eroded, soil quality deteriorated.

The first European owners didn't live there, and the second, the MacDonald family, were the first Europeans to occupy and farm. They were kinder to the land, although they ran more stock.

Above Panaki (left);
Hohepa Epiha

The island was sold to an absentee owner in 1954 and managed by Janet White, an Englishwoman who'd not long been in New Zealand and left an account of her life on the island in her book *The Sheep Stell: The autobiography of a shepherd.*

She called the island 'Aroa', and described its owner as a well-meaning doctor from Palmerston North with dreams of forests, bird sanctuary, lake, pheasants, prize-winning cattle. She drove out to look at it from the mainland and there was her island, 'aloof and golden. Isolation gave it a veiled enchantment.'

The word 'golden' hinted at the dry country farming the island had reluctantly given itself to, but all of her descriptions of the island were opaque, overlaid with a gauzy Englishness which did not fit a subtropical island in the south seas.

White was a sheep-farmer. She lived in the 'homestead', the hut which still stood near the sea in Papatara Bay, patched, a couple of chimneys sticking up like a toasting fork.

Alone, she wrestled the spectres of island farming: transport, accidents, sickness, isolation, none of them the reason she quit.

She was moderately successful, in that she survived, and it was not the island which sent her packing but a man called Jack she'd met on the immigrant ship bringing her to New Zealand.

Jack would have been called a stalker in later years. He tracked her to Motukawanui, twice stole boats to get to the island, begged her to marry him (she did not say so, but she was not that much of a fool, for Jack was clearly a no-hoper) and eventually attacked her with a rifle butt putting her in hospital and him in prison. She left the island before he was released from jail, returning to England.

After other owners, and more farming, the island was abandoned in 1973. The only trace of European settlement now, except for some fruit and shelter trees, was the hut at Papatara. They left less tangible evidence of their stay than their stone-age predecessors, not counting environmental damage. Andrew Blanshard, a Department of Conservation (DOC) archaeology ranger, described Motukawanui's Maori archaeology as 'mindblowing', and ached to spend more time on it.

———

Hohepa took us to Panaki, a little island to the north of Motukawanui. The channel between Panaki and East Hamaruru, like many in this group, was created by the caves beneath giving way to the faults and cracks in the rock and collapsing.

Hohepa's father and his brothers would row here all the way from Matauri in what Hohepa called their banana-boat because of its shape, turned up at each end. They'd row all day to reach the island before nightfall, put into this tiny bay, haul up the boat and sleep under the upturned craft. They'd wake in the early hours and set out again for the fishing grounds at Wiriwiri to the east, loading their little boat with giant hapuka, so heavy the boat would sit very low in the water.

Then they'd have to get back through the surf at Matauri, sometimes dropping the hapuka back into the water to give them more freeboard, pulling the fish back in when they were safe.

For all of this work his father sold the fish for three shillings a dozen of whatever species he had. This was how he fed and raised his huge family of 28 children, Hohepa being the twenty-sixth, for after his first wife died of leukaemia his father remarried. Fourteen girls, 14 boys. 'A miracle!'

His father had spoken no English, only Maori, the language they'd been brought up with, comfortable as a Pakeha family with English.

But schools of the time were having none of it. They tried to whack te reo

Above The Cavallis:
a family of islands

out of the child, to force children whose nature was Maori to speak only English at school. For his first couple of years at school Hohepa would go home with his hands running red from being strapped. Dover Samuels, who lived at Matauri Bay and was once Minister of Maori Affairs, was beaten with a length of supplejack vine for speaking the only language he knew, as the Whakarara Native School at Matauri tried to whip his language out of him.

Panaki looked bereft now. An indestructible poly fishing net lay bundled above the high-water mark. His father might have regarded it as space-age technology.

Hohepa talked of the great schools of trevally and maumau that once were common here, crayfish running so thickly they turned the water red.

He reached for a canvas briefcase he'd brought onto the boat. He laid it in his lap, flicked the catches, opened it gently. Inside was a red tartan bundle. He lifted it out, a karakia rumbling deep in his throat.

In the bundle lay a mass of feathers, white, brown, blue, tawny, flaxen, speckled, delicate as roses, each one of them carefully laid to form a soft composition, a fragile portrait reaching deep into the past.

It was a feathered cloak, a korowai, a taonga of thousands of feathers chosen from so many birds that when someone asked the question Hohepa shrugged it off. 'It would take days to count.'

He cast it over his shoulders and it was a magic cloak, for he changed immediately. He became taller, more noble. His face was graven, his eyes deep in shadow. It was one of the most beautiful objects I'd ever seen.

———

We went down to Motukawaiti, the only privately owned island in the Cavalli group. As a mother the poor island was in dire need of counselling. It was also the only inhabited island in the group, although nothing moved there.

I'd already approached the owner, by a roundabout route, for permission to go ashore. The answer trickled back: no.

An architect's project report set out the work that had been done on the island: a turn-of-the-century farm cottage had been restored, and four pavilions built to house guests, sauna, spa, complete with gymnasium and underground cellar.

A central summer pavilion boasted walls of glass louvres and a glazed roof allowing guests to sleep under the stars. Everything was sited for the superb views over coastline and surrounding islands and, in that way of architects, was claimed to provide 'an elegant dichotomy'.

Dichotomous it might have been, but just at that moment it fell short of elegant. Given over to its recent, sad, history. A dubious paradise, it seemed to me.

The island was an example of New Zealand's procedures for selling property to foreign buyers.

Wenning Han, resident in New Zealand since about 2001, bought the island for NZ$10 million and sold it a week later for $12 million to his company St Morris, of which he was the sole director. The vendors were a Northland family.

Mr Han's purchase was financed by a loan from a Mr Zhang, who was living in China and would own the island if the loan was not repaid. By February 2013 the loan, and interest, had not been repaid as required. Mr Zhang applied to have St Morris put into liquidation and in August that year became the owner of the fine island kingdom of Motukawaiti.

A long investigation by Land Information New Zealand (LINZ) set out to unravel the island's ownership for the Overseas Investment Office (OIO) and decide whether anyone should be prosecuted in connection with its purchase.

The law required that 'overseas persons' needed permission from the OIO for investment in sensitive land, and LINZ was in no doubt that Motukawaiti was very sensitive indeed.

The government agencies investigated their suspicion that Mr Han and St Morris bought the island intending that Mr Zhang would be the eventual owner, despite Mr Han's insistence that he'd bought it for his own purposes. In short, that Mr Han and his company St Morris, not 'overseas persons', were fronts for Mr Zhang, who *was* an 'overseas person', getting around the need for government permission.

The investigation took fully five years. Those who had followed the role of the OIO in overseas land purchases were not surprised by the investigation's conclusion: smoke but no fire. There was not enough evidence for a criminal prosecution. Civil penalties might have applied but the time limit had run out long before, in 2012. So, in February 2016, the OIO announced that nothing was to be done.

The island was now on the market, price negotiable but last listed as NZ$30 million.

Matauri Bay elders were enraged: Hohepa Eripa's brother Nau threatening that the Ngati Kuta were considering occupying the island and had banned its owners from using their Matauri Bay boat ramp, and Dover Samuels, who lived at the bay, suggesting the government return the island to the hapu through its Treaty claims.

Hohepa shrugged. What was the point, he asked, of claiming something that had never gone out of their ownership, had always been theirs?

Meanwhile the island lay idle. Nigel Atkin and Fiona Powell, part of that intriguing network of island guardians who I later met taking care of Pakatoa Island, spent a short time on Motukawaiti and found its buildings and equipment in a sad state of repair. They mended wind turbines, put in solar panels, repaired the washed-out jetty . . . and returned to Pakatoa.

Today Motukawaiti's buildings looked fine from the sea, but the little white house and the spa and the sauna and the glassy pavilion had the air of resorts

Right The pohutukawa
marae: *Te Kahi Paihau,*
The Bearded One

that were no longer resorts, as abandoned as the terraces of an old pa high on a headland.

The island's website remained up, luring guests with 'your very own 72ft luxury motor launch', promising a traditional Maori welcome, therapists trained in traditional and Maori wellbeing therapies, perhaps a game of golf over at Kauri Cliffs on the mainland.

I filled in the form for prospective guests and sent it off. There was no reply.

———

Piraunui Island lay nearby. It was a rock hump, riven with caves at its base. It was just another island in the archipelago and I would have taken no notice of it but for Hohepa.

Piraunui meant the smelly island, he said, stinking, foul-smelling, putrid.

Only chiefs were buried there, he said. Their bodies were hung from trees until the flesh rotted off their skeletons.

Then their bones were taken down and placed in holes, where they still lay. The dark eyes of the caves peered out. We shivered and went on.

'Over there, to that little rock, a titi island,' he directed. 'Stop. You'll see a track from way back, going back to the 1700s and still used today. For catching muttonbirds. [Grey-faced petrel chicks; southern muttonbirds were the chicks of sooty shearwaters.] All the kai was here, fish, mussels, paua, titi. We're still getting them, in September. You don't go and rape and pillage. The family get together on the beach and do their karakia before they come here. Sometimes when the tide is low and it's three o'clock in the morning. That's the time when the birds are leaving the chicks.'

The island looked unscalable but closer, stone steps appeared, leading up an almost vertical cliff to the top.

To the north boats carried divers to the wreck of the *Rainbow Warrior*, the Greenpeace ship sunk after it was blown up in Auckland Harbour by French agents, its last resting place near the Cavallis.

The rocks for the *Rainbow Warrior* monument on Pukepika, the headland at Matauri Bay, came from cliffs near where we sat in the long swells sweeping past the Cavallis. The great basalt pillars, the biggest of them weighing six tonnes, were pulled carefully from the shore, a massive effort.

Along that coast also were said to lie the remains of Hongi Hika, the great Ngapuhi chief who died of bullet wounds in 1828 at Whangaroa. His final resting place was secret, but some said his body had been separated and buried in several places, and one of them was a cave along this coast. We went no closer.

Opposite Muttonbird fortress

BAY OF ISLANDS

'Once, this was the centre of New Zealand
civilisation, crucible of our small universe.'

T he Bay of Islands was so crowded that the best place to see the trove within it was not from the sea at all.

The grandstand was a point high in the hills where old New Zealanders first came face to face with the future. From there, with sharp eyes and a little imagination, you could see almost every island in the Bay of Islands, 144 of them.

Once, this was the centre of New Zealand civilisation, crucible of our small universe.

In Rangihoua Bay below this viewpoint stood the Marsden Cross, where Samuel Marsden took the first step in his divine plan: a mission in New Zealand, a place where the rich soil of the Maori mind could be improved 'fit to rank with civilised nations'.

He'd met a young rangatira, Ruatara, who'd been to London to visit the King and failed, and was left naked, beaten and ill. Marsden nursed him back to health and took him back to Port Jackson, now known as Sydney. There, news of the burning of the brigantine *Boyd* and the massacre of its crew in Whangaroa reached them.

Marsden was horrified. Ruatara was close, possibly even related, to the Bay of Islands chief Te Pahi.

Te Pahi was a well-travelled man of great mana. He'd been to Europe and Australia. He was intelligent and anxious to learn Pakeha skills and technology. He was to have been Marsden's patron in the Bay of Islands.

Governor Philip Gidley King had even given Te Pahi a house, the first known European building presented to Maori, and Te Pahi erected it on his island fortress, Te Puna. This was shaping up to be a fine relationship.

Then, in late 1809, the *Boyd* was attacked by Maori, its crew killed, the ship burned in revenge for the flogging of a young chief, Te Ara, who'd joined the crew. Te Pahi was wrongly named 'chief of the murderers', a treacherous old rascal who had been architect of the massacre. In fact, he had tried to save the *Boyd* survivors.

Previous Bay of Islands

Following Black rocks (left); the tall ship *R. Tucker Thompson*

Marsden believed he'd been mistaken for Te Puhi, a chief who had been involved.

It was New Zealand's most tragic spelling mistake. A vengeful bunch of whalers, drunks and skunks not given to reading the fine print of any situation, then descended upon Te Pahi's island, burned his village, razed his European house, and killed about 60 of his people. Te Pahi, wounded by a musket ball, escaped by swimming to the mainland but was later killed in a fight perhaps precipitated by the *Boyd* disaster.

He'd gone from honoured guest whose son met royalty in England to a man who was maltreated by the crews of visiting ships, whose daughter and son-in-law had been taken away from him in a European ship, whose son had died of a possibly European-inflicted disease. So Marsden's protector died, ignominiously.

Ruatara succeeded to Te Pahi's mana, fortunately for Marsden, for the chief was interested in Pakeha methods, particularly farming.

Against the odds, Marsden's mission was built in 1814, gazing over its fine bay to the islands beyond, which were home, then, to a fair proportion of New Zealand Maori, Ruatara its new protector.

In 2014 a small piece of Te Pahi's history came home. Governor King had presented him with a silver medal inscribed 'to Tippahee, a chief of New Zealand, during his visit at Sydney, New South Wales, January 1806'.

Someone — a whaler? a sailor? an early surveyor? — had raked it from the ashes. The medal was not seen again until it resurfaced in a Sotheby's auction in Sydney. Auckland Museum and Te Papa paid more than $300,000 to get it back.

———

You stand reverently in this rare spot with the islands of the bay spread below.

Te Pahi and Ruatara had two pa here. Te Pahi's favourite, the place where he was attacked, was Te Puna on the Te Pahi Islands directly below, four of them arranged like the stumpy legs of some ancestral table. They looked tiny and uninhabitable.

But from the sea, later, they were not so. One had a cottage and another looked like a turtle and was called, of course, Turtle Island by locals. Its back side boasted a tiny beach and a sheltering reef and in the morning sun looked like a miniature island paradise. Te Pahi agreed, for he spent much of his time there. The islands were guarded by rocks rising like fangs from the sea, the old chief's teeth.

I walked to his old mainland pa Rangihoua, perhaps 700 years old, treading thigh-deep through thick spongy grass which clung like tentacles. The track to the pa once ran up from a beach in front of Marsden's mission, along a sharp ridge. The pa ended in a twirly top like a turban, or an ice cream, a fantasy where palisades once spiralled upwards. I climbed terraces and followed palisade lines and saw that several hundred people could have lived here looking down on Marsden's little mission.

Hohepa Epiha's great-grandfather trod the earth here at the same time as Te Pahi and Ruatara.

Hohepa recited, again, his paean to continuity, 'I am the land and the land is me, I am the water and the water is me.'

———

Motuarohia was the place where Captain Cook first dropped the *Endeavour*'s anchor in New Zealand. His ship drew up before the loveliest island his crew could have hoped for. A rock stood up like a blade, flanked by three lagoons, all but severing the island in two.

Here Cook first set foot on New Zealand. The island was now divided between private owners and public, and the spot where Cook first landed, known as Cook's Cove, was private: the great navigator might have mulled over that one. The two hundred and fiftieth anniversary of that event was to be celebrated in 2019.

The *Endeavour* was immediately surrounded by waka, about 35 of them arriving in the space of half an hour, huge craft carrying 100 or more. The arithmetic was interesting: 3500 people, at least, within easy reach. Rough estimates gave the Bay of Islands a population, then, of 50,000 people. The whole of Northland now accounted for some 160,000 people, a third of them in Whangarei: obviously the Bay of Islands was then the centre of this South Pacific cosmos.

A small altercation, a little gunfire, and the great navigator sailed away.

Now this nearby, broad bay on the island with its rocks and its lagoons had its own population statistic: one of the most photographed places in New Zealand, tour boats constantly arriving, disgorging, departing.

Somewhere in this bay lay the site of another first for New Zealand, the place where the tangata whenua got their introduction to British law and order through judicial murder, or capital punishment.

Motuarohia was also known as Roberton Island. Elizabeth Roberton farmed the island heroically after the death of her husband John, a former whaling captain who in 1839 bought Motuarohia from the Ngapuhi.

She had two children of her own and a third lived with them, Isabella Brind, granddaughter of a Ngapuhi leader, Rewa. Thomas Bull also worked on the farm.

At some point in 1841 Maketu Wharetotara, aka Wiremu Kingi Maketu, joined the family. Maketu was the son of an important Ngapuhi chief, Ruhe, and according to contemporary accounts wanted to learn about Pakeha first-hand. He became a family favourite.

But the abusive Bull offended his mana and in November 1841 Maketu had had enough. Maketu turned on the man and split open his head with an axe before Mrs Roberton's eyes. She protested. Maketu killed her too, then slaughtered the two girls.

The little boy fled but Maketu caught up and threw him over a cliff which became famous among early tourists. Maketu then set fire to the house and went home.

His father, Ruhe, faced a dilemma. Maketu had killed the granddaughter of a chief who might demand utu and go to war.

Local Pakeha authorities, such as they were, foresaw the same problem, perhaps with consequences for the young settlements nearby, and were reluctant to act. Instead, Ruhe turned in his son to Pakeha justice.

The colonial government's new justice system faced its first real test. A Supreme Court was established in Auckland and Sir William Martin, an impressive judicial figure 'whose talents and integrity rendered him singularly fitted to fill an office at once so high and so difficult', took his seat on the bench in March 1842.

Maketu pleaded not guilty, but the evidence was overwhelming. As he'd previously confessed, the guilty verdict was not surprising especially in a young colony anxious to impress its authority upon the people.

Auckland was a crude little place then. According to a contemporary account: 'The authorities were well aware of the necessity of exercising firmness and severity to obtain and retain a hold upon the native mind . . . the Maoris came from far and near, filling the streets of Auckland with crowds of solemn, awestricken, inquisitive aboriginals, awaiting the course of British justice.'

Above Whitiora Marae, papakainga of Te Tii Mangonui

Chief Justice Martin issued New Zealand's first death warrant. 'We require and . . . command you that upon Monday, the seventh day of March instant, between the hours of eleven in the morning and two in the afternoon of the same day, him, the said Maketu, you forthwith convey to the front of the common jail of the said town of Auckland, and that you do cause execution to be done upon the said Maketu.'

According to one account: 'The Maoris could not believe that so awful a sentence would in reality be carried out. It was considered, according to their customs, most unmerciful to permit the victim to know of his approaching doom. The punishment of death should, in their views, be dealt unexpectedly and without warning. They protested to this effect, but their pleadings were not heard.'

Whether this was correct or not, Maketu was speedily dispatched at Mount Eden jail, his execution watched by a large number of Maori who were deeply impressed. The teenager became the first person to be legally hanged in New Zealand and his trial might even be seen as the first tic in the judicial cheek given the continuing high rates of Maori imprisonment.

The same account described Chief Justice Martin's new image: 'The judge was looked upon with very great awe after such a terrible exhibition of his power. In his future travels on circuit crowds used to collect to see the man who had,

Above In Whitiora Marae

according to their ideas, power to dictate this deed of vengeance and cruelty.'

The scene of the crime was a quiet place now, although what did I expect? Spectres and quadrilles?

Andrew Blanshard, the DOC archaeologist, was still looking for the exact site of the murders, slowly narrowing the list of possibilities. It was somewhere near the beach, he thought, but those early settlers left so few signs of habitat. Yes, they burned the bush, yes, they loosed the rats, but in that way that New Zealanders still had, their houses were temporary things. Ancient Maori left more: their pa sites, terraces, pits and gardens could still be found.

Now the bay was in kikuyu grass flats while the surrounding hills were slowly regenerating and might return one day to something close to the scene facing Cook as he peered over the rail 250 years before.

––––––

Moturua had a complete record of habitation. Sliced open it would reveal 800 years of human history from early Maori to rich Pakeha paradise.

Mangahawea, one of the four main bays, had a midden site which Andrew Blanshard knew went back to around 1280, giving up moa and seal bones, even a tuatara jawbone. Out on its southern end, on private land once owned by whalers, lay the houses of people such as Craig Heatley, Sky TV founder, and the Goodfellows, owners of an extensive business empire. Heatley's place included a helicopter hangar and a tunnel joining two bays. Only God knew what archaeologists would make of that in 800 years' time.

Two strong pa once guarded this island. One of them, Hikurangi at the north, was revived in World War II as an Army observation post, Pakeha finding the site as useful as Maori. From the bay below, Waiwhapuku, soldiers controlled minefields laid through the Bay of Islands.

Saddlebacks, the rare North Island robins, rescued kiwi, regenerating bush, the island's conservation success stories seemed overshadowed by its history, which was unrelenting: when the 1984 film *The Bounty*, a remake of the famous mutiny starring Anthony Hopkins and Mel Gibson, was being filmed in 1983, the crew stored their explosives on shore. According to Andrew Blanshard they exploded all right: 'The fire burned half the island.'

When Captain James Cook and the botanist Joseph Banks landed on Moturua they estimated a third of it, 60 hectares, was under cultivation. The place was a garden.

Yet Cook was not the biggest news on this island in the eighteenth century. That honour went to the French explorer Marion du Fresne who landed here, disastrously, in the winter of 1772.

His two ships anchored in Waipao Bay, later known also as Frenchmans.

Above Bay of Islands: isles of despair

He established a camp there, and another at Clendon Cove on the mainland, where his crew set about cutting timber for his ships, which had been badly damaged in a gale at Spirits Bay.

They needed to fix leaks, replace timbers and spars, and they were having to go 20 kilometres or so inland to get good kauri; the Bay's considerable population was making inroads into the supply. They sometimes dragged the logs over ice, for this was the late 1700s, and much colder. Du Fresne had grown fond of Maori; he explored their life and customs, regarded them as friends, and for the weeks the French had been in the Bay of Islands relations were good.

Yet on 12 June, he and two boatloads of officers and crew, 25 or 26 of them, fishing in Manawaora Bay just across the water on the mainland, were attacked and killed by hundreds of Maori.

One theory, the most popular, was that they'd broken a rahui, or ban, by taking fish from an area where people had drowned. They'd caught fish which had fed upon the mana of the dead. As du Fresne and his crew were cooked and eaten, that raised the prospect of a more complicated sequence: they'd eaten the men who'd eaten the fish which had eaten the mana of the drowned men.

But the most popular story was not always right. Other theories jostled for position. Why had they been attacked on that particular day? They'd fished there often before. Perhaps they'd unwittingly upset Maori in the past and something had triggered the violence. Or they'd offended by cutting down trees without the proper ceremony. Or they had intruded upon a political standoff caused by Ngapuhi hapu incursions into these eastern Bay of Plenty islands, displacing local people.

Whatever they'd done, they were swiftly clubbed to death. Their assailants took their clothes, brandished the Frenchmen's cutlasses and pistols and, according to one account: 'The bones of the foreigners who had been killed were made into forks for picking up food, and the thigh-bones were made into flutes.'

The surviving French retaliated swiftly. They left their timber camp and fired upon their Maori pursuers, killing and wounding several of them.

Slowly local Maori grew bolder. They surrounded the French camp in the bay on Moturua. A greatcoat vanished, an anchor, other things. Du Fresne's second-in-command, Julien Crozet, decided he should attack.

On 14 June they marched up the hill and attacked and burned the nearby headland pa killing between 250 and 300 inhabitants, the first time muskets had been used to kill Maori.

'The story goes,' Andrew Blanshard said, 'that they buried the dead on a sandy beach not far from the Goodfellows' property, buried them with one hand sticking above the sand to show they hadn't been eaten.'

Locals returned later to that bay, Hahangarua, and re-interred the bodies.

The French rushed to repair their ships. Then they left, hurriedly. Before they went, Crozet took possession of New Zealand for France, recording the seizure in an official document which he sealed in a bottle along with ship's papers and buried above the high-water mark on Moturua. Many searched, none found it. Nor did they find any other trace of the French.

Hahangarua looked like any other bay, if a little richer. Everything from that time had vanished, as if it had never been.

———

Urupukapuka Island was the most visited in the Bay, ferry services to Otehei Bay becoming cheaper and more frequent. Some 110,000 people a year were trooping across to the island, 10,000 of them campers on the three campsites maintained by the Department of Conservation. This was a publicly owned island, only the area of tourist facilities in Otehei Bay leased to a private company. Zane Grey, the American author and renowned game fisherman, established a base there in the late 1920s.

For archaeologists the island was rich. Every terrace, every pit, every pa site on the island had been recorded, and there were some 2000 of them.

Ngapuhi expansion into these eastern Bay of Plenty islands pushed out the local inhabitants and there were enough battlefield sites to satisfy the most bloodthirsty historian.

One pa site even showed earthworks designed for muskets, although no one knew whether they were actually used. Human remains found at Otehei had been re-interred.

To the north of the island lay the rocky Waewaetorea passage, narrowing to a point where two pa faced each other across the water, half a world away from the north but as perfect a set of fortresses as ever guarded a European strait.

The island had been farmed for many years, and DOC still ran sheep to keep archaeological sites from becoming overgrown.

Otehei was the perfect waka harbour and beach, as sheltered and calm as any modern tourist arriving by ferry, having a coffee and a look around, could dream of. Stingrays loved the bay, especially as a refuge from orca.

On the other side of the bay lay the Black Rocks, dark platforms rising sheer from the sea. The only other place in the world with rocks like this, locals boasted, was Easter Island. They were flat-topped, covered in short stubby vegetation.

Hohepa Epiha's father used to play rugby on this rough field, the teams battling the ground as much as each other. 'Blood was spilled during the game,' he said. I wasn't surprised. I'd as soon have played on broken glass.

At the end of the game the teams simply dived off the edge into the sea and climbed into waiting boats. The rocks ran vertically, deep into the water.

Today as the swells rose and fell they revealed layers of colour, sealife and growth, turning purple as they disappeared into the deep.

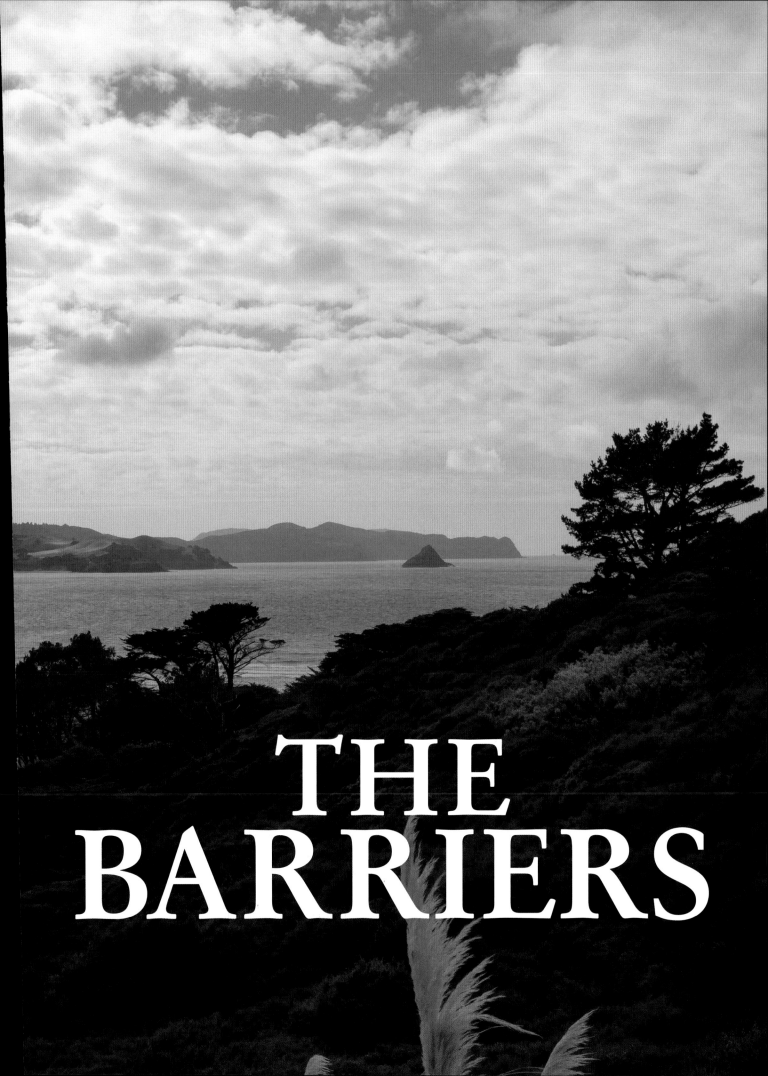

THE
BARRIERS

GREAT BARRIER

'There was no past nor present on Great Barrier Island, just lives continuing. What happened yesterday was more or less what was going to happen today.'

48

A rattling aeroplane carried us to Great Barrier Island. Almost immediately we stopped talking about arriving and started worrying about leaving.

There was a gulf between this place and the rest of New Zealand, literally. Passenger services had only a tenuous hold on the place. The island was other-worldly. It felt dark, and strange.

To press the point, Greeny had our aging station wagon waiting. The only rules for driving here, he said, were:

Don't cross the white line
Don't hit a power pole
Don't run over a possum

Well, all right. We wouldn't. We couldn't. No white lines, no power poles, no possums. None of them existed on the Barrier. This was as basic an explanation of the island as you could get.

Not so long ago there was another rule: first find your road.

Roads were also a fragile amenity on the Barrier. They remained uncertain, bored and scraped through rotten rock, prone to slips and likely to be covered in so much water that at one point on the main highway flood marker poles seemed to be graded in fathoms.

A sign near the ferry wharf at Tryphena urged care: roads, it said, were also footpaths. To a visitor it sometimes seemed the other way round: footpaths were also roads.

Not far from the ferry terminal lay a Standard Vanguard, early 1950s. On the long driveways leading off public roads the timeline was recorded by dead cars.

Even remarking on this was to miss the point: there was no past nor present on Great Barrier Island, just lives continuing. What happened yesterday was more or less what was going to happen today.

Pages 44–5 Barrier prospect

Previous Great Barrier

Here, aristocracy equalled the length of time your family had been on the island multiplied by the place names you'd left on it. Except for Sven Stellin, who was a real count, but with only a half-century on the Barrier reckoned he was more a Johnny-come-lately. 'We've been here fifty years but we're still newbies.'

That evening, in the bar of the Claris Sports and Social Club, Greeny delivered what became a standard warning about getting off the island again: keep a check on ferry sailings, he advised. The weather could turn. The usual ferry was not on the run, he said, and the substitute, well, who knew.

———

The island's European history lay as much in absences as anything. The great kauri forests disappeared in the twinkle of a sawmiller's eye. The delectable oysters went, with much of the fish. Many of the farms torn from the bush disappeared.

A couple of churches, a few early houses struggled on. Old Maori pa did better.

The Medlands' great enterprise, slaving over a farm cut from the bush and swamp, started in a whare at what was now Medlands Beach and full of expensive holiday houses.

Early Medlands were led to their place by the one-legged patriarch of the Blackwell family riding a bull. He'd arrived in 1865 with his wife, baby daughter and brother-in-law. Their little girl died on the voyage.

At their peak, Blackwell holdings ran back from the harbour right to the tops of the main ridges.

Les and Beverley Blackwell still lived on Walter Blackwell Road.

Beverley belonged to the fifth generation of the Sanderson family, going back to 1863. She grew up on the family farm a short distance from her present house. Her brother still lived there, her parents and grandparents were buried in the family cemetery in a nearby field.

The Blackwell's house felt solid, which was just as well. Hauraki was thought to mean north wind, and the island stood in its way, the barrier to the Gulf.

A macrocarpa hedge ran alongside the house until kaka stripped the bark and it died. Then an angry gale stamped across the dunes and ripped out the trees' corpses. Imagine the strength of it. Macrocarpa are tough, the reason they dotted the landscape as shelter.

Inside, the house had the feeling of sanctuary, the couple in their cosy, comforting living room, light years away from the Blackwells' first, awful two years on the island in 1866. Les rocked in his chair, tapped his hands on its arms.

Beverley was sent off the island once, to Auckland Girls' Grammar. 'It was such a shock. Traumatic. Coming home to the island is a freedom which I've never lost.' Most children on the island knew the feeling; even now, there was no secondary school.

Above Towards
Medlands Beach

Les did correspondence school, and his day of reckoning came when he was called up for compulsory military service. For many young men it was an unwelcome intrusion into their lives. Les liked it. 'It was the first and only time I've been away from home for so long.'

For many years only a rough track joined the two main harbour communities, Tryphena and Fitzroy. When Les was a child he fell out of a tree. It took three days for the district nurse to get her horse through all the rivers between them. By the time she reached him Les had recovered.

When she was 25, Grace Medland found a Fitzroy resident born on the island, her own age, who she'd never met before.

But the rough, raw roads were good enough to take Beverley to Les's 21st birthday party. So they met and married in a ceremony attended by almost all the 200 people on the island.

And, oh, said the Blackwells, keep an eye on the weather. That ferry . . .

Great Barrier's relationship with Auckland was fraught. Young people struggled for work on the island. Many had to leave. The island was growing older: at last count the median age was 54.6 years compared with 38 for New Zealand as a whole.

Yet unlike other cities and towns in New Zealand there was no resentment towards the city that was slowly sucking the life out of the island. One reason was that Auckland *gave* the island its life: its transport, hospital services, goods services, most of its income from tourism which was now the island's biggest industry. Although, as someone remarked, 'Tourists are a vital part of the economy. But we don't have to *like* them.'

Even Les wanted to leave the island, once. Beverley talked him into staying. I asked if he ever regretted it. 'No,' he said, unconvincingly. Beverley said, 'Yes you have.'

What if he *had* left? 'I think I'd have gone farming.'

Les thought about that. 'But we probably wouldn't have been able to survive as well as we are now. We don't buy any vegetables or fruit. We have over one hundred fruit trees in the orchard. Beverley bottles all the apricots, we had lots this year, peaches.' They bought everything else they needed from a Devonport supermarket which took it to a ferry for the run to the Barrier.

The telephone rang twice, then stopped. 'June,' said Beverley. If it had rung three times, it would have been Jeanette, another daughter.

Communications here had always been, well, eccentric. For 14 years the island relied on pigeons for contact with the city. Even when telephones arrived early last century islanders had to put up with interruptions, delays and party lines for more than 80 years. A single gale could cut everyone off.

One glorious day, 20 April 1991, an automatic telephone exchange was opened. The last toll call on the old manual exchange was made to the Governor General, Dame Cath Tizard: her line was engaged.

There was no cellphone reception in Tryphena, port of entry. A woman at Claris airport said, 'Go down to the Mulberry Grove store then walk across to a big pohutukawa on the foreshore. Stand underneath it and your phone should work.' It did.

———

The Barrier skyline stepped down on either side of the ancient volcano Mount Hobson, in spikes and turrets, spires grooves clefts shafts canyons, so that its outline looked like a cardiograph, its heartbeat marking a war here, a massacre there, a shipwreck, a wave of destruction.

Simply existing had always been hard on the Barrier. The earliest European settlers scraped a living cutting firewood or digging kauri gum.

Industries had come and gone, leaving relics like gravestones.

Copper was mined at Miners Head from 1842. A great deal of exaggeration

went on. After three years the mine closed. Mining resumed a few years later amid more chest-beating ending in tears for investors.

Two Sanderson brothers found silver in their creek in 1892. They started a silver rush which lasted a decade. Up to 700 people lived in Oreville. The town was just a name on a map now. Beverly Blackwell née Sanderson showed me a finely worked bracelet made from the silver.

Gold was found too, the most successful company, the Barrier Reefs Gold Mining Company, building a long wharf at Whangaparapara and stamping batteries in Oreville. But quantities were small and no one made much money. Interest revived briefly in 1967 but proved nothing more than a burp. Mining was banned in the 1980s.

Kauri was mined also. Unlike copper, silver and gold, the island was thick with it. First it was cut for spars on sailing ships. Then it was burned as owners cleared their land for farming, or gumdiggers burned scrub.

Then it was logged.

Huge kauri dams were built high up the creeks, water and logs packing up behind them until the dams were tripped and spouted the whole caboodle down to the coast in a spectacular roar of destruction. The great kauri forests were finally destroyed between the two world wars of the twentieth century.

At the end of it all no one made their fortune. That was the Barrier way.

———

I waited for Sven Stellin at the Port Fitzroy wharf with Pete, a railways enthusiast. He'd heard of a signal box, a very rare one, being used as a house in a commune deep in the mangroves. Sven had agreed to take him there.

Everyone climbed into his open aluminium dinghy and set off. The morning was quiet, the water calm.

The journey seemed long, the water grew rougher, we got wet. Eventually the boat slowed. Sven steered into a channel, passed between mudbanks amid teal teetering on the edge of extinction.

He pulled into a small jetty surrounded by mangroves and dark water. Pete spotted his signal box and leapt off in delight.

Sue Reusser came down the valley to see what the fuss was about. She was one of the original 20 people who formed the Wairahi community 20 years ago.

She met Bruno Reusser when he was helping build a house further up the valley, and married him in his native Switzerland. How did Bruno handle that? He said, 'I'm happy here. I leave here less than my wife does.'

'We both really like fishing, being self-sufficient, working outside and gardening,' Sue said. Just as well, for there was a lot of that in the community, along with building their own houses, growing, catching and making all their own food, running their mussel farm and getting to and fro. Their lovely old launch lay at its mooring in the bay.

They raised three daughters within the community and shared the Barrier experience of watching them leave. Now grandchildren came — to visit.

Sue said rather sadly, 'When we all had young families here it was different. Then, all the kids played together and people looked after them.

'There are no small children here now. But we get together for meals, casual meetings, we've had a lot of working bees, and we always have a nice picnic sitting on a field or in the bush somewhere.'

Back into Sven's boat, out through the mangroves, past the teal, past poor Annie Flinn's grave standing behind a white picket fence on a little headland.

Annie was a Sanderson, born on the ship *Tybernia* carrying her large family from England. She was christened Annie Tybernia and married Thomas Flinn. She died in 1893, of measles and diphtheria. A few days later her daughter, Ann Winifred, died too. She had measles and could not survive without her mother's milk.

The Flinns were among the earliest settlers at Port Fitzroy and Flinns lived on the island still, Con Flinn famous for an escapade of his own.

Once he was sailing the 500-kilometre passage from Napier to Great Barrier in his old cutter *Ruakuri* when his boat was damaged in a fierce gale near East Cape, and blown 500 kilometres off the coast.

The gale raged for three days and at the end of it Con was able to make some running repairs and aim for land. He was even able to dry out his transistor radio and, on the midday news, heard that an official search for him had been abandoned, and that Great Barrier locals were organising a search of their own. Seventeen days after leaving Napier, unseen by searchers of any stamp, he limped into Port Fitzroy just as a Barrier search committee was meeting to discuss their next move. Someone looked out of the window and noticed a yacht sailing into the bay. He telephoned down to the committee: 'I reckon we've found him.' Con had sailed into his own rescue.

———

We went over to Sven's house. It took a little while, because we had to pass alongside his property and there was quite a lot of it.

People said he lived on an island. He didn't, but he might as well. His property was the end of a peninsula, cut off, boat access only. The house settled in a pretty garden beside a very large shed.

His father bought the property, against the wishes of his family. Sven's wealthy, aristocratic grandfather owned a grand house in Lower Hutt — Casa Loma, now listed as an historic place.

His mother, the contessa, used to servants and comfort, cried.

The farm was surrounded by water and small islands, 43 kilometres of coast with no road access, no telephone until 1996, a 90-minute trip along Fitzroy Harbour by open boat then a 5-kilometre walk to school.

'Sometimes by the time we got to the wharf the school bus had gone. So we had to walk. It'd take us all day to get to Okiwi, ready to hop on the school bus and come back home.'

The old homestead burned down and they moved into a one-roomed hut. Then his father was thrown from his horse while he was mustering and lay in plaster for months, leaving his unfortunate mother, the contessa, to do the hard work. When Sven's father recovered, his entire flock of 2000 sheep had been stolen.

Sven was sent to boarding school in Auckland, returned to the farm at 17, saw his father die of cancer, and found himself the owner of a ruined farm. At 21 he received a legacy from his rich grandfather. He spent it, he said, on sex, drugs, rock and roll. With more family money he and his mother began redeveloping the farm.

'But it got to the stage where we realised that it was a big black hole.'

Then he had an idea. At the end of a day's clearing scrub he'd get off his bulldozer and the air would be fragrant with the aroma of crushed kanuka and manuka.

Now, a young man from nearby had had a manuka splinter in his eye for days. Finally a doctor removed it and the eye healed perfectly.

The doctor wasn't surprised. He said ti tree had known antibacterial properties.

Sven had some expertise in distilling oil. He confessed to once growing cannabis and serving three months in jail for it.

He thought about the boy with the splinter in his eye, and the aroma. Then he made a few stills, experimented until he was producing 5 millimetres of ti tree oil a day.

The big shed beside his house now accommodated a giant kettle and a condenser which coiled from it like a python, into twirly tubes, through valves. Ti tree leaves went in one end and oil came out the other. It was selling well.

Sven inherited his title, count. Asked about it, here on his peninsula on a faraway island, he just shrugged. How would you measure the distance between Swedish aristocracy and this man in his spotty overalls and his wide Kiwi accent and the competent air of someone who'd wrestled his living from the wilderness?

———

Great Barrier's worst disaster was the SS *Wairarapa* sinking in 1894. Under the command of the veteran Captain John McIntosh the ship was steaming from Sydney to Auckland.

Right Gravesites, Katherine Bay

Despite uncertainty over her position, and dense fog, the ship slammed into Miners Head at full speed. Between 121 and 135 people died. The real number was uncertain.

Survivors clung to the cliffs for 36 hours above an awful soup of wreckage, cargo, bodies and the corpses of the horses. Two crewmen battled their way south for help.

It took three days for news of the tragedy to reach Auckland, but the Ngati Rehua people at Kawa responded immediately. They found the wreck and with settlers rescued the survivors, who they clothed, fed and housed, some for two weeks before they were taken to Auckland.

Now well-kept white fences surrounded two gravesites at Katherine Bay, one small, one a little bigger. Such tiny things for so much tragedy.

There was only one headstone, a memorial to Father Seraphim McIvor, who drowned. No one knew exactly how many people were buried there. Some bodies were later dug up and taken away by relatives, including that of a young woman found clutching her baby. Another gravesite lay at Tapuwai on the island's east coast.

The ship's cargo of oranges was washed up on beaches and trees grown from their seeds flourished.

I was interested in another famous Great Barrier wreck.

One spring night years before, I'd received a telephone call at my Christchurch home from a man named Rick Hellriegel. He was then one of the four most famous men in New Zealand.

They were the crew of the trimaran *Rose-Noelle*, which had been missing for 119 days on a voyage to Tonga.

They'd been given up for lost. In fact, their yacht had capsized off the Wairarapa coast, drifted for four months, and by some act of grace washed up in Little Waterfall Bay near Rosalie Bay on Great Barrier Island.

It took another day and night to climb the cliffs to a house on Windy Hill. They found food and clothing, and beds, and a telephone in a neighbouring house, and from there told the world of their survival. First to reach them was the Great Barrier constable, Shane Godinet.

I was writing for the *NZ Listener* then. Rick and one of his crewmates, Jim Nalepka, wanted to tell me their story. It took weeks, for they were both still weak, both physically and emotionally exhausted, and could only talk in short bursts.

The Great Barrier house had been their salvation and they described every detail of it.

Much later I read Shane's account of their arrival on the Barrier. A writer rarely finds two people telling the same story of an event, let alone several. I was amazed that the three accounts fitted each other exactly.

Only the house was different, a quarter-century on. Its garden had grown, and it looked settled. It lacked the gravitas of an historic place. But it was.

Eileen Ngawaka grieved for her guavas, stripped from her trees by kaka and kereru. A real loss on an island where self-sufficiency was a way of life.

She and her Uncle Charlie were descendants of those Ngati Rehua rescuers.

After generations of intertribal warfare followed by the customary settler land grab, the tangata whenua had lost their land and were given a 2400-hectare reserve at Katherine Bay to call home.

Uncle Charlie lived in a bach up a long track lined with dead vehicles. He'd just returned from Auckland. He went there quite a lot, but seldom further. You've got to travel, he said.

Eileen Ngawaka sat in her living room lined with family photographs and mementoes. She ticked them off: five children, nine grandchildren and a great-grandchild on the way. 'They like to come home often, but there's no work for them here.'

Her son Brownie lived next door and was working on Raoul Island for the Department of Conservation. One island to another.

She was 84 years old and had lived on the Barrier for all but five of them, when she was sent away to escape a typhoid epidemic. Her four-year-old sister had died and on the day of her funeral her two-year-old brother died too. She was already a Ngawaka before she married her cousin. 'I didn't want to lose the name, see.' She laughed.

Above Uncle Charlie Ngawaka

She had grown up before she knew her island properly. When she was a child people walked tracks or rowed boats to get around. To her the southern end of the island had been as mysterious as New York.

More cousins lived on Flat Island, a fishing settlement off the coast, but she said, with a gesture like a wave of farewell, it wasn't like it used to be. Most of the family . . . 'Some have passed on, the younger ones have moved off the island.'

Now she spent her days knitting. Her favourite patterns were horses and reindeer, but penguins were creeping in, and surely that was . . . ? Yes, Scooby-Doo. She was looking at diversifying into cats, foxes, elephants. A whole menagerie waited to be knitted.

———

The ferry company in Auckland phoned. The ferry had broken down two and a half hours into its voyage to Great Barrier. The sailing we'd been booked on was cancelled. There'd be no sailing the next day nor, possibly, the day after.

Flights had been cancelled too, because of the weather. A few passengers stood in the little airport terminal, looking confused. When . . . ? How . . . ? No one knew. A nice woman at the desk, who seemed experienced in this sort of thing, booked us on a flight but said it probably wouldn't take off. If it didn't, well, there was always tomorrow.

Every islander we met simply shrugged. That was life on the Barrier. By then we were starting to get the swing of things. So we went to the Irish pub. And later, just as it was almost too late to go, the airline called. The pilot was prepared to try a last flight. We hopped smartly aboard and went home.

Opposite Eileen Ngawaka

Above Sisters

Rakitu/Arid

'The island seemed to rise from the sea in cliffs crowned with a wisp of bush, a thug in a wig.'

Captain Cook named this island Arid. It was a good description. The island seemed to rise from the sea in cliffs crowned with a wisp of bush, a thug in a wig. But Maori knew it as Rakitu. They found it fertile, and so did the European settlers who farmed it for more than a century.

The island may have looked barren but a wide green valley divided the land in half, as if it had been chopped with a blunt instrument.

Even by 1868 an expedition was reporting that 'Arid Island certainly does not deserve the name bestowed on it by Captain Cook. The high, rugged, desolate-looking cliffs, that encircle the greater part of the island, hide within them, beautifully sheltered valleys, covered with luxuriant fern and bush, and watered by streams which, uniting,

empty themselves into the small boat harbour on the west coast . . .'

That small harbour was its one landing, all but invisible. It snuggled into Rakitu from the northwest, a chink in the cliffs. Inside was a sandy beach and still water and a happy escape from the wild winds. This was the centre of Rakitu civilisation.

Maori cultivated these valleys for centuries. Rehua, the ancestral figure of Ngati Rehua/Ngati Wai, lived on Rakitu. They left pa and kainga sites.

European settlers followed. The Rope family farmed Rakitu for more than a century.

One of its most famous stories, still told on its near neighbour Great Barrier Island, was of the day Bryce Rope delivered a spare part for his bulldozer. Rope had been a Mosquito pilot in World War II

and another wartime pilot, Fred Ladd, ran an air service in the Gulf. Together they planned to drop the heavy part from Ladd's aeroplane into a paddock on Rakitu. They duly shoved it out the door, but instead of landing on the grass it killed the Ropes' prize bull.

In 1993 the government bought the island from the Ropes, who had insisted their island remain in New Zealand ownership. The family continued to farm it until 2010.

The Crown planned to hand over ownership to Ngati Rehua but in the meantime Rakitu was managed by DOC, open to the public, or at least those who could get there.

HAUTURU
/ LITTLE
BARRIER

'It looked steep, and riven, and wild, and stranger than any part of New Zealand I'd seen.'

At last, Te Hauturu-o-Toi, Little Barrier Island. Six months of negotiations had gone into getting here. We were allowed to stay one day only. This was not just a barrier to north winds rollicking down the Gulf. It was a bastion, fortress, refuge.

Every morning I made a cup of coffee, sat on my sofa and looked across the Gulf to the forbidden island. Often it was only the suggestion of an island, hazy below a bonnet of cloud. Sometimes the cloud shot straight up so the island looked like the volcano it once was.

Now, at last, here we were bounding across a big easterly swell, the island growing huge in front of us. It looked steep, and riven, and wild, and stranger than any part of New Zealand I'd seen. A crooked top cocked a snoot at all comers. Great cliffs repelled boarders, belittling the permits, regulations, cultural induction, quarantine, and minute inspections we'd gone through to get there.

All our clothing, shoes and gear had been inspected for creatures and seeds, minutely. Food was checked for banned substances, notably cucumber. Everything was packed in sealed containers.

Hauturu is 80 kilometres from Auckland, 27 kilometres from Leigh. Only an authorised boat could land you on the island, and it could only get you there if the weather allowed.

At the end of it all lay an island which was as close as you could get to the original New Zealand.

The island was not just an ark for endangered species. It was a place where some species had always lived without *being* threatened.

No harbours sheltered visiting boats. The single landing place allowed people ashore in fine weather and even then was precarious. Most humans had simply found Hauturu/Little Barrier too difficult and left it alone, allowing the forest and everything that lived in it to survive and sometimes even to flourish. This was one of the nation's few remaining vaults, at 3083 hectares a large one and arguably the most important.

Previous Hauturu/Little Barrier

Opposite Liam's museum, Hauturu

It was not entirely virgin, of course. Maori had been coming here for centuries, since the great navigator Toi te Huatahi nosed down this coast in the twelfth century.

Early Europeans had dabbed and jabbed. Rats and cats and the usual prowlers had had a crack at doing what they did so well, predating. But they were all gone now and the flightless, unprotected animals that had evolved in the absence of predators, those creatures which made New Zealand unique, were taking a cautious leap of faith.

A good two-thirds of the island was very much as it had always been. Those parts of the forest that had been cut more than a century or so ago were regenerating vigorously. Wildlife flew, hopped, crawled and slithered.

————

Steep shingle beaches lay on either side of Te Titoki, the only safe landing place on the island, although it stretched the meaning of 'safe'. Huge signs on both sides of the point announced '*No landing*'.

One of the two DOC rangers on the island, Richard Walle, had run his strong aluminium boat on its cradle down rails into the sea, where he sat just beyond the shore break. The idea was for our boat, skippered by Grant Sneddon, to pull alongside and transfer us and our gear into Richard's boat which would then be hauled back up to its shed, and safety. It worked, although the weather gods were kindly that day.

Richard lived on the island with the other ranger, his wife Leigh Joyce, and their children Mahina and Liam.

Immediately beyond the beach lay Te Maraeroa flat, where Maori had once lived and died.

Deep ruts had been gouged in the stone bank where waka had been pulled beyond the sea's reach.

Overgrown stone walls enclosed what had been gardens, acting as storage heaters. An old pa sat further along the flat, another on the headland high above, four more on top of cliffs that rose sheer from the sea. All of them had stone fortifications, very rare. Battles had been fought here, people had died, much of Te Titoki Point was tapu, urupa or burial grounds within.

Civilisations had been and gone, Maori and European, leaving only a few remnants. Now, DOC buildings huddled on the flat.

One of them was the rangers' house. I was curious.

What sort of coincidence was it that brought two people together, prepared not just to work but to live and raise a family in one of the most isolated places in all New Zealand?

Their story ran like this. Richard was a carpenter on the West Coast, working

Left Inside the cloud forest

on restoration projects for DOC such as Donovans Store in Okarito and the Fox River bridge.

Leigh was working on the rowi, the Okarito brown kiwi.

She was camping on the beach at Okarito when Richard came along. He invited her to dinner. They picked mussels on the way home.

It was a match made in conservation heaven. Leigh said: 'We had this amazing walk, up to the trig towards the mountains, we went up there for breakfast, had pancakes, watching the sun touch the mountains, then we walked down to the Three-Mile beach, and on the way we saw Hector's dolphins surfing on the waves and he'd never seen dolphins before, and cooked up billy tea, and he'd never had billy tea before, and we walked around and saw seals, and he'd never seen seals before, and we walked back to the beach, and it was such a beautiful day we thought we'd go kayaking up the lagoon a couple of days later, and we had another bonfire, and cooked tea over the fire in one of the little islands, and he'd never had tinned sardines before, and we kayaked back down the lagoon in the moonlight, and as we paddled there was a silver wake of phosphorescence. Then we went to Okarito, and stirred up the embers of a fire someone had left on the beach and got a big bonfire going, and we saw an aurora. And Richard was completely blown away.'

Oh, the romance of it, the beauty! Could anyone have resisted such magic? Not Richard. He had only one fear.

'I was too scared to ever come back because it was such magic.'

They worked on Stewart Island, then on Codfish Island off Stewart's west coast, centre of kakapo recovery. Leigh did her PhD on kakapo. They went to Bougainville, Papua New Guinea, with Volunteer Service Abroad (VSA) then returned to DOC work on Maud Island in the Marlborough Sounds for several years, then the rocky remote Stephens Island off the northern tip of D'Urville as relieving caretakers, then Hauturu.

They'd spent the night before we arrived on the island high on a ridge watching a kakapo nest. It looked to me a tough tramp up there but they were both rangy specimens.

Once, the island was home to half the world population of kakapo, the ground parrot. As their environment changed the birds faded away. They were transported to Codfish and Maud islands for safety, but later some were returned to Hauturu.

Now there were ten on the island, four females and six males, and the long-term plan was to have a self-sustaining population. The watchers hoped to see them raising chicks without outside help.

So they'd been waiting for Heather, the kakapo, to leave her nest so they could 'candle' her egg, the ancient technique of shining a light through the egg to check the embryo's health. The egg was small for such a big bird, like a pullet's.

Around dawn they thought they'd got lucky; Heather beeped one of the light beams which told the watchers she was off the nest. They made ready. Then, beep-beep-beep. Heather was like a kid before a sliding door, hopping back and forth across the beam. They gave up. They'd had enough fun for one night.

———

Leigh had grown up by the sea, the long, long beach running north from the Christchurch estuary, rowdy surf and sandhills, a free life of adventure that she wanted for her children. She seemed to have succeeded, all right.

The kids were home-schooled, of course, but all of those areas of child development in textbooks, cognitive, social, emotional, language, motor skills and so on lay just outside the door.

Both children had created little museums.

Mahina had a collection of abandoned nests and eggs, bellbird's, robin's, fantail's, a whitehead's nest so rare that not even Te Papa had one, as a visitor from the national museum noted enviously.

A kaka egg, kakapo and long-tailed cuckoo feathers, white kiwi feathers. ('Two people here have seen white kiwis.')

A bigger museum in the living room with Liam's favourite, a big piece of kauri gum with insects trapped inside. A little lava ball, broken open like a nut. A kaka skull, with beak. Bits of old crockery found in a creek. A giant centipede, Liam's favourite animal on the island not just because of its rather nasty bite but for its wave-like walk. A fibre ball left by a kaka which sucked the juice and spat out the rest.

Mahina told me of the day she'd seen 12 kokako feeding on the daisies in the lawn outside their house. If you were very quiet, she said, they'd stay, unless Liam came charging out of the door and scared them off. Said with an older sister's affection. Mahina could tell an entire story, in detail, without once using the word 'like', much less 'oh my god'.

Leigh said: 'And it's not about . . . stuff. When these guys were little on Maud Island we got given a bicycle for Liam and Mahina, that is, given to Mahina and passed down to Liam, already second-hand, and they were zipping around the farm tracks there and one of the training wheels broke. So Richard and Liam sat down and made a wooden wheel for his bike. I love that. It's all about making do with what you've got. When you're on an island you can't just pop down to the shop to buy something; the next service might not be for three weeks. So you just make do and improvise a lot. I really love that about living on an island.'

Liam was building a yacht with his dad to add to his fleet: one little boat he'd built himself sat on the beach, the *Sun Skipper*, bright and pretty, alongside his raft. His parents bought him the timber and left him to do whatever he wanted.

These people called themselves islomaniacs.

Following Images from Hauturu

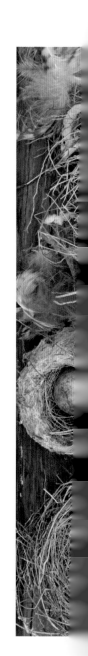

I'd heard island people call themselves island-keepers, or island hermits, or just plain islanders, but it was the first I'd heard of islomaniacs.

When their time on Hauturu was up they wanted to go to . . . another island.

———

Hauturu was a lifeboat, floating the pillaged and the endangered.

The hihi, or stitchbird, was down to a few survivors and all but unknown to most New Zealanders.

Andreas Reischek, who was a taxidermist for the Canterbury Museum, went searching for hihi in the 1880s in the virgin bush of Hauturu, 'resolved to seek him out or die in the attempt', he wrote in his book *Yesterdays in Maoriland*, amid 'giant kauri trees reaching skywards like mighty cathedral towers'.

Maori were then settled on the southwestern side but Reischek believed hihi might have survived on the precipitous, all-but-impenetrable other side of the island. There, in this primeval paradise, he found his bird.

'At last, after months and months of patient search, after traversing every part of this rugged island, and climbing up and down ranges 2000 feet above the level of the sea, in the deep and silent recesses of the Hauturu bush it suddenly appeared before me, like the blue flower of romance which at length crowns the efforts of the believing seeker.'

After shooting a few, and taking specimens for his boss Sir Julius von Haast and the naturalist Sir Walter Buller, he left the tiny hihi population even tinier.

But he'd found the birds, and they were saved from extinction when Hauturu became a bird sanctuary in 1894 and later a nature reserve. With care — there was a reason for the six months it took us to get onto the island — the unique stitchbird population had grown enough for the birds to be moved to other islands such as Tiritiri Matangi and Kapiti, and to wildlife sanctuaries. Now there were some 400 on Hauturu.

The new nature reserve was a wonderful thing for rare birds, but a tragedy for the Ngati Manuhiri who lived there.

The Crown had first tried to buy the island in the 1840s. Ngati Manuhiri and other residents objected. Negotiations stalled.

The great kauri forests of Hauturu sang their siren song to the empire-builders. But who owned the island? The cutting rights? The Native Land Court dillied and dallied and meanwhile the Crown was still banging on the door, not because of the stitchbird, but because of the late-nineteenth-century fear of Russians attacking New Zealand: the island was a strategic asset. The sanctuary came later.

How the people fought for their island, and how the Crown resisted. Many court hearings, years of petitions to Parliament.

As the people living on the land, winning sustenance from it, Ngati Manuhiri claimed manawhenua. Other iwi, Ngati Wai and Ngati Rehua, also claimed ownership.

The Crown had its way, of course. You couldn't fight Parliament Buildings. In the end they just took the island.

More than a century later, in 2011, Ngati Manuhiri got their island back — for one week. After seven days the island was gifted to the people of New Zealand, but not to their old adversary, the Crown. Ngati Manuhiri kept 1.2 hectares for themselves.

It's possible that the hihi's long whistle was one of relief.

————

We walked up a ridge track with Richard, Mahina and Liam. Ancient Maori pits lay on either side, amid regenerating forest: this was the easiest part of the island to reach and the side where kauri had been felled.

Virgin forest lay on the other side of the island, out of reach of all but the very fit and highly authorised.

Here we were walking where Maori had trod for centuries. Once someone had stopped to tie his bootlaces and seen a glint beside the track: a beautifully polished adze lay there, shining through the ages.

Thickets of regenerating kauri lay all around amid flourishing bush, fallen leaves coppering the forest floor. The cushioned feel of the deep forest. I could hardly believe my luck. On any world scale Hauturu was amazing. I was walking into something relatively untouched, as close as could be to what New Zealand was once like.

This place had shed its cats in the 1980s, its rats early in the new millennium, and its wildlife was celebrating. Endangered species had found refuge here. The long, haunting cry of the kokako rang in the tops like an organ. Robins silently watched us pass. I heard the kik-kik-kik of kakariki, saw the dark shapes of kaka.

Somewhere in the understorey kiwi and tuatara ran about, kakapo boomed in the tops. Giant earthworms burrowed, native bats hid. Out on the rocky shore lay the only known breeding ground of the New Zealand storm petrel.

We climbed towards the cloud forest, where that cap of cloud I could see from my sofa on Waiheke had created its own rainforest. The kauri grew bigger, and fatter. One hundred and twenty years of protection had made some very big trees. Epiphytes dripped.

We headed towards the four-person kauri, so-called because four people could just clasp hands around it, where the remarkable, untrammelled, original, perfect Hauturu truly began.

Following Richard Walle and Leigh Joyce with Liam and Mahina

It began raining, hard. We walked back down, to the old village site among its rock walls on the flat.

Many things had happened here. People lived, fought, died.

Te Ao Rosieur told me one of the strangest stories I'd ever heard.

She was a direct descendant of Hauturu's last Maori resident, Rahui Te Kiri. Rahui and her husband Tenetahi had fought for her home to the end.

Up to then, I'd thought of the island as an ark, or New Zealand's safest, soundest wildlife vault. But as I listened to Te Ao it came alive, a place of magic.

Rahui was the daughter of Te Kiri, paramount chief of the Pakiri, Matakana and Tawharanui areas. She and Tenetahi had rescued Maori imprisoned on Kawau during the Waikato war. She was a formidable woman who was not going to be pushed around.

She and Tenetahi lived on Hauturu and raised their six children there.

When the Russian scare made the Crown eye the island as a fortress, several hapu contested ownership, expensively. Many years of court hearings followed. At last, one day in 1886, Rahui and Tenetahi were named among the list of owners.

Now Andreas Reischek took the stage, literally. That same day he presented his research on the island's birds to the Auckland Institute. There was a surge of support for the island to be set aside as a refuge for endangered birds, the plight of the hihi, stitchbird, propelling the campaign.

One of the many ironies of this whole business was the fact that Reischek and Buller were lamenting the demise of the stitchbirds, one of the most important reasons for turning Hauturu into a reserve, and at the same time helping the birds on their way to extinction by killing many of the remaining hihi as specimens and exhibits. That the birds survived the ravages of both enemies and friends was miraculous.

The government offered to buy Hauturu. On behalf of the owners Tenetahi agreed to sell, for £3000, plus costs.

More wrangling with the Crown followed.

The government's dealings became so murky that the owners withdrew their offer to sell, and called tenders for felling the kauri. The government then bought the island compulsorily, and paid Tenetahi's and his family's share into the public trustee.

Tenetahi, Rahui and their children refused to accept it. The money was never taken and was one of the grievances only accepted and addressed by the Crown in the Ngati Manuhuri settlement of 2011.

Meanwhile in one of the dawn raids that a later twentieth-century government found so useful, a mixed force of bureaucrats, soldiers and police on 20 January 1896 forced Tenetahi, Rahui and remaining Maori off the island. Rahui was last to be manhandled into the boat.

Rahui returned to her home on Hauturu three times. The amazing thing about that story was the way she got there.

At least once, for accounts vary, she swam from the mainland. A distance of 38 kilometres through the ocean. A very long, hard swim. Once, as she was being removed yet again, she jumped overboard and swam back.

According to Andreas Reischek: 'Rahui, I may say, is five feet ten inches tall, and the possessor of a fine if muscular figure.'

The government finally gave her a choice: stay on the mainland, or go to jail.

Rahui had become legendary since. She was said to have had her sight restored, at 100 years old, by Tahupotiki Wiremu Ratana, the faith healer who founded the Ratana church.

She was taken to him by two chiefs, carrying her so her feet didn't touch the ground, and at the end she rose to her feet and walked out. She died soon after in her pa at Leigh.

The photographs accompanying her obituaries showed an immensely strong face, hair cropped short like a helmet, a formidable woman.

Tenetahi died in 1927. He was 97. Rahui died in 1930, aged 100.

————

I raised the lid on a box, revealing a tuatara. He looked indignant, I thought, but stayed exactly where he was. The species didn't get through the millennia by taking fright easily.

In 1990 only nine adult tuatara were found on the island. Now there were a couple of hundred, at least, raised in a captive breeding programme run by Leigh and Richard. Usually the eggs were sent to Victoria University for incubating but this year all 19 of them had been kept on the island, and incubated in the kitchen cupboard. All of them hatched, Mahina and Liam doing their schoolwork while baby tuatara broke out of their eggs on the kitchen table. They were kept in an enclosure for a year, then a bigger enclosure for another year, growing big enough to escape ruru, or moreporks, and predation.

Some of the original adults found in 1990, saviours of their species, were still there in their plywood refuges. We were looking at the last of the *sphenodons*, essentially unchanged for 240 million years.

We searched for Rudolph, one of the originals from the 1990 search. There he was in a corner, a wise old eye slanting up. A third eye somewhere inside checked circadian rhythms and seasonal cycles.

I dropped him a worm. Two rows of teeth on his upper jaw and one row on his lower snapped over it. He grunted faintly.

Above Pohutukawa forest,
Te Maraeora

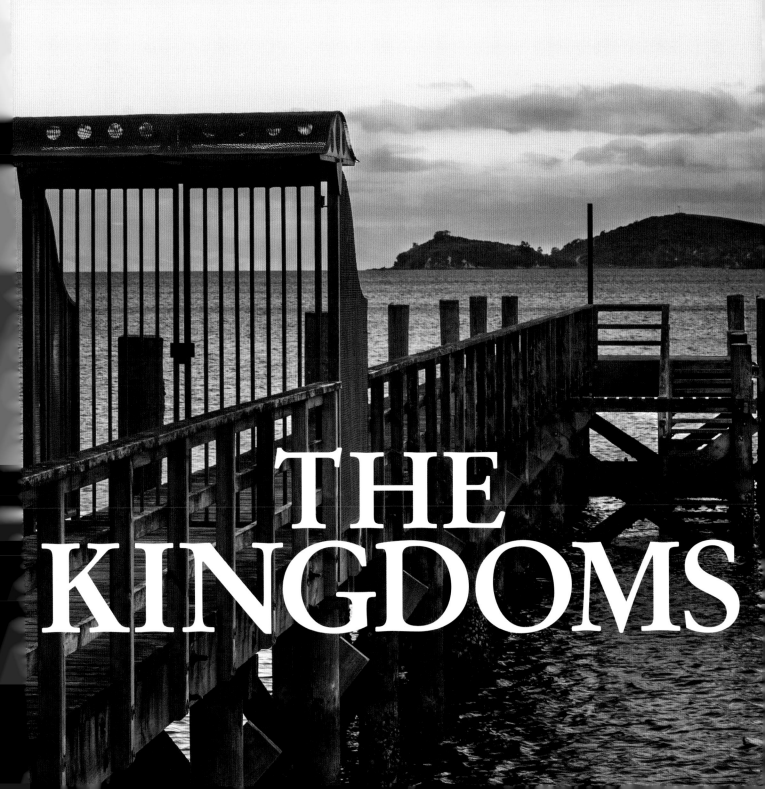

THE KINGDOMS

PUKETUTU

'It was not a huge house by modern
New Zealand standards, but grand enough in
a more egalitarian era when even a business
baron lived comparatively modestly.'

Early maps, circa 1853, showed Puketutu Island deep in the Manukau Harbour, thin channels threading the soft mud surrounding it. The mud became a sandbar which became a causeway. The path to the island grew from low tide only, to half-tide, to any tide.

Yet this was still an island in every sense. Once, natural attrition kept people out. The island was simply too hard to get to. Now you could drive onto it, but not *into* it. Puketutu was private property, and when the road stopped, so did you. The island had been turned over to the public; but just when the public would be able to go there remained unknown.

Most people didn't care very much, because Puketutu remained largely unknown, even in Auckland. If you said you were going to Puketutu, people said, 'Where?' Outside Auckland they simply looked blank.

This was once the private domain of one of New Zealand's best-known business figures, Sir Henry Kelliher, whose most famous venture was Dominion Breweries.

Puketutu started life as a series of volcanic eruptions some 25,000 years ago. The eruptions formed an island of 197 hectares. It was occupied by Maori for centuries.

The island was originally bought from Maori, Te Kawau of Ngati Whatua and three others who claimed to own it, at what any businessman would see as a good price, five pounds and ten blankets. A subsequent owner, Henry Weekes, paid two hundred pounds for it barely a year later in 1846 and Puketutu became known as Weekes Island. One more owner later, Puketutu became the property of John Logan Campbell, so-called 'father of Auckland'.

Campbell was the man who gave Auckland its Cornwall Park, the 172-hectare park so close to Puketutu in size that the island was often compared with it in terms of what it might become.

According to *Puketutu and its People*, by Paul Goldsmith and Michael Bassett, the island played another part in New Zealand history: Te Pu-rakau, a mighty puriri tree on the island sacred to Maori, was felled for fence-posts. That night,

Pages 88–9 Pakatoa

Previous Baronial paradise

Opposite Entrance hall, Kelliher homestead

a mighty storm wrecked the naval corvette HMS *Orpheus* on the Manukau bar, the nation's worst shipwreck with 189 lives lost. Were the two connected? Maori thought so.

Henry Kelliher bought Puketutu in 1940, as farm and sanctuary. The former drover, Gallipoli and Somme veteran was a wealthy man of varied business interests by then. Most famously he was boss of Dominion Breweries whose brand name Waitemata Ale was on everyone's lips, literally.

Why would Sir Henry have chosen Puketutu, in the teeth of the westerlies, rather than an island in the more Pacific gulf?

Goldsmith and Bassett said only: 'Its natural beauty and proximity to Auckland have long made it a desirable asset.' He bought it for weekends and holidays, but it became first a wartime refuge then a permanent home. He developed the island as a farm, then established plantations, and later quarried rock: Puketutu's volcanic history lived on in Auckland airport runways and city motorways.

His lasting monument was the homestead. It was built by previous owners, the Bull family, after their old, two-storeyed wooden homestead burned down, apparently when a fur coat was left on a heater.

The Bulls, with that New Zealand penchant for importing northern architecture into the South Pacific, went for the Spanish Mission style. They built a two-storeyed hacienda on a flat piece of land sheltered by the biggest of the volcanic cones.

The Kellihers made it their permanent home, added a library, redesigned and redecorated, surrounded the house with exotic and native gardens, fountain, ponds,

Above and opposite Inside the Kelliher homestead: Sir Henry's portrait; a crest in the door; a hidden bar

paths, even a Samoan fale. The place became a social centre, glittering with names, everyone from the German raider Count von Luckner to the actress Vivien Leigh.

By far the most famous, however, walked on all fours: Cardigan Bay, the racehorse which was showered, deluged, with honours. He featured on postage stamps and cake tins. He retired in 1968 at a ceremony in the United States attended by the New Zealand Prime Minister, Sir Keith Holyoake, and was put out to pasture on Puketutu, living on Sir Henry's stud farm for the next 19 years until he died.

Cardigan Bay, celebrated in obituaries around the world, was buried at Auckland's racecourse Alexandra Park near the Hall of Fame with its special sections devoted to the horse.

Gavin Steiner, who now looked after the homestead, was given the last surviving horse on the island, Hammer, as a gift. Hammer shared Cardigan Bay's paddock.

Sir Henry raised prize cattle too. What happened to his prize bull? I asked Gavin. 'He's on the floor, in the cigar room.' Hammer, still going strong, cruised the green pastures behind stone walls near the old stables.

Gavin had lived and worked on Puketutu for 20 years. He loved the island, breathed it, only crossed the causeway to the mainland when he had to. 'If you took the causeway away,' he said, 'I wouldn't know it was gone for a few weeks.' He offered a glass of island water: 'The most beautiful water you'll ever taste.'

He loved the company he worked for too, Dawsons (whose principals were godfathers of his children), and saw them as saviours of the old homestead, deserted and deteriorating after Sir Henry's death. Dawsons, an Auckland firm, ran the place as a venue for weddings and events, leasing the house and its 3.6 hectares from the Kelliher Charitable Trust.

It was not a huge house by modern New Zealand standards, but probably grand enough in a more egalitarian era when even a business baron lived comparatively modestly.

All of the original furniture and most of the art had been removed, but the house had been carefully maintained as it was. Its hardwood floors glistened, panelled walls glowed.

Yet the place was surprisingly modest, for a Spanish Mission-type house.

Upstairs, the sun-filled main bedroom opened on to a terrace. Lady Kelliher's make-up room was as big as the average suburban bedroom and complete with mirrored walls and curved vanities all looking like a 1950s film set. But the house preceded the days of endless en suites. Lower-floor bedrooms were now kitchens and workrooms.

There was a big dining room, and a withdrawal room for the men after dinner, and a sitting room and a nice, shadowed refuge with an inlaid walnut slide screen which lifted, Bond-like, to reveal a bar behind. The story went that Sir Henry believed his wife knew nothing about the hidden bar and he and guests would slope off for a secret drink. 'You can't fly on one wing,' Sir Henry would declare, a saying heard over ten thousand jugs of DB in a thousand public bars.

I said, 'A lot of people don't know about this island.'

Gavin: 'I think it's to do with the fact that the Kelliher family kept quiet about things and why not? They didn't feel they owed the public an explanation. It adds to the mystery of the place.'

Sir Henry died in 1991. He'd had a strong social conscience, supporting Labour's social security policies, and certainly would have approved the Kelliher Charitable Trust's resolve to restore the island to its original condition and turn it over to the public. The old quarries were to be filled in with biosolids from Watercare's waste treatment plants, and yes, biofill was exactly what you'd imagine it would be.

The island was still not open to the public and there was no telling when it would be. Gavin Steiner was punting decades. Hoping for decades too. Yes, the island would make a wonderful regional park. But oh, the people, the rubbish, the graffiti. Instead of just leaving stuff alone.

He said: 'I wish there wasn't a causeway out here. I wish that Puketutu was somewhere up north, out of the public eye. Because then the council wouldn't care about it.' He sighed. 'The day the council turns up and says, you work for us now, will be the day I leave.'

Causeway, public or not, Gavin in every respect was an islander, an island-keeper, feeling the beauty, revelling in the solitude, grateful for his life.

One of the original paintings still hung in the entry foyer. It was a portrait of Sir Henry, by his daughter Pamela. Sir Henry was sombre, dark hair and widow's peak looking patrician, as if he were holding audience.

Which he did, every morning and evening, to a loyal following of one. Then, Gavin Steiner paid his dues.

'When I leave at night, I've done my check, I come down from my office, I always walk past his portrait and say, "Good night, Henry, I'll see you in the morning."'

'I guess it sounds a bit weird.'

Probably not to Sir Henry.

PAKATOA

'Paradise met the fate of many businesses
in the late twentieth century, an era of
silver tongues and sharks' teeth.'

n the 1960s and 1970s there was a cinema routine called 'intermission', known down in the stalls as half-time. It filled the gap between the shorts and the feature film. Having stood for 'God Save the Queen', customers filled intermission with various activities. Mainly, everyone rushed outside for a fag.

Those who stayed could watch advertisements, often for cigarettes: Du Maurier, full of elegant women in white, were my favourite, the smokes hidden at home in the tallboy.

The best was an advertisement for an island paradise, full of women in two-piece bathing costumes around a blue pool. Men in polo shirts and two-toned wing-tips played golf, palm trees swaying overhead, azure sea lapping golden sands. Everyone sighed. Those Pacific islands. Fabulous.

Hang on. This was . . . New Zealand. Pakatoa? Where on earth was that? (We were down south.)

Sir Robert Kerridge, who at one point owned a cinema in every decent-sized New Zealand town and city, had added tourist hotels to his portfolio. Kerridge Odeon built a resort on Pakatoa Island in the Hauraki Gulf and introduced a hydrofoil to the Waitemata to carry guests across the water.

A friend of mine went to Pakatoa for her honeymoon. She returned with convincing descriptions of paradise. Had she held on for a few years she might have met Russell Crowe, the film star, who at 17 became entertainments officer on Pakatoa.

Now, this was a reverse in Pakatoa's history. Never more than a stopping place for Maori, for it had no fresh water, it was bought by the Salvation Army as a lock-up for inebriates, first for men, then for women. The purchase took place in the early 1900s and a contemporary article in the *Otago Daily Times*, based on a story from an elderly man who was one of the first to be sent to the Inebriates Home there, set out the flavour of the place.

Twenty people lived on the island then, in a self-supporting community.

They gardened, fished, cooked, and when they were not working, wandered the island at will, swimming, sleeping, reading. 'The life was in many respects ideal.'

Others . . . well. 'They were, if not criminals, men of arrant laziness . . .'

How like the tourists Kerridge longed to attract.

Men were transferred to the neighbouring island Rotoroa in 1911 and Pakatoa then became home to wayward women, to the delight of passing sailors. The women stayed until 1942, when Pakatoa became a retreat for aged men until sold in 1949.

For almost half a century Pakatoa was used for drying out its inhabitants.

Kerridge put the plan in reverse. For a quarter of a century Pakatoa was known as the party island, replete with competitions for the biggest bar tab.

But the resort business was hard when you were out in the Hauraki Gulf, a long journey from Auckland and even longer when azure seas turned nasty. Everyone faced the same hurdles: guests, staff, suppliers. Easier and often cheaper to hop on a jet plane and wing away on a trip to Fiji.

Paradise met the fate of many businesses in the late twentieth century, an era of silver tongues and sharks' teeth. Kerridge Odeon merged with a company called Pacer Pacific headed by David Phillips. His empire did not survive the sharemarket crash of 1987. A German, Ralf Simon, and a Briton, Giovanni Di Stefano, both revealed ambitious plans for the island. Both proved dodgy and exited the country, hurriedly. Simon promised helipads, an international golf course and even an unlikely English country garden for Pakatoa but spent many subsequent years in German jails, once breaking out of the allegedly impregnable Oldenburg Prison. Di Stefano was a convicted fraudster once described by a judge as 'one of life's great swindlers'.

Poor Pakatoa sailed on, decaying but beautiful.

———

The island was bought in 1994 by John and Bernice Ramsey, who owned Mt Pember station, a conglomeration of stations and runs in Canterbury, and Crusader Meats, a big meat, pelts and wool exporting business.

Surprisingly John, Bernice, their two sons and daughter and partners had a go at running the resort themselves. John said: 'I went out at the weekends. I was caretaker and barman.'

They ran their own ferry from Auckland and Coromandel but getting staff to work on the island was always a problem. That was another island quandary: guests stayed for days, but staff had to spend weeks at a time there, and evidently the island idyll could not withstand the battering.

The Ramseys' resort business lasted six years. It was, John said, hard work. 'And you didn't make any money.'

One Sunday evening Bernice got fed up and dropped a letter of resignation on her husband's desk. The family packed up and left.

Pakatoa was back on the market, 24 beach-side cabins, 38 two- and three-bedroom units. Nine-hole golf course. Pool, landing strip and consents for development.

When I visited it, the island was still for sale and I got the impression that John was not all that keen on selling. He and his family used it as a holiday home, each with their own favourite unit. Quite a luxury: perfect beaches, lots of sunshine, plenty to do, no crowds on the golf course, and your choice of where to spend the night.

'It's our holiday home,' said John, who'd once bought the Benneydale pub after its latest owner shut it down. John became a local hero.

'If someone has a big chequebook, a very big one, they can buy it. I don't care what happens. People pay more for a holiday home than we paid for the whole island.'

Opposite The stage is set, Pakatoa

On Pakatoa everything was left as it was.

It was a private island, closed to the public. Nothing intrigued people more. Boaties took no time at all to realise the island was untenanted and unguarded, no one around to chuck them off. Open slather followed, 'rape and pillage', according to Nigel Atkin, who became one of Pakatoa's two guardians.

He and his partner Fiona Powell came to the island in 2010, the result of a random telephone call. They stayed for several years before they were headhunted for a stint on another rich man's island in the Cavallis, for they were now members of a select profession.

Fiona, the businesswomen, called them island-keepers, rather like lighthouse-keepers, people willing and able to look after their equipment and live or even thrive on their own.

Committed professionals were hard to find: many dreamed of an island to themselves, not so many could take the isolation.

Motukawaiti in the Cavallis was developed as a spa but no one had been there for a year and it needed work. Buildings needed maintenance, the jetty was washed out, the generator broken down . . . Nigel was one of those handy men who could do anything: overhaul engines, rebuild his own boat. He'd once done a spot of surgery on the dog under a vet's direction, and even repaired his own teeth with Araldite.

He'd fixed much of the island when John Ramsey called and asked them back. So he and Fiona returned to Pakatoa.

———

Nigel picked us up from Man O'War Bay on Waiheke Island in an aluminium boat less than 3 metres long. The day had a metallic look about it, threatening to get worse, and the chop was building out in the channel. He was unworried, sneaked along Waiheke's lee as long as possible then made a run for it, beaching near the jetty where the hydrofoil once disgorged hundreds of expectant tourists.

For a moment Pakatoa looked just like those ads in the intermission. Holiday units shone in the morning light. Golf carts stood ready to carry players to the course up the hill. Restaurant windows gazed out on the sea. The reception desk lacked only a perky person with a smile. It just needed people to bring back the half-time commercial.

They were absent. Not a soul but ourselves. For the very first time, I felt like Jack Nicholson. In *The Shining*. Curing his writer's block by taking on a job as caretaker in the deserted Overlook Hotel. Nigel, whose role was a bit closer to Jack Nicholson's than mine, loved it.

'I'm as happy as a pig in muck.'

Through reception. Wood-panelled. Four couches and a Space Invaders machine. A Benson & Hedges mirror: *Discover Gold!* Souvenirs: Pakatoa Island caps, polo shirts, postcards. Ancient flyers: 'The golden beaches and relaxing island lifestyle are ready and waiting . . .' And waiting.

Golf clubs out the back ready for the course, tennis racquets for the court, cricket pads, sun umbrellas. Uniforms on hangers, white short-sleeved shirts and brocaded waistcoats. The shop ready to serve ghostly figures populating the pool court, cash register open, cartons of crisps and sno-cones at the ready, bundles of the special Pakatoa currency available for exchange.

A pool with a few centimetres of water in the bottom. Barbecues rusting beneath a collapsed pergola. Spa pool in an octagonal building, bowling green in front with balls ready in its gutter. Restaurant ('licensed') gazing over lawns to a perfect view of sea and islands. Conservatory now missing. Kitchen with metres of stainless steel glinting dully. Bar menu, hot dogs (battered), $2.50. Yum. The dance floor now crusted with bird poo from the weka waltz. A disco ball glittering above. A wall featuring a lurid sunset through palm trees, looking like a film set. ('It *was* a film set,' Fiona said. 'More like *Hi-de-Hi* than *The Shining*,' said Nigel.)

The bar set with bottles, Pepe Lopez, Galliano, Campari, blue Curaçao. There used to be more, but, said Nigel, 'Twenty years of people raping and pillaging, wandering off with televisions, radios . . .'

He said: 'Every day is a good day. If you can't be happy out here you don't deserve to be out here. You can have the worst day with machinery failing, or banging your toe, and you've only got to look out the window. It wouldn't work if your partner didn't embrace it.'

Above A palmy paradise

Following Inside the island idyll: just add guests

Fiona did. A self-employed publisher who had started the magazine *Her Business* and was once named business editor of the year, she maintained a strict routine on the island, in her office every day from 10 am to 6 pm.

Outside, holiday units lay brazen in the sun, like another film I once saw, everyone lazing around on a beach in sunglasses and striped hats until one of them toppled sideways and it turned out that a nuclear explosion had petrified them all.

Fiona said: 'I never made a bed. Whenever the room was a mess we just moved into the next one.' She was joking, but it could have been true.

Pohutukawa Lodge, the most expensive rooms in the resort, and right on the beach, gazed vacantly over the sea. The owners and their families still came to stay there at Christmas.

We walked over to the conference centre, spreading comfortably against a hillside. Two storeys, Tui Room, Kakariki, Fantail, Kiwi rooms. The carpet smelling like a vege garden and an easy walk over to the squash courts and gymnasium, exercycles with that abandoned look of gym gear in a thousand suburban garages.

Two tennis courts. Neat staff quarters that once accommodated 28 people in the glory days before cheap weeks on Plantation Island killed it.

Mainland electricity and telephones in every room of the resort. The mains cable to the island was severed and never repaired. Diesel generators powered the island now.

Yards full of everything from mysterious machinery to concrete kiwis. Floats from wartime submarine nets. If you needed anything here, you just fossicked. You were bound to find it, somewhere.

How strange all this was, one thought; but strangeness was in the island's genes.

Nigel and Fiona were getting rid of the phoenix palms, yes, those swaying palms that once were Pakatoa's signature, but they seeded like grass on the island, so invasive they crowded out other species. They were keeping only the most iconic. Without them, pohutukawa were flourishing.

They got rid of the rats, too. They would have got rid of the weka transferred to the island by DOC, probably, if they had not been protected. An aversion to weka was common on Gulf islands, where they were seen as pests.

The two were encouraging other species. Geckos and skinks would be fine. More shore birds. Rare dotterels once nested there, until weka came.

Nigel said: 'This island is pest-free. We didn't need scientists, DOC, plans, we just did it. You can do it without involving 25 committees. Just do the bloody thing.'

———

The Ramseys closed the resort in 2000. Family members ran it as a party island for a while, but it had been stagnant since 2001.

Everything had been for sale since.

You could not help but look at the island and get ideas. All those buildings, the cabins and bars and restaurants and conference centre and gym and everything, and all going to waste, why, wouldn't it be wonderful if . . . ? Most had been tried.

The weekend resort. The party island. The boaties' paradise (Warning: boaties found on the island after midnight, asleep, say, under a palm tree, would be charged a full night's accommodation.)

Most of them were stymied by a single problem: getting people, guests and staff, onto the island and off again. Various ferries, varying degrees of success, the overheads, the expense, the uncertainty. Nigel summed it up: 'You don't know if you're going to get twenty people out for the weekend, or two hundred, or none.'

Yet the island itself remained as it always was, close to perfect.

Nigel and Fiona dreamed of environmental rebirth. Perhaps something like neighbouring Rotoroa, bought by a wealthy family and handed over to a trust as a publicly accessible reserve.

Meanwhile, said Nigel: 'It is a privilege and a pleasure to be out here. We have carte blanche on a beautiful island in the Hauraki Gulf, just Fiona and I.'

Fiona: 'The reality is, it's really isolated, there are events we miss out on, or have to rush away from, even going shopping on a bad day, getting wet.'

Nigel: 'It's an adventure, so cool, just so cool.

'The best thing that's happened to Pakatoa in the last twenty years is that nothing's happened to Pakatoa. It deserves a bit of respect. It's a tribute to John, if he's done anything he's done nothing. It could have been a casino or full of gated communities with people in hundred-thousand-dollar yachts but nothing has happened. The island's had time to catch a breath, be respected, get a bit of mana back. Rotoroa is not about money. And Pakatoa will never make money. Its value is as a piece of the Hauraki Gulf.'

We walked down to the beach, followed by their crippled pet seagull Kate. The bird couldn't fly. Nigel was making her a helium balloon with a basket underneath to carry her into the sky: 'Because she'd enjoy it big time and she shouldn't be deprived.'

Then we crammed into his little boat and banged off into the channel. The south wind had got up, the boat bucked, spray flew. Nigel shouted through the noise. 'Could be worse. We could be on the Northwestern motorway.' It was dusk, but he had to get back. A French friend was leaving Auckland to sail across the Pacific. He was calling by with a bottle of champagne.

THE
NOISES

'This was the house that Captain Wainhouse
built. It was white with green window
surrounds, cute as a button, with a little
verandah in front, small as a playhouse.'

Early in 1827 the French explorer Dumont d'Urville was feeling his way into the Hauraki Gulf. He'd had a truly appalling voyage from East Cape, almost losing his ship several times. He'd rounded the northern tip of Great Barrier Island, calling the sharp rocks there the Pointe des Aiguilles, The Needles.

'As we got beyond The Needles,' according to d'Urville's journal, 'we discovered one by one the many islands scattered across the entrance to Shouraki Bay [Hauraki Gulf], a view that produced the most picturesque, vivid impression.'

Deep in the Gulf he came across a sprinkling of islands and islets, some no more than rocks. Searching for something homely half a world from home he named this group Les Noisettes, hazelnuts. That name didn't translate as well; it became the Noises.

The islands did not look at all like hazelnuts. The Noises fitted them better. The tides running through them, the waves smacking them, composed their own symphonies.

The group lay 2 kilometres northeast of Rakino. The biggest of them, Otata, was only 21.8 hectares. Then came Motuhoropapa (9.5 hectares), with a hut built by the old Wildlife Service. Then Maria (Ruapuke), whose light flashed thrice in the night, 2 hectares. The David Rocks lurked in the sea.

It was not easy to believe people could live on any of them, but they did, for this large group of islands was privately owned.

The owners were not rich families or individuals seeking to create private domains. Instead, they went back more than 80 years and were happy for the public to visit.

A Captain McKenzie, master mariner, owned the Noises in the 1920s. He sold them to his friend, another master mariner, Captain Frederick Wainhouse, in the early 1930s, for £200.

Captain Wainhouse, clearly a man who liked his own ship, bought them to retire onto. His family described him as a classic old sea-dog with a cap and a pipe hanging out of his mouth.

Captain Wainhouse married Margaret Neureuter. Their family spent summers on Otata, shepherded through surrounding minefields by the Marine Department during the war. Then nine months of the year. Then all year round.

They had no power or refrigeration or any kind of communication. They grew vegetables, an orchard, kept chickens, brewed their own beer.

Captain Wainhouse died on his island. A fire on the beach signalled his death.

His widow handed the islands on to her nephew, Brian Neureuter.

He and his wife Marlene lived there in summer with their three children, Sue, Rod and Zoe, and when the parents died, their ashes were scattered on Otata.

———

Now, the Noises were owned by Sue, Rod and Zoe Neureuter; safe hands.

Some islands around the country had been bought by people who then declared them exclusive and repelled all boarders.

The Neureuters took another approach, summed up by Sue like this: 'If you'd gone as far as getting there, and wanted to go for a walk, you should be able to go for a walk.' Her brother Rod said: 'If people make the effort to get there they're probably going to like the place.'

For getting there wasn't easy, a long way by boat from Auckland, a difficult anchorage and a tricky landing when you reached Otata, the only island where a casual visitor would want to stroll. Closer, the little islands were covered in bush. Orangey cliffs glowed on Otata.

The island ended in a scrawny neck topped by a rocky head, a steep shingle beach on each side. In any sort of wind one or both beaches were tricky. A flat calm was best.

Glimpses of white showed through bush as we approached the beach.

This was the house that Captain Wainhouse built. It was white with green window surrounds, cute as a button, with a little verandah in front, small as a playhouse. Bedroom kitchen living room and all. Penguins lived beneath the floor. The old captain must have been careful when he stretched.

A later lean-to at the back extended it from tiny to very small. It was filled with holiday stuff, snorkels lamps longlines nets pumps ropes tarps tubs. Simple table, board bunks, nostalgia, that particular shade of bach-green everywhere.

The bach was never locked. Once, when they were young, every single window in it was broken. Only the odd vandal had visited since, but they counted themselves lucky. They loved their bach, its simplicity offering no temptation to thieves.

Outside, under a corrugated-iron roof, sat a dining table, a sink and bench,

Above Tricky landing on
Otata and (left) a dot of
white: the cottage

a cooking fire, mostly built from driftwood and flotsam, lovely to sit under in the afternoon sun.

They baked bread there, and this primitive kitchen could turn out a whole Christmas dinner, from turkey to pudding.

Family campsites were scattered around, for most preferred tents. Zoe's camp was a little further down the track, with her own composition of canvas and old iron. They were self-sufficient there, getting together with the rest of the family for the occasional dinner, which sounded odd to me, because this habitable part of the island was pretty small. They were talking about an area perhaps the size of a rugby field.

A fisherman's careless blaze set fire to the island in the early 1930s. Half the island was laid waste, but now a newcomer would scarcely notice.

Birdlife was restored and vegetation flourishing as much as it could on these rocky outcrops. Sea and land birds, lizards, skinks and snails roamed the islands. Tuis and bellbirds sang from pohutukawa. Giant weta had been released on Motuhoropapa.

The family had so carefully restored the native cover that one visiting group of botanists commended the Neureuters for keeping the Noises in such good condition: 'It was both refreshing and reassuring to see an inner Gulf island with a fully-functioning ecosystem.'

An 800-year-old pohutukawa, 70 metres across the crown and big enough to see on Google Earth, squatted on its throne above the house.

Water was a worry: they collected rainwater and by mid-summer it was running low. They didn't wash towels or sheets, took enough clothing for a month, restricted themselves to a few little bits of handwashing, and when Rod's wife Sharon opened the wash bag back home, she said, '*Pooooh*!'

Rod, Sharon, Sue and Zoe Neureuter now spent their own Christmas holidays on the island with their children, continuing the long summers of their youth as if the world had not changed one bit. The island was part of who they were, inside them forever. The Neureuters still arrived with as much food and as little clothing as they needed, lived on fish and shellfish and rainwater, played on the sea and in it, and were as happy as anyone could hope for.

Some things were different. The islands were healthier.

The Neureuters had taken care of the place, kept them free of weeds. Sue said: 'If you've grown up with a place, and you were taught to love it from when you were very young, you're better owning it, with that continuity. Otherwise, people come and go. I don't doubt their intentions but they don't have the same deep-seated love. We hope now to instil it in the next generation, which seems to be working.'

Rabbits and stoats were cleared from the island. Rats were deadly: on the tiny Maria/Ruapuke, once used for bombing practice then mostly cleared to make way for its lighthouse, rats had killed a thousand white-faced storm petrels.

The war against them was joined by DOC and conservation groups as well as the family and was won slowly, over years, Maria Island and the David Rocks becoming the first of the New Zealand islands to be declared rat-free. But rats could swim long distances. Puzzled conservationists discovered they were swimming from Rakino, 2 kilometres distant, until that island had its own rat eradication programme. The battle had been constant, but the rats were destroyed.

Except for Razza.

Razza the Rat was deliberately set loose on Motuhoropapa with a radio collar, to see just what he'd do, and how hard he'd be to get rid of. He proved as cunning as, well, a rat.

He quickly circumnavigated his new island then disappeared. His collar went dead. Oh dear, the search!

Quite by chance, Sue, walking on Otata, spotted a rat dropping. It was DNA tested. Razza. The first *scientific* proof that rats could swim long distances.

His place in history did Razza no good at all. He was trapped underneath the Neureuters' kitchen sink and that was the end of him. But he lived on in Witi Ihimaera's children's book, *The Amazing Adventures of Razza the Rat*, in which Razza was marooned by scientists, escaped, and became a (live) hero.

There'd been other dramas, including this curious story:

Zoe, very pregnant, had gone to the island with Brian and Marlene for the weekend. Unexpectedly, she'd gone into labour. They called a helicopter, lighting a signal fire on the beach to guide it.

Since then the rescue helicopter had been called twice more, once when Rod lacerated his foot, and again when he suffered a more serious accident. He'd been windsurfing when his kite whisked him out of the water and slammed him headfirst into a rock which, covered in oysters, was rather liking hitting a bunch of knives.

His head was split from front to back. Later, it was held together by 50 internal stitches and 30 staples.

The helicopter pilot by this time had a long experience of the Noises. He was the same one who'd taken Zoe to hospital 26 years before.

————

That Christmas, fine and calm, the Neureuters had counted some 200 boats around their islands. They were worried. Many of the boats were fishing but there weren't any fish left to catch.

The family, without refrigeration, had only ever caught what they could eat on the day. When they were children they had a ritual: in the evenings they'd go out with their father in the dinghy, only 100 metres or so off the beach, fish for 20 minutes to an hour, and come home with enough for the next day.

Zoe: 'Fish for breakfast and dinner.'

Rod: 'There were times when there was so much snapper on the plate . . . we weren't allowed to leave the table until it was all gone. Dad was not one for wasting anything. If we caught it, we ate it. Now they're catching small fish, if they're lucky. Basically for every legal snapper you're taking this year you're catching at least five undersize. It's the worst snapper fishing I can remember out there by a long shot.'

That summer they came across a fire left burning on the beach (there'd been a total fire ban on the island) with undersized snapper wrapped in tinfoil.

'Most people are only talking snapper and crayfish but other fish are suffering too. We've seen a huge proliferation in recreational spearfishing. They're going in and shooting territorial fish like red moki. Gill nets are set over the reefs. They're becoming barren of those fish.'

Boats were dredging for scallops and turning the seafloor to rubble. 'Death by a thousand cuts,' Sue said. Seabirds were disappearing, once-noisy colonies falling silent.

The Neureuters worried that if they plugged for a marine reserve around the Noises they'd meet the same resistance as a proposed reserve met on Waiheke and be shouted down.

'But something has to happen,' Rod said, 'a whole or partial marine reserve, and a general change of fishing practices. Recreational fishing is doing as much if not more damage than commercial. The commercial guys have to report their catch, why not recreational? If we don't, there won't be anything there. We're seeing a major decline in the marine health of the Gulf, and you just can't be quiet about it. You have to speak up and start doing something about it.'

So, they were campaigning for no-take zones over at least part of the group.

Rod Neureuter said: 'People automatically think we're millionaires but we're not. The islands are very close to my heart, and Sue's heart. We want to keep them pristine.'

The family trust which owned the island was due to divest in 2020, and the family was intent on long-term protection. 'We want to wrap them up in some way,' Rod said. 'We don't want them developed. They're little jewels. They're so valuable, not in terms of dollars, but in terms of the Gulf.'

Rabbit

'He said: "The tuis are back. The place is overrun with weka, little blue penguins nest everywhere. It's a different island now and it's amazing."'

Rabbit Island was a dot of a place between Kawau and the mainland. It was a second home to David and Sydney Lumsden, who bought it for $43,500 in 1976; islands were not so much a desirable accessory for arrivistes then, and cheaper.

'Rabbit' was one of several names for the place. It was one of a group once known as the Mayne Islands, after Edward Mayne, who was said to have been connected with Kawau's copper mining era. He owned a farm on Hobson Street, Auckland, now part of the central business district, which was then still prime grazing country. Mayne went on to become Sergeant of Arms in the New Zealand Parliament.

Rabbit Island's proper and much more musical name was Takangariki, or the short casting of the net. Its neighbour Takangaroa was the long casting of the net.

It had also been known as Pine Island, after the trees which made the tiny island look rather like a pin cushion.

When the Lumsdens bought the island they vowed to fell the pine trees, and so they did.

A local historian noted that the island then appeared to have had a haircut.

The Lumsdens promised to replace the pines with natives and turn the island into a wildlife reserve.

They did that too.

David Lumsden was Mayor of Newmarket then, and wore the chain for five terms, 15 years, until his borough became part of Auckland City in 1989.

Now he lived at Manly on the Whangaparaoa Peninsula and commuted across the water to his other home on Rabbit Island.

Three houses stood on the little island, one for the Lumsdens and one each for their daughter and son and their families.

Where grey pines once grew, pohutukawa and puriri now flourished. 'The tuis are back,' he said. 'The place is overrun with weka, little blue penguins nest everywhere. It's a different island now and it's amazing.'

David collaborated with Jim McAlpine on Kawau to start each New Year with a bang. He owned four cannon, two big, two smaller. ('I'm a bit of a buff.')

On the stroke of midnight each 31 December, following a tradition established by Governor George Grey on Kawau, he fired a cannon from Rabbit Island. An answering crash came from Jim's cannon ('medium-sized') on Kawau, then another blast from Rabbit. Very satisfying.

'We used to put tennis balls in,' he said. 'Now we just use gunpowder. Proper gunpowder, and it's not easy to get, either.'

ISLAND STATES

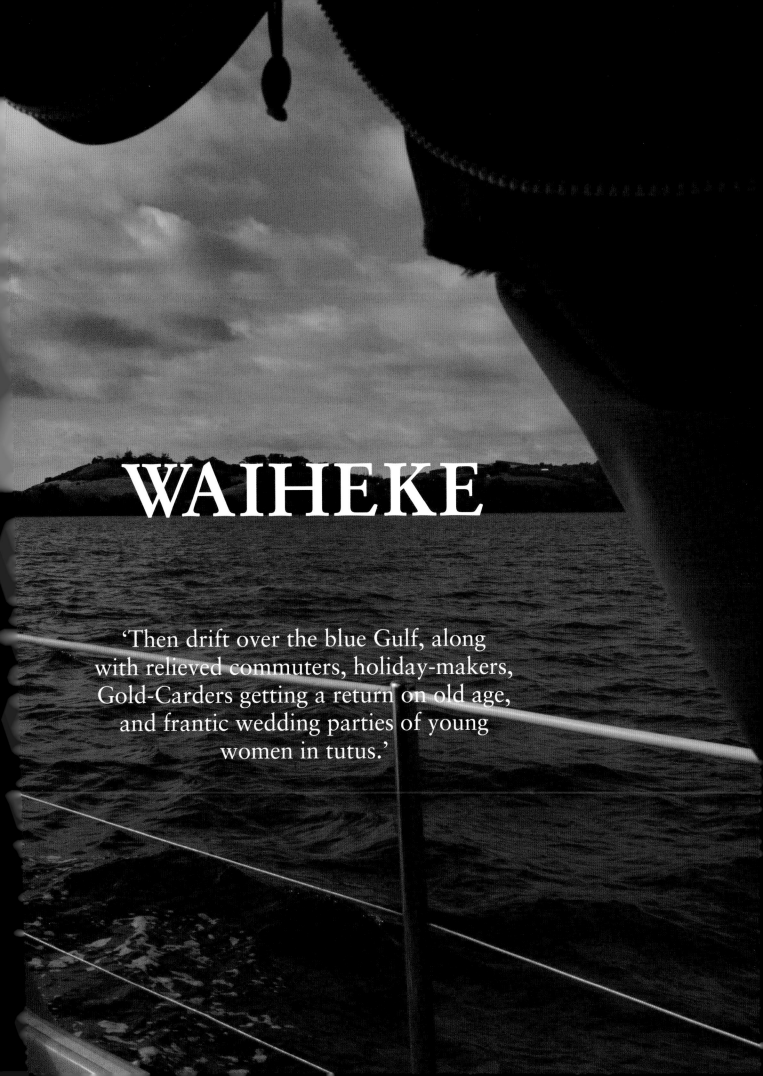

WAIHEKE

'Then drift over the blue Gulf, along
with relieved commuters, holiday-makers,
Gold-Carders getting a return on old age,
and frantic wedding parties of young
women in tutus.'

Some people were terribly excited when *Lonely Planet* named Waiheke Island as the fifth-best holiday destination in the world. Café owners, restaurateurs, vineyards, tourist bus operators, accommodation people and every shopkeeper who could sell so much as a straw hat, knelt down and felt the sun.

I lived on Waiheke Island and didn't much care.

The peace of the island, the fun of the place, the strength of its community, were more important. But in a place as beautiful as this one, they had to be fought for.

Developers had wanted to build a marina in Matiatia, where the ferries berthed. The idea didn't fit well on an island where small boats lazed on moorings. The community spent $430,000 batting the idea away. Another proposal immediately took its place, growing back like a flatworm's severed head. That was what being fifth in the world meant. Beauty was a business opportunity. Everyone wanted a piece of it.

When I first visited Waiheke many years before, it just seemed small, and hemmed in. I was from the South Island, where things were neither small nor hemmed in. I loved its mountains and its big skies, and its loneliness, and had a South Islander's distaste for the north.

I felt trapped on the island, and thought the people smug.

Thirty years on, one of my friends from those days still lived on the island, and no one felt smug, for the world had intruded.

Once my family spent our time in Golden Bay and Christchurch. Life was wonderful. Then floods wrecked our Golden Bay home. Earthquakes ruined our city. We decided after 10,000 of them we'd served our time and could move north with clear consciences.

Our twin sons lived in Auckland with their families. Their friends were dubious. Disasters seemed to follow us, they said. We settled on Waiheke Island. Two months later we had two earthquakes. See, they said.

Waiheke Island was a good choice. Its pace of life, its island-ness, its eccentricities, its accepting nature. Easy to get onto, and off. If you'd had enough of the city, it was easy to produce a ferry timetable, look at your watch, and announce, 'My god, is that the time . . . ?'

Then drift away over the blue Gulf, along with relieved commuters, holiday-makers, Gold-Carders getting a return on old age, and frantic wedding parties of young women wearing tutus and fascinators, throwing back stubbies of pinot gris and always hoping to beat the odds against the Big Day being the happiest of somebody's life.

I lived on the island still, and had grown to love its peculiarities.

Here you did not curse other drivers, out loud at least, nor honk your horn at them.

I was showing a city visitor around the island once when a car pulled out from a side road right in front of us. Both cars were going scarcely faster than a walking pace, and there was no danger. My passenger leaned over, beeped the horn and yelled out of the window. The poor man looked both apologetic and hapless, and I hoped I was looking like that too.

You did not speed. Most of the island's roads were limited to 50 kilometres per hour. The speed on the Onetangi straight, the island's longest, was raised to 60 kilometres per hour, and the top speed way out in the country was 80.

Few locked their cars. What would a car thief do? To steal a car on an island you needed to get it off, and there was only one escape route.

Once, when a car was stolen from a rather vulnerable woman and wrecked,

Above Textile artistry

people, including the thieves, clubbed together to buy her a new one.

I was stunned to read a real estate advertisement for a house in a 'gated community'. In god's name, why? Many didn't bother locking their houses either.

I went to the street leading to an expensive subdivision of houses. The gate stood at the end of it and yes, it was locked. But a public walkway ran beside the gate. You could simply walk around it.

Here, locals argued over whether a sign painted on a concrete wall constituted graffiti. The sign said: 'All you need is love.'

Very little crime bothered Waiheke. The weekly police reports published in the island newspapers told of a gentle community.

A typical week might produce a brief list of youthful yahooing, drunken driving and the occasional break-in, usually with official exhortations for the community to be more security-minded. The community didn't think so. In the statistically unlikely event of a robbery, it was a small price to pay for freedom from fear.

Islands had natural defences: very large moats. At the Waiheke ferry wharf a noticeboard published photographs of undesirables: 'Not to come to Waiheke.'

But why an island at all? That, really, was the question behind every island resident in this book.

People chose to live on islands for all sorts of reasons. A defined domain. Plenty of sea. A simpler life. Commonly, a sense of freedom, which was surprising, because you were confined in a much smaller land.

For me, when the ferry set out over the sea, threaded its way through other islands with the Auckland lights merging with the sunset behind, I simply thought the world beautiful and the island a dream.

———

'Waiheke's bohemian and hippie past,' *Lonely Planet* declared, 'is not far from the surface. The island continues to have a thriving artistic community.'

But was it true?

Tanya Batt was every magazine writer's idea of Waiheke.

She looked like a flower on a bike. No, the whole posy. She lived in a community, an eco-village of 15 homes, in a house she built herself, mostly.

She spent her first night there on a mattress on the concrete floor under a tin roof and when she woke up in the morning there was a horse outside the window. In her mind it was a white horse. Like a unicorn in her garden. Its owner reckoned it wasn't white, it was dappled, but Tanya had seen its soul.

She made a living as a storyteller. Of course.

When I met her she was working on the subject of islands. She was part of a charitable trust, Once Upon an Island, setting out to create a network of island communities based on stories, and she was getting ready to go to Norfolk on an island-to-island exchange.

'I love islands,' she said. 'Wherever I go in the world I seek them out. I have a theory that we have the opportunity to resolve all kinds of social and ecological issues on islands. We feel them first because of our limited resources and our finiteness. It's one of the things I love about living on Waiheke, the parameters of it. I can feel the edge of where we live.

'Some people don't like that. They feel claustrophobic. I like the idea that no one else can reach me. I like that about islands, the distinct isolation you get. They're their own little kingdoms, queendoms.'

She said things about living on her island which seemed to me to be true. The quite rare feeling of wanting to be at home, instead of being somewhere else and dreaming of it.

She lived simply, her little house beside a huge vegetable garden dotted with fruit trees, a Garden of Eden without snakes. It gave off a strange, half-remembered sound which after a while I recognised: lots of bees.

Here, she had to grow her own food, build her own shelter. A minaret housed her composting lavatory. A half-built mud-brick house stood on the section next door. A cold wind sneaked in from the south, a thief in the light. She put down a plate of fat walnut brownies. 'I think of myself as a storyteller. It feeds me and puts a roof over my head.'

Quite a nice little roof too, starting with a simple structure like a farm shed,

Above Tanya Batt

Opposite Storyteller's garden, with minaret

and slowly growing into a fairy's home. Its colours struck me between the eyes. Blues yellows purples greens reds and everything in between. It was an Aladdin's cave of mermaids, fairies, mediaeval queens, antique operatic costumes. She put them on for storytelling sessions, hopped on her electric bike and danced over the hills.

——

Visitors disembarked from the ferries at Matiatia and were driven into Oneroa township by the world's most patient bus drivers. The first proper building they saw was the Waiheke Library. It was right on the leading edge of town, the finest public building in all Waiheke.

The building showed that someone in the drab city council offices in central Auckland had style. As you approached, the library waved like a woodland in a gentle breeze, flickering in the light. The essence of Waiheke was carved into its curving wood: 'Lots of rain, lots of sun, lots of wind, lots of day, lots of night.'

Designed and crafted by Kazu Nakagawa, who carved the letters into the wood, one a day.

He'd been a boy in Japan who lived by the ocean and started designing windsurfers. The fibreglass and resin made him sick so he moved on to something more natural: wood.

He began making furniture in a place near Yokohama. His chairs didn't always quite work: too small and too fragile, he said. One was still in his workshop, beautiful, uncomfortable.

Then he came to New Zealand with his former wife, first stop in a world tour which never happened. He got as far as Waiheke and stopped. Someone thought he might fit on the island. That was 1988. He applied for permanent residence and eventually got it. 'In Japan I saw people, cars, buildings, and that's how I grew up. This is completely different. Everything is so exposed. I see lots of sun. I feel lots of wind, and rain.' Lots of day, lots of night and so on.

Was he an artist? Mmmmm. He was hesitant. In Japan people respected artists so much, separated them from ordinary people. He was wary of the term here. On Waiheke a lot of people had hobbies and called them art. The word didn't have the same gravitas.

His house stood in a garden of kanuka, punga, lemons, a big totara, a simple wooden building that somehow contrived to be . . . different, coloured glass and small frames like a child's drawing. The house, he said, was half-owned by the bank, an enviable average. But yes, he was just about making a living.

I'd seen his work first on one of Waiheke's biennial 'Sculpture in the Gulf' headland exhibitions. He'd built a catwalk jutting out from a cliff. People dressed in black and white clothes, all made from other clothes, an assemblage of others' lives, a patchwork of the past. Then they walked out into space along the catwalk. It was a transforming experience.

The black and white clothes were created by Rose McLeod, a textile artist. Rose was a celebrated artist, but not a thriving one.

She and her husband, a potter, and her son came to Waiheke in 1978. She travelled from Auckland on the *Iris Moana*, an old Navy Fairmile launch converted to a ferry, and the journey took an hour and a half, sometimes two hours. There weren't many day-trippers, then.

She was creative. She'd worked in film, and with the Mercury Theatre.

'The island was very empty, hippy-dippy. We didn't have any money. It was lovely but very hard to make a living so we moved back to the mainland after a year.

'I married a man who didn't think income was important, back then. That marriage did five years. Then I came back to the island for another period. I was doing art, making quilts, doing fabric work. We all do some things in our lives we'd rather forget about. I was a little wild. It was adventurous and fun. I'm glad I did it but I'm glad it's over.'

Rose had owned several homes, at Palm Beach, and down the island near Orapiu. She fixed up an old fishing hut there and built a studio. Amazing gardens, beautiful.

'I was doing bits and pieces, wedding flowers, exhibiting, piecemeal. Barely making a living. I lived very simply.'

She moved back nearer to town, Oneroa, now lived in a pretty old house with a studio, but she couldn't afford to stay. She'd been hoping for a stroke of good luck, or good fortune. She got neither.

Rose was leaving. She was not alone, she said, in being pushed off the island. She talked of other artists. They could no longer afford to live here. Waiheke was simply too expensive, falling victim to its own fame.

———

Waiheke was slightly warmer and a bit drier than Auckland.

No one was quite certain what the name meant. The most common guess was 'cascading waters', although the only falling waters on the island were the Cascades, hardly more than a trickle. Most thought of the name as a mistake.

This was the third most crowded island in New Zealand after the North and South Islands.

Seasons worked on the island like a bellows. Around 8500 people were thought to live there permanently, blowing out to several times that number in high summer.

The people on this island were whiter than Auckland, older but poorer. That was according to Census figures, although the poorer bit was open to conjecture. Were all of those mansions squatting in their bays a façade?

Someone had bought a disgraced financier's palace in a bay whose palms could be seen peeking when you were standing on Palm Beach, but was otherwise private. The new owners didn't like the manor, so they did the logical thing: they burned it down.

I'd like to have reported that the financier's victims joined hands and danced around the flames.

But the bay was exclusive, all right. A few boaties watched from their vessels, a few people from the hillside. Perhaps people were torn: the palace of the damned going up in flames (cheers) versus the waste (groans). Otherwise, it was, like so many things that end in fire, just an end. For the moneyed it had a cold hard logic.

But why weren't these people pushing the average income statistics sky-high?

For two reasons, probably. First, because their numbers didn't fit the space they occupied. Or rather, they fitted very loosely. They took up a lot of ground but there really weren't all that many of them. Secondly, because most did not spend very much time on the island, and probably weren't there on Census night, when a third of all houses on Waiheke were unoccupied.

Many of the island's houses were holiday homes. Beachfront settlements in winter looked barren as their Japanese maples. At night they were swathes of black.

Waiheke was as susceptible to property myths as its big city neighbour, but one of them was certainly true: in the previous year it had become much more expensive to buy a house.

Where did this leave those bohemians and hippies who, according to *Lonely Planet*, were the reason for so many people nipping over the water? The island paradise was busily pricing them out of the market.

Two communities of houseboats lived a precarious existence on the island, dodging bureaucrats intent on running a standard rule over the way people lived, laying down plans like shrouds.

One of them survived in the Bay of Lost Dreams, alias the Causeway.

Until the Causeway was built, getting from the western end of the island to the east was a lengthy, winding undertaking. The Causeway ran over a swampy inlet almost severing one part of the island from the rest. The new road created a bay which dried at low tide, and became a resting place for old and eccentric boats. They perched and lurched all over the bay, pretty, crafty, some like waterborne caravans, some reeking of northern traditions, some of ages long gone, a polyglot collection of satisfying vessels.

Its many supporters reckoned that old boats needed a place to die. Alas, under the officials' beady eyes they were tidied up, and some disappeared. But enough remained to make up a maritime museum of their own.

Among them were houseboats, and on two of them lived Steve Martin, Mary Christie and families.

They met as conservation volunteers, did good work, looked for somewhere to live, but even then found Waiheke too expensive.

Then they saw an open fishing boat lying near the Causeway. 'I could do wonders with that,' Steve thought, and he did. Mary borrowed the money, and they built a cabin on the boat with enough bedrooms for themselves and four children, two boys and two girls.

People called it the *Tardis*.

They went around the Gulf in it. It could still move. Later, Mary moved onto a boat near it, the nucleus of a fleet.

But the island was changing.

Steve said: 'New money has come from overseas, bought houses here. We believe a handful of these people are the ones who don't want us down here so they've been to the council to force everyone out.'

Mary: 'I think there are people out there who don't like us. We've had a lot of issues; in Anzac Bay [the next bay over] the houseboat community there had people complain they were spoiling the view. Whereas we've always believed we are the postcard.'

So they were. When I first moved to the island tourist brochures boasted of them. They appeared in every television and film documentary made about the island.

Well, the houseboats had survived the purge, so far, although bureaucrats buzzed around them like wasps. Many, like me, hoped they would live on as an antidote to the suburban life that greyed even a paradise like this one. Listening to Bach on a quiet evening as Mary practised her violin had an amenity value that should have found its way into the district plan.

———

The sea here was so *usable*. You could sail on it, swim in it, fish it, live on it and most of all, love it.

We lived in Onetangi, walked, swam in the warm sea and looked over the Gulf to the islands. Looking was my main recreation. I was very good at it.

One evening we went to Palm Beach for a nude swim. The evening was hot, the clothes-optional end of the beach crowded. We walked back through black rock still pumping out the day's heat, went down the opposite end for some of Palm Beach's excellent fish and chips. Beside us a big group of Argentinians were using the community barbecue, grilling something that smelled delicious.

French was the second most-spoken language on the island, followed by Maori, German and Spanish in that order. Every summer Argentinians working in the vineyards and cafés filled the island with life and colour.

But the language coming from the single public toilet was robustly Anglo-Saxon.

A woman was locked in. The electronically operated door would not let her out. Her calls for help had an undertone of desperation.

Several people gathered outside, tugging at the door, trying to be soothing. I called the city council. Yes, they could call a technician, but he might be some time.

Maybe even tomorrow.

Everyone agreed we needed tools. Modern Japanese cars didn't have any. The woman in the toilet wanted to know where her husband was. He should have been in the fish and chip shop, she said.

I went down to the fish and chip shop. Her husband wasn't there.

But a woman was holding a sheep on a lead while she asked people to sign a petition objecting to road works. The sheep looked interested.

Sure, she said, she had a screwdriver. She opened the back of her car. Inside was a box, the kind I imagined hauled gold bullion. Certainly it was heavy enough.

It held tools for every occasion. Dozens of them. Hundreds perhaps. She had to go home, she said. I should take the box, then leave it with Peter in the fish and chip shop. She pushed the sheep into her car and shoved off.

I wrestled the box back down the track to the toilet. Several helpers then attacked the door with a fine selection of screwdrivers, crowbars, spanners. It wouldn't budge.

A smallish man strode up the path. He announced himself as the missing husband. He called to the woman inside. She told him she was stuck. He watched the action for a moment then seized the door handle. To everyone's astonishment the door swung open. The woman flew out. The husband puffed with triumph. Off they went.

I lunked the toolbox back to the fish and chip shop, which was full of people, and told Peter he was to be the guardian of the sheep woman's toolbox. He didn't so much as look surprised.

Ah yes, *Lonely Planet*. This, to me, was the real Waiheke.

Above Houseboat community, the Causeway

KAWAU

'One hundred and seventy years later Grey's influence could be seen and felt by anyone taking a walk on the island.'

There'd been an unusual frost that morning and the steps on the Sandspit wharf were slippery with ice and mud. The tide was out and the water was still between mudbanks.

Michael Marris picked us up and his powerful boat sped across the quiet water, past Rabbit Island and Takangaroa and Martello Rock and over to Kawau.

We stood on Michael's jetty in the fine morning light.

A man and a woman came by on stand-up paddleboards and stopped for a chat.

They were wearing sporty land-happy clothes. They didn't intend getting them wet. They were simply out for a paddle, as others might take a walk, but walking wasn't so simple on Kawau. In the city people might meet over their back fence. You couldn't do that here, but you could meet in boats, so that's what people did.

We climbed a couple of hundred steps to Michael and his wife Gabrielle's eyrie and watched a big red barge carting spoil dredged for the new marina at Sandspit out to sea to be dumped.

A fence kept wallabies out. Some here loved them, some did not. The fuzz of kanuka forest was just about all the native cover left on the 2000-hectare island, because the wallabies ate everything else.

This was a generally cohesive island but wallabies could tear it apart. People got very excited about them.

They chewed the understorey down to the ground, eating out most native species except weka.

Two-thirds of the North Island's weka lived on Kawau, and they were everywhere. The Marrises had even found them in their bedroom, three storeys up. 'I threw a couple out the bedroom window and moved evolution on several notches because these things flew. They were soon back.'

Locals were reputed to be trapping them and carting them over to the nearby Pembles Island at night in rubber dinghies with muffled oars. One (pro-weka) resident had photographed a bird swimming back to Kawau. People got very excited about weka, too.

Ah George, I thought, you had a very long reach.

For me, this island had two distinctive features.

The first was its relationship with Governor George Grey, the enigmatic, eccentric ruler who didn't so much stamp his personality on the island as cast it in stone.

The second seemed boring by comparison: a quirk of land development which was to affect the way islanders lived from then to now.

The two together, the grand house and the exclusive sections, made the island seem wealthy and aloof.

———

Grey was appointed Governor of New Zealand in 1845. Born, probably, in Portugal, educated in England and soon enough a more or less permanent expatriate. He revelled in New Zealand but thought a few exotic touches would improve it.

He wanted a private home on an island. He bought Rakino and began building a house but abandoned it in 1862 when Kawau came onto the market, its earlier sale to the copper miner John Taylor by Maori having been allowed to stand.

What was to become Mansion House Bay, in Bon Accord Harbour, had housed 400 miners working copper in the undersea mine a short-ish walk away, until the mine was flooded and the enterprise became so hazardous and unprofitable it was abandoned. The good times were remembered in the company's name: Bon Accord.

Grey bought the whole island, for £3700. He spent much more, £5000, rebuilding and extending the mine manager's house in the bay. Then, much of the island had been clear-felled, kauri and totara for building, kanuka for firewood.

Grey planted exotic gardens, created a zoo park and stocked it with emus, possums, kookaburras, zebras, monkeys, deer, peacocks, wallabies.

That alone was enough to change the island forever. The possums and wallabies chewed their way through the remaining vegetation. Native flora and fauna were destroyed. Silt from the denuded land washed into the sea. One hundred and seventy years later Grey's influence could be seen and felt by anyone taking a walk on the island.

His more immediate legacy was the house he built, a grand affair. His library ceiling was supported by four kauri trees cut on the property and sent to England to be turned and polished.

It was Grey's sanctuary. He returned here whenever his career hiccupped, as it did rather often.

Grey liked to run his coach and horses up to a vantage point called Grey Heights, where he could see other Gulf islands and almost all of his own.

Branches of the road ran down to other bays around his island. The roads had since become tracks but except for the reserve around the mansion they now often crossed private property.

Grey sold the island in 1888 to Eliza Thomson, an Australian, and never returned to Kawau. He left New Zealand for the last time in 1893 and ended a 36-year impasse with his wife Eliza in 1897, which said something about leaving things to the last minute, for both died the following year.

Later, in 1904, the island was bought by Andrew Joseph Farmer, once Mayor

Above Inside Mansion House: colonial decor

Following Governor Grey, omnipotent

of Te Aroha. Farmer made the second, permanent change to the island.

He set aside land near Mansion House Bay for a township. It was never built.

Farmer used Mansion House as a boarding house, not very successfully. He faced the usual problem of island hosts: transport, or how to get guests, staff and supplies on and off the island.

Farmer's fortunes worsened when a grand annex he'd built was burned down.

He turned to subdivision for a solution. He carved the island into sections which had one enduring feature. New Zealand law demanded that every section had access, either by road or water.

The island had no roads. Except for the area around Mansion House Bay Grey's were either truncated or non-existent.

So Farmer's sections were big, and long, and their access was from the sea. They ran down to the water's edge at high water, and except for sections in more modern subdivisions, they stayed that way.

Now you could see the consequences of all of this.

Almost all of the island was now privately owned and the Department of Conservation had the rest of it. Grey's wallabies had eaten out most other species and, if you accepted DOC's view, had laid waste the island.

Kawau was big, but you couldn't get around it unless you were in the know. The islanders' own tracks ran down to their jetties and there were more of those here than anywhere else in the country.

People landed on their own properties and walked up their own tracks to their homes.

If you did not want to, or need to, you did not have to have any contact with neighbours, much less the tourists and visitors who came to the island.

To reach your house they would need to have a boat, land on your jetty and find their way up to your house. As one islander said: 'It's not easy to pop over to a different part of the island. Unless you're on the same ferries or water taxis coming out to the island you just don't know others.'

To visit someone else's house, unless it was very close, you walked down to your jetty and took your boat.

The jetties had caused fuss in the past: some islanders had posted signs warning people off; these were private jetties, they said. In an era when ownership of the foreshore and seabed were nationally contested, this did not go down well; they were seen as usurping, if not the foreshore (for they had riparian rights) at least the seabed, public property.

Court hearings resolved that argument, the signs disappeared, but not very much changed. As Michael Marris said, why would you want to tie up to a jetty? It only led on to a house.

The result of this was a rather exclusive atmosphere, reflected in the island's reputation. Visitors went to Mansion House, or walked over to the ruins of the copper mine, but otherwise only glimpsed island homes. Some were modest,

POETICAL WORKS OF THOMSON BEATTIE &c.

Grant by Purchase under Land Regulations of 1st April, 1856.

SIR GEORGE GREY:

HIS FRIENDS AND FOES.

—

A POLITICAL SATIRE.

—

BY ALEXANDER STUART.

—

"Prepare for Rhyme—I'll publish—right or wrong;
Fools are my theme—let satire be my song."—Byron.

PRICE — — — ONE SHILLING.

CHRISTCHURCH:
Printed at the "Lyttelton Times" Company's Printing Office, Gloucester Street, and published
by Dudley and Co., 81, Madras Street South.
1882.

d, by the Grace of God, of the United Kingdom of Great Britain and Ireland, Queen:

To all to whom these Presents shall come, Greeting:

Know ye that for good consideration, Us thereunto moving, We, for Us, our Heirs and Successors, do hereby grant unto *Samuel Greenwood and Thomas Enoch of Hokitika, in the Province of Canterbury New Zealand, Boatmen, their* ——

Ths Heirs and Assigns ALL that Parcel of Land in the Province of Canterbury, in our Colony of New Zealand, containing by admeasurement *Eight Perches more or less situate in and fronting on Brittan Street Hokitika and numbered 640 on the map of the Chief Surveyor of the Province of Canterbury setting out and describing the Town of Hokitika aforesaid.* ——————————

as the same is delineated on the Plan drawn in the margin hereof, with all the Rights and Appurtenances thereto belonging: To Hold unto the said *Samuel Greenwood and Thomas Enoch at Sonnet or common* ——— **his Heirs and Assigns for ever.**

In Testimony Whereof We have caused this our Grant to be Sealed with the Seal of our Colony of New Zealand.

Witness our trusty and well-beloved *Sir George Grey, K.C.B* Governor and Commander-in-Chief in and over the Colony of New Zealand, at Wellington, this *Twelfth* —— day of *October* ——— in the Twenty-*Thirtieth* year of Our Reign; and in the year of Our Lord One Thousand Eight Hundred and Sixty-*six*

No 5031.
Reg C. 23

more were substantial, and Grey's legacy lived on here too. His taste in houses had been inherited by some of the island's more grandiose house-builders.

Yet in Mansion House Bay where Governor Grey's house still stood grand, I'd sometimes anchor my boat, and in the evenings after the ferry had carted the last tourists home, sit alone in the quiet gardens at the back of the house surrounded by wallabies and white peacocks. Next morning the sun would rise on a brand-new world.

———

Ruins of the copper-smelting house still stood in Smelting House Bay, alongside the Lidgard boatyard with an ancient boat named *Mystery Girl* inside.

The old Lidgard house was nearby, a sort of English country house that seemed to have run out of steam halfway through its building.

Nearby I found another island relic, George Zylstra.

George was born in Amsterdam, was hunted by the Nazis in World War II but survived. He did an apprenticeship in restoration work after the war but despite high demand for his trade remained suspicious of his nation's ability to keep living below a rising sea level, and came to New Zealand instead. George claimed to be 80 but locals had worked out that he must have been a good deal older. Still, he hopped off the roof he was working on, to a shaky ladder underneath, nimble as the steeplejack he'd once been.

For a man who'd once repaired church steeples this was nothing. He was in great demand on Kawau's lofty roofs. Back on level ground he walked with a

Above Inside Mansion House

Following Governor's bedroom (left); mementoes

stick. He needed a hip replacement, he said, but he kept putting it off because there was always another roof to fix. Besides, he said, 'I like to hang on to my own bits. I don't believe in all this nylon stuff.'

He believed in the power of wood. George claimed to be able to do anything, and according to all reports that was true.

He took off his cap to show a wild bird's nest of hair and ears that stuck out like Delft jug handles.

Today he was not just repairing the roof. He was installing a spa bath in a new bathroom he'd created, turning the en suite bathroom into a wardrobe, putting in walls, adding a new room and fixing up the plumbing. The owners of the house knew nothing of this. They'd hired him to fix up a couple of things, but George had his own ideas on what should be done. He reckoned they needed a spa bath and he'd found one on Trade Me. He reckoned they'd be happy.

———

Kawau's permanent population was marked by an almost total lack of resident children. Education never went well with islands.

I met a man who reckoned he, his wife and neighbours were about 60 per cent of the island's young people, defined here as forty-ish. They batted that one around for a bit. What about X . . . ? And Y . . . ? Hard to tell. Maybe a little less than 60 per cent, they agreed.

Michael was intent on community. His magazine, a resurrection of an old island masthead called *Kookaburra*, was filled with community events and chatter. The Music in the Gardens concert, large on Kawau's calendar, was getting a good spread.

Issues needed to be discussed. Lots of tensions between the Kawau community and mainland bureaucracy existed. Islanders generally resented the growing power of bureaucracy, but Kawau was going one step further than any other island.

Michael said: 'We are a unique community with special demographic requirements and geography, that is, an island. That means we deserve and require considerations unlike those of Mount Eden, or Queen Street or even Waiheke Island. As a community we have a common interest, to keep mainland New Zealand at a distance, to manage our own affairs as completely as we can.

'As a community we're careful custodians of this environment. The less influence and control we have from central and local government the more we're able to exercise our own discretion in favour of the island. Not for us, but for the island.'

Waiheke Island, to the south, was also forging a breakaway movement, petitioning to get out of the Auckland Council's grip and strike out on its own. Islanders were self-reliant by necessity, they argued.

Waiheke, though, had roads, council services.

Kawau liked to think it could take care of itself.

Lin and Larry Pardey, who were famous blue-water sailors, anchored in Bon Accord Harbour, Kawau Island, one night in 1985.

In the dark hours of the early morning, a gale blew in from the west. It smacked against their boat *Taleisin*, the boat the Americans had built themselves in California, of timber they'd milled from bare logs.

Their boat had no engine. They knew Bon Accord in an easterly gale was dangerous, no place for them. Kawau Island was strewn with reefs which were unmarked then, traps in the night.

The Pardeys sailed back and forth outside Bon Accord in the dark until there was enough light to find their way across the reef at the entrance to North Cove, the island's next harbour to the north. They anchored their boat and went back to bed in gentler waters.

In the bright new day Larry climbed into the cockpit and looked around. Holy cow. He declared the place perfect.

So the Pardeys decided that when they retired from the sea, they'd live in North Cove.

The house they found there had been on the market for eight years. It had a wharf, and a boatshed, but Lin thought it a wreck.

'At first it was just an interesting interlude. Then it became our home base. That was 1986. We worked on it for five years. We tidied the house, built the sea walls, Larry unbolted every plank from the jetty and pulled every piling

Above George Zylstra

slowly upright. Then we sailed to Australia then to Africa for eight years.'

They came back to Kawau to live.

Lin didn't look like a woman who'd wrassled a boat out of raw timber then faced the best and worst the seven seas could heave at her over the course of a lifetime and some 320,000 kilometres. The last time I'd seen her photograph was in a book called *Bull Canyon, a Boatbuilder, a Writer and Other Wildlife*. It was an account of the two finding an abandoned stone hut in a canyon 80 kilometres from Los Angeles and building their boat.

The new Lin was a model senior citizen: after 11 books she was now a publisher in her own right, still working on several projects and looking strong.

The Pardeys' rebuilt house shone on the water's edge, the jetty straight and true against the blue sea, the boatshed housing a boatbuilder's museum, old navigation lights, ancient bronze cleats, canvas buckets, wooden spars, oars, a hundred clamps, boxes of chisels with worn handles and sharp as razors, knives, gauges, planes, lengths of exotic timber.

Everything had a patina of age, the house, the buildings, Lin herself and probably her lifelong companion Larry, too, but he was sick in bed this day. Every part of it looked at ease with every other part.

They suited New Zealand, New Zealand suited them, especially its do-it-yourself tendency: Lin liked to show friends abroad a local advertisement for a DIY coffin.

The *Taleisin* had gone, sold to some young people in Auckland. Its space on the jetty was occupied by a beautiful little Herreshoff yacht. Larry bought it for Lin as a sixty-eighth birthday present.

Especially, Kawau fitted them. The islandness of the place appealed. 'Living on a sailboat for years, you live on an island. There are no roads, people don't just hop in a car, they have to work to come and see you, they have to care. When they get here they put the other world behind them. Most of our guests slow down over a day or two and get to the pace where you can actually be with them.'

I wondered what made this island seem the best place in the world to live for a couple who'd seen an awful lot of islands.

Lin Pardey answered obliquely: 'What's special about this small island is that it is an active community,' she said.

Although . . . 'It would be nice to have another thirty people on it. When I first moved in there were about a hundred and twenty. Now we're down to about sixty although it's going back up again.'

On the other side of North Cove Peter and Erin Hyde, the managers of Camp Bentzon, named for a Dane who immigrated to New Zealand, bought 12 hectares of land and donated it for public education and recreation, were getting ready to leave the island for their annual holiday.

Where did people who ran a recreation camp on a holiday island go for their holidays? To a city, said Erin. Of course.

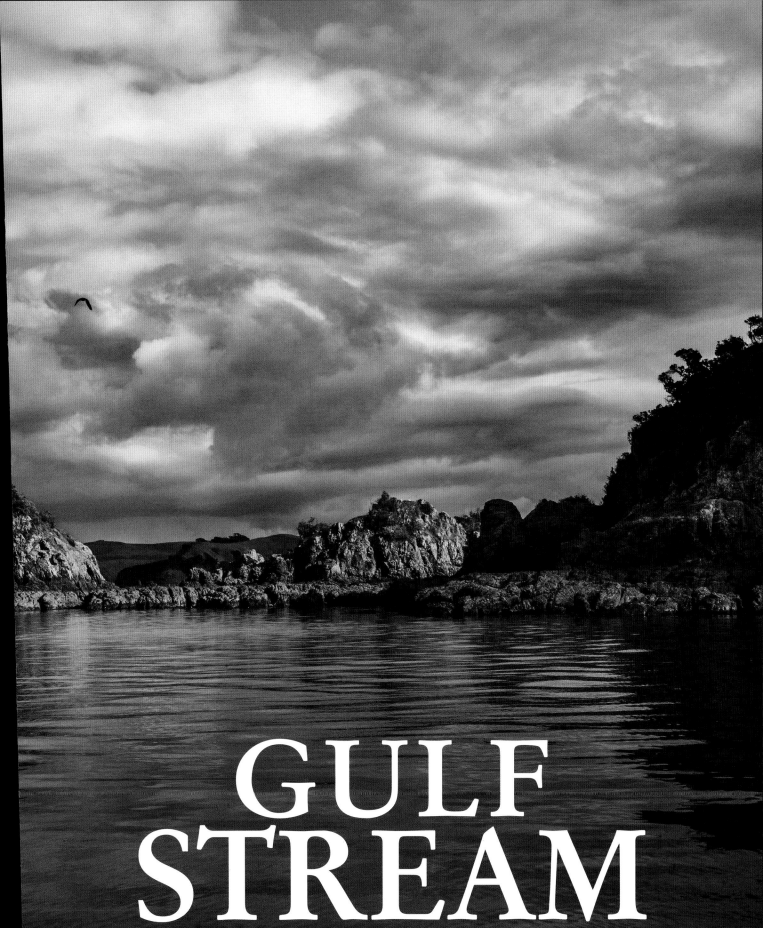

GULF
STREAM

RANGITOTO

'They lacked the tyranny of money, showed
a disregard for cash and flash. Their simplicity
declared that stuff was transitory, they
made do and wasted nothing, and only
beauty remained.'

O n the country's best-known small island sat the survivors of its Kiwi bach community and on this hot Saturday morning it was hard to know which was the bigger attraction.

Ferries to Rangitoto were awash with tourists. They overflowed the decks and flooded onto the jetty.

Lots of them trickled into the Collins' bach and Alan Collins said, 'This is private property,' and they said, 'Sorry,' and Alan said, 'Have a look in the door if you want.'

'It's beautiful,' said a tourist, 'such an amazing kind of place.'

Alan said, 'She's a bit rough here and there, but you know . . .'

'That's what gives it character,' said the tourist.

'Sure does,' said Alan. 'This one's a hundred years.'

'A *hundred*?'

'Yes, pit-sawn kauri timber, you can see the saw marks, one guy sat in the pit, the other guy above, pit-sawn.'

'Good stuff,' said the tourist, and took off to see lesser sights, such as the crater 260 metres above which only 600 years ago was spewing lava and creating the Queen City's brand, the perfect shape of Rangitoto.

They could thank the military for the roads on the island. Soldiers left their mark on the landscape, none so useful as their roads and, oh, the causeway which linked Rangitoto to its neighbour Motutapu.

The track from the wharf to the summit went right back to 1897, and on this island even crime paid. From 1925 to 1933 prisoners built roads, paths, the swimming pool near the wharf, tennis courts, a community hall at Islington Bay, once known as Drunks Bay where drunken matelots sobered up before sailing from the Gulf.

Rangitoto was a big place once. Reg Noble ran a shop, post office, a bus which was now in Auckland's Museum of Transport and Technology. Shirley Collins could order meat once a week, bread and milk every second day. There

Pages 152–3 Rakino welcome

Previous Rangitoto

Opposite Bach 36, the Collins' bach

were dances and films and fishing contests and sports days and a band and Father Christmas arrived punctually by boat.

Across the island lay the leftovers of unwanted ships, rusted by salt sea and eaten by worms.

But I was interested in the baches. This was one of the best-preserved Kiwi bach communities in New Zealand, and the biggest remnant of a way of life. The blinkered had tried to do away with it yet here it was, diminished but alive, all the more startling for its contrast with the plastered paradise across the water.

This whole island was built on the cheap. The Crown paid only £15 for it in 1854. Possibly Maori thought they got a good deal. The place was too rocky and barren to live on and there was no water. The neighbouring Motutapu was much classier real estate. Even the Crown was a bit squiffy about buying Rangitoto despite the price.

People still came, though, for the moonscape, for the peace and the fishing.

Soon there was a Rangitoto Domain Board, and they were leasing campsites for a couple of pounds a year, then 'shack sites', four quid a year with board approval for the shacks.

Mr Jones used to row over from Mission Bay for the fishing. He and his wife Edith applied for one of them, on 8 August 1911. They got Site No. 36, and they built a tiny bach on it, beautifully simple, of pit-sawn kauri, the same timber that tourist was marvelling over today. But Mr and Mrs Jones soon moved to

Christchurch, for the drift north was unknown then, and the bach was used by Edith's sister Nora Ryan.

Nora married Alan's grandfather Alf Parker, who was already a Rangitoto enthusiast. The Parkers had two daughters, Elsie and Violet, and they married two brothers, Bill and Fred Collins. Bill was a 1935 All Black who played seven matches. 'Uncle Bill was a big big guy and dad was a shortish guy and they looked like Laurel and Hardy,' Alan said. So Bach 36 became known as the Collins' bach.

Shirley Collins went there first at Christmas 1957. The bach was now pretty much as it was then. She and Alan married a year later and since 1960 they'd lived in the bach every Christmas, every Easter, and most weekends.

After all, she said: 'What sort of holiday is it when all the woman's got to do is a lot of housework?' As, she thought, was the way in modern, faceless holiday homes. 'All I do is the dishes and I sweep out. And that's it, that's my day. You sit and read, and knit.' And talk, and laugh, and take comfort from your neighbours, who popped in and out as if their lives were a conversation joined only with commas.

It was a fragile idyll, of course.

The baches were built at a time when anyone with enough enterprise could bang up a roof over their heads on their piece of paradise.

By 1937 there were 140 baches, and that year the Minister of Lands decided there would be no more. The existing leases were given a deadline: in 20 years they'd be gone. That took them through to 1957, when the leases were renewed for 33 years, no sales allowed, no exchanges or renting or altering the baches, and when owners died their baches died with them.

The shop was arbitrarily destroyed in 1982, the ambulance hut, the children's playground, all that community work vanished in despair. The baches began disappearing so rapidly that by 1990 only 34 were left in three settlements, Rangitoto Wharf where the Collins' bach was, Islington Bay, and on the far side, Beacon End. They were given a further 33 years, a number that seemed to have lodged permanently in someone's pigeonhole.

'What on earth am I going to do?' Shirley Collins wondered. 'Every Christmas holiday of my entire married life I've spent down here. Kids and grandkids. And I thought damn it. I was sitting here one day and a girl came along, and I thought I've a good mind to call all the bach owners together and have a meeting and she said, I'll help you. I rang half them up, she did too. We had the meeting at our place and it got too big for our place. I was the troublemaker.'

So the Rangitoto Island Historic Conservation Trust was formed, and soon the gongs were clanging, and the bach communities were registered as historic places by Heritage New Zealand. It noted the baches had had an axe hanging over them for the best part of a century, that Kiwi baches were disappearing along with other artefacts from a former life, such as the great New Zealand weekend, that the more they vanished, the more New Zealanders appreciated them, that they were now cultural icons and that anyway, they were very fine buildings.

They lacked the tyranny of money, showed a disregard for cash and flash. Their simplicity declared that stuff was transitory, they made do and wasted nothing, and only beauty remained.

None of that stopped the government from trying to evict them in 2004. Someone had decided that a few baches, appropriately consented, disinfected, and tidied up, could stay. In short, the Kiwi bach culture could be bottled. The rest, those without lifetime leases, would go. The Rangitoto baches, like Kiwi baches the country over, were seen as subversive.

The bach owners took Chris Carter, the Conservation Minister, to court. They won, the judge agreeing that the government had acted illegally and declaring: 'I prohibit the minister from taking any steps pending his decision which may have the effect of forcing owners or caretakers to vacate their baches.'

Well, phew. Kiwi baches were as rare as tusked weta. They'd been torn down all over the country and replaced by grey ranks of dismal holiday houses where fun was ordered. The way of life represented by baches, simple, appreciative, friendly, was becoming so rarefied as to need its own protection order. Now the survivors peeped out from under the skirts of Rangitoto's dress circle. All the uncertainty had had one positive effect: the baches had remained pretty much as they'd always been, and no one would think of getting rid of them now. Any one of the misty-eyed tourists walking up the Collins' path that day would have beaten off the apparatchiks with sticks.

So here sat the Collins' bach, inviolable for the moment, as far from Omaha Beach's weekend palaces as you could possibly get. We sat outside, on benches arranged around scoria sculpted by prisoners who'd carefully flattened many bach sites on this island. The bach community now looked after the island in much the same way that those prisoners once did, but rather more cheaply for the taxpayer.

The Collins' bach, No. 36, was perfect in its simplicity. Pohutukawa trees shaded the spot. In their century or so here the family had seen bush grow to giants. 'In my time,' said Alan.

The main bach contained a living room and two bedrooms. 'A lot of people have got their places more modern,' Shirley said, 'but I like it just the way it is. Why not? We've got all mod cons at home.'

To get to the kitchen you walked through the living room, out the back door, past the old corrugated-iron smokehouse where they once did all their cooking in a blackened dixie sitting on two iron rungs. 'We used to eat fish straight out of the smokehouse,' Shirley said, 'a bit of vinegar, oh gorgeous, on fresh bread and butter.' And along to the kitchen door. It was a big room, with an open fire, the hub of the place.

Uncle Bill's collection of walking sticks, some made of old fishing rods, some driftwood crooks, sat against a wall. Chairs painted that particular shade of bach-green. A two-burner gas stove, crockery in a cupboard behind leadlight doors along with games and, oh, bach stuff. An antique Electrolux kerosene fridge, salvaged from a trawler, had taken over from the meat safe and kept their stuff cool. It burned silently, its little icebox frosted over.

This bach had grown from a way of life and Shirley wasn't about to change anything.

'We had to paint the kitchen. It would have looked really good cream but that wasn't right and that's why I painted it grey. But the pink ceiling in the living room, I'm not touching. Nora, Alan's grandmother, did that.'

Alan: 'She was a tyrant. My grandfather was an English gentleman who came out from Croydon. A government analyst who lived in Herne Bay.'

The community was doing up the few houses abandoned in the purge. The bach next door to the Collins' was now a little bach museum.

Two others in Islington Bay were being tackled by the community. 'But it just ruins everything,' said Shirley, 'we've painted them up, you've got to have this, and that, all the rules and regulations, you have to have power, somewhere to do their phones.' For the places would be rented.

Above Bach colours

Younger ears vibrated to the siren call of dishwashers and wide-screen television. No television in the Collins' bach, just an old radio and solar power for the lights. A curtain around the concrete out the back for a shower. Shirley said it was the closest they could get to nature although when I looked at the sea, crashing over the bach roof in storms, the pohutukawa growing huge and blotting out the mountain, I thought nature was doing a pretty good job of getting closer to *them*.

The average age of the bach owners was rising. Every bach had to be passed on to someone in the family or be abandoned. It was an awful choice. They'd slowly fade away or be preserved as artefacts, like skeletons under glass.

Fewer people used the Collins' bach now. The Collins' three children were all in their fifties. When they were kids they lived in the water, spent the night up the mountain on New Year's Eve. Summers rang with the laughter of children and teenagers. With families of their own they did not come so much now. The other Collins family stopped coming.

They used to sweep out the swimming pool every night, keep it in good shape. It was filling with rocks now, didn't hold water.

———

Scientists now believed that Rangitoto was an active volcano long before its last roar around 550 years ago. That must have been awe-inspiring, blasting rocks in an almost perfect circle, shooting ash into the air and across to neighbouring Motutapu, perfectly preserving Maori footprints. Certainly it established Motutapu as the neighbourhood's residential centre: Rangitoto was simply too hard to walk upon.

That most recent eruption raised the question of whether Auckland's icon might yet turn on its glittering neighbour and cover it in hot ash. Experts said it would not, or that it might, depending.

The last eruption left caves all over the island. 'Quite big ones,' Alan said. 'Some of them go down thirteen metres, you break your neck. There's quite a lot of bones and skeletons. Once the tide was out for miles and miles and I found a skull sitting on a rock. Only on a real spring low you'd see it. Another chap said the rest of him was in a cave, on a platform. I left his skull there, I thought he might like it.' Rangitoto caves were once burial places for the people on Motutapu.

Over on the wharf the ferry was filling up. I could see Alan was looking forward to the last ferry leaving at five o'clock so he and the bachies could get together on the green near the old swimming pool, have a drink, or a couple, talk, reminisce, laugh.

Opposite Scene from the front window

RAKINO

'On the way down to the wharf, Maurice
sang and honked at the pukeko, and
laughed his head off.'

Rakino appeared as a low, even island in a spread of them, Motutapu to one side, Tiritiri Matangi through the Rakino Channel, the oddly named Noises and an entourage of islets on its other side, its own rocks and reefs all around. The first reaction from a boat crew pushed toward the island by a south wind might be, oh dear, do we have to go in *there*?

With cause. Old newspapers are full of stories of uncharted rocks, strandings, sinkings, wrecks, the worst of them the scow *Rangi* which went down with all four hands on the night of 14 January 1937.

The wind blew directly into Sandy Bay, chopping the sea into sharp little waves. It seemed to have been misnamed. An islet joined to the island by a reef guarded the bay on one side, Rakino's community hall crowded onto the ferry wharf on the other, and a lot of hard rocks lay between the anchorage and the soft sands of Sandy Bay.

A narrow road ran away from the wharf up the hill to a scattering of houses.

There were no shops. One brave fellow who obtained a hawker's licence and did his best to provide people with what they needed was exhausted by the sheer difficulty of his enterprise.

The Rakino community hall beside the wharf still had a price list on the wall of its main room, a glass of beer $6, bottle of wine $25, water $2. They were the days when locals gathered once a month for a chat and a drink. Those days were gone, ending when the long finger of liquor licensing pointed even at Rakino.

Now the hall itself was in danger. The sea was beating up the shelf it was built on. Its deck was closed and the main hall could bounce on its foundations in a heavy sea. It was a comfortable, handsome building spilling onto the wharf. The building accommodated hall and library downstairs, art gallery for classes upstairs, yoga classes over Christmas.

No one quite knew the population of the island. People came and went. Twenty permanents, a recent 18 per cent population lift, was the best guess. Some

137 houses. Locals sensed a sea change in the island's fortunes as Aucklanders cashed up and moved. The first amphibious Sealegs had just arrived.

Cars were parked nose to tail near the wharf, door to door along the road's lower length. Wait a minute. Was that grass growing from important parts, such as the engine? Were they cars or garden ornaments?

Their most important body part seemed to be the duct tape holding them together.

Maurice Brown answered.

They weren't abandoned, and all of them were goers, he said, except for perhaps one or two. They were simply the cars people had on this island.

After all, they didn't have to go far, for the island was only 2.4 kilometres long and 1.2 kilometres wide. Nor fast: the few roads were steep and narrow.

Maurice was the authority. He was the city's man on the island, the person who took care of wrecked cars, along with roads, rubbish, mowing, right down to spare parts and good advice, ran a de facto, free taxi service for people who needed a lift, cleaned the toilets.

For anyone who wanted anything done Maurice was the first port of call. Wherever he went he checked lights, picked up bottles and cans left by disrespectful visitors. He was an island-keeper in the most practical sense. In this paradise bay.

'He's like Mitre 10,' his wife Norma said. 'People need a washer or a bit of plumbing or something and they come to Maurice and he's got stuff everywhere. He rummages around and nine times out of ten he's got exactly what they're looking for.'

———

Long ago Auckland City held an option to buy the island for a marine park. The *New Zealand Herald* objected: 'Its disabilities are easily stated. It is too far away, too difficult of approach because of shallow water and exposed landings.' Besides: 'The island is not of a character to make it attractive to holiday-makers.'

Not, that is, until Dr Maxwell Rickard and the United Peoples' Organisation came along. Rickard, a psychologist and nightclub owner who toured New Zealand as a hypnotherapist under the name 'The Great Ricardo', bought the island as a refuge for the nervous, disturbed, orphaned, unwed with babies, and the elderly, or any combination of the same. The refuge was to be financed by interested persons, and Rickard advertised for 100 of them. They were required to donate all their worldly goods to the cause, and to live on the island.

Meanwhile, he asked the United Nations to recognise Rakino as an independent country.

Neither the 100 persons nor the United Nations came forward, and Rickard

Above Governor Grey's
first bay

then reached for the next best option: subdivision into 25 four-hectare blocks and 125 sections. To house holiday-makers, contented old people, and probably the nervous, disturbed, unwed, orphaned et al.

The Great Ricardo moved on, but I couldn't help feeling that his legacy lingered.

———

We went back to Maurice's house, the industrial centre of Rakino, its beating heart. Pukeko lined the route. He accelerated, honked. They scrambled away, squawking. He pushed back the brim of his purple AC/DC cap, laughed. We

passed what was said to be the world's first solar-powered telephone, in an old-fashioned red telephone box, calls to Auckland free.

Did someone say Maurice's house? More his wife Norma's wonderland. Green and gold, and pink and blue. A painted nymph, the goddess of love, gazed down at her shell-full of white flowers. Grecian statues stood around looking nobly at yellow and blue pots and pillars, gold garden seats, a bath with waves painted inside, a blade from a boat's propeller that gonged when you struck it, pink and red hibiscus flashing all over the place, the colour spilling over into the house, into every room.

The interior décor was leopard-skin. Leopard-skin sofas, ironing-board covers, table mats, bedspreads, chairs, coffee mugs.

A giant tui, bright green and blue, feasted inside a yellow cage hanging outside, its door open. The bird was real. I'd never seen one like it. Other tui shared a

Above Rakino's community hall

Following Maurice and Norma Brown, at home

tree with bellbirds. Had Norma and Maurice created an island within an island, a paradise in paradise?

The two of them met when Norma, 12, had been staying at her aunt's house and Maurice at the place next door. When Maurice and his cousins came home from church on Sundays, oh, said Norma, they'd look so smart in their white shirts and dark trousers and she really liked the smiley one. She leaned over the fence and said hi. She was 15 and being chaperoned by her sister when she went to a dance and Maurice went too.

He was her one and only. They married when she was 17, he 20. Her father told her: 'You've probably made the right choice but as a father I think you're far too young to make that choice. But I can't stop you.'

The Great Ricardo himself could not have produced a more magical marriage. When I met them they'd been married for 52 years.

Maurice was first to fall in love with Rakino. He visited it often, fishing and diving. He was the assistant manager at the Onehunga Tavern then. A customer had a Rakino section for sale. Maurice and Norma stood on the land, admired the view, felt good, saw the bank manager, bought it.

When the man who had the city council contract on the island retired, Maurice took it on.

They had only one room then, an outside shower, no toilet. They built their house bit by bit, until the building inspector cried enough.

Colin Maclaren came over. He was the local historian, also owner, publisher and editor of the island's newspaper, the *Rakino News*. He lived on the island permanently and reckoned to die there. He rated a permanent resident as someone who had burned their bridges and didn't have another home in the city.

He told of Governor George Grey's house, down on the foreshore in Home Bay.

Grey wanted an island of his own, the first rich man in a long line of island emperors. He bought Rakino in 1862, imported exotic birds and animals.

Colin's account had a party of Maori prisoners sent to the island by the government which then had to house them. They stumped up £50 for a weatherboard house, Grey's. 'I think what he did was, wanted something on the island, got the government to pay for it.'

The original was two rooms by two rooms, lean-to at the back. Then Kawau came onto the market and Grey preferred it. He built a mansion there instead.

The Sanfords, the fishing family, later bought the Rakino house and it grew.

Now Grey's place had grown into a single-storey house, perhaps not a mansion but big by any city villa standard, cream with olive trim.

According to local newspapers, its most recent owner had put it up for sale. There were various outbuildings, and a relocated church.

The history of the Te Akitai Waihua people said the rangatira Ihaka Takaanini was arrested following Grey's invasion of the Waikato. Ihaka and 22 others were taken by the colonial military forces and later imprisoned at Otahuhu. Ihaka's father and two of his children died there.

Ihaka and his fellow survivors were then exiled to Rakino. He died there in 1864.

From the Appendices to the House of Representatives Journal: 'Ihaka did not thrive much on the island, and died there, it is presumed of homesickness and a broken heart.'

Grey's was a nice house, now, but was there a shadow of its dark history? Maurice didn't like it. 'Too many ghosts.'

But he remembered the church well enough. As a child he'd sat in it for Sunday sermons in Northland. Hard pews, a hard life for Maurice. His grandfather and Dame Whina Cooper, the Maori land rights campaigner, were brother and sister. Whina would make him sit in a corner and not move his head until she let him, declaring, 'This will make you think of God.'

Maurice grew up on the sandspit across from Ngunguru. His name was Morris then, but he changed it when he got older. 'I wanted something more flash.'

His father died three months before he was born. His stepfather was cruel. Once the children hid in the forest for three days.

Finally his stepfather left home — taking it with him. He hitched a bullock team to the house and towed it off the property, leaving seven children homeless. Maurice went milking when he was 12, getting out of bed at 2.30 am and going to school when he finished.

He'd fall asleep at his desk and the teacher, knowing his family depended on the five pounds a week he brought home, would let him nap. He remembered the church, and the stepfather, and the watch his mother gave him as a reward for keeping the family afloat. 'I was the only one in school who had a watch and my mates would chase me around shouting, "What's the time Maurice?"'

On Rakino he had a wife and a happy home and Northland was just a bad memory.

Then he saw the church arriving at his island. His church, his old life, was catching up with him. 'Too many ghosts.'

———

A knock at the door: someone dropping off fifty dollars for a load of wood Maurice had delivered.

Another knock: someone dropping off a bottle of Jim Beam, a gift to Maurice for towing her car.

A third knock. Jim McIvor, a neighbour. His hand was bandaged. He'd burned it, badly, in unexplained circumstances except, 'It displayed what an idiot I am.'

No doctors lived on the island, but three midwives did. He found one of them and she broke out an emergency delivery kit and dressed the burn.

Three days later it was much worse and Jim was in serious pain. He called the hospital. Nine minutes, *nine minutes*, after the call, a helicopter landed nearby, and flew him to hospital. If you seriously injured yourself, Rakino was the place to do it.

Jim's hand was healing, slowly. He was a former accountant who made beautifully designed and engineered fountain pens. Norma showed me one he'd given her. It glowed in her hand, like a jewel. I said so. He was pleased. 'But I still won't tell you how I burned my hand.'

Another visitor. No knock this time, just a hand coming through the door. It was holding a glass cake pedestal with an iced chocolate cake, looking splendid.

The hand retreated, and so did its owner, so quickly I caught only a glimpse of him. 'That was Brent,' said Norma. 'He knew we had visitors so he baked a cake. He made us one yesterday too.' (Yesterday's cake stood on its glass stand on the dining table, also looking splendid.)

Far in the distance the curved white finger of a Takapuna apartment building gave the island a benediction. Auckland City was across there, Takapuna Beach full of people walking dogs, and it was a very long way away.

On the way down to the wharf, Maurice sang and laughed and honked at the pukeko, and laughed his head off. As I got out of the car I noticed the duct tape holding its parts together. It was in a leopard-skin pattern.

ROTOROA

'He said: "This beautiful place, with all my childhood memories, in a matter of months looked like the Somme. I thought, this island is *stuffed*."'

On a chill Monday morning, before the sun was up, a tough-looking aluminium boat nosed around and headed for the ferry wharf. Half of the Rotoroa Island population had arrived at Orapiu, Waiheke Island. Two men and two boys, immaculate in school uniform, popped out of the boat.

The boys looked clean and pure and full of the joy of life. Cody and Aron Salisbury, 11 years old, were just starting their working week. A taxi would take them from Orapiu to Onetangi, 13 kilometres away. From Onetangi a school bus would take them to Waiheke Primary School, the name embroidered on their maroon school jerseys. When school was over they would reverse the journey. So far the week was going well: the boat had crossed the water without drama.

Big bins of groceries and hardware went back onto the boat, enough for two families for a week. All had been carefully packed and sealed, and would be as fastidiously unpacked on the other side. Rats and pests would be fatal to Rotoroa's new enterprise, its rebirth. Two rats had been caught on the island recently, causing consternation and delaying the release of rare and endangered takahe; no one knew where the rats came from.

Rotoroa was separated from Waiheke by the Waiheke Channel. When the channel was good it was very very good. When it was bad you'd be much better off somewhere else.

The first decision Phil Salisbury had to make every morning was whether the weather was going to behave itself, not just that morning, but for the whole day, for there wasn't much point in the boys going to school if they couldn't get home again. Phil had spent some of his own childhood on Rotoroa but in those harder times school at least was easier. Kids had their own school on the island.

In those days Rotoroa was the Salvation Army's home for alcoholics, refuge, hospital, jail, sometimes even salvation. Closed to visitors. They weren't a tourist destination, the Army said.

In summer now, ferries brought hundreds of people to Rotoroa. According to Gennene Salisbury, some of them disembarked and asked where the mud pools were. They thought they were going to Rotorua. She preferred the original name. It was known to its original owners as Motu Te Rotoroa before they sold it to a settler for blankets and some breeding sheep.

Most visitors, though, knew exactly where they were, on the once-forbidden Rotoroa whose intriguing history and glorious beaches were now open to anyone who cared to make the trip.

I'd been there before, in mid-summer, and thought it the most beautiful of islands. Gentle waves caressed Ladies Bay, its flanks soft and warm.

Some former visitors, sentenced to Rotoroa, had plotted to reverse the trip; instead of escaping to paradise, they dreamed of escaping *from* it. According to the United Press Association of 19 October 1926, one even made it as far as Sydney: twice escaped from Rotoroa, he was found wandering the streets and arrested. Whether he was carted back across the Tasman to serve his time in the heavenly kingdom remained unknown.

By then Rotoroa had been a Salvation Army 'treatment centre' for 15 years; it opened in 1911, closed in 2005. The Salvation Army didn't dodge any bullets: this was to become New Zealand's most enduring addiction treatment centre, taking those cast out of mainland, mainstream New Zealand. Habitual drunks could then be sent to jail, or, alternatively, sent to Rotoroa or, for women, Pakatoa. So, they were inmates.

Phil Salisbury's dad was a taxi driver who'd had a spiritual awakening in the midst of a sickness and resolved to change his life, and inevitably his family's. He found a newspaper advertisement: 'A Christian person wanted to work with people with addictions on an island.'

He applied. The Sallies didn't care about qualifications; they simply wanted willing people, and there could not have been a surfeit of those. Both work and religious duties were rigorous, the island was even more isolated then, when boats were slow, and the Sallies' pay, well, as Phil put it, no one ever did it for the money.

Mr Salisbury, senior, got the job.

The family had grown up in Mangere. Rotoroa was . . . different. Very English. All the men worked and every house had a gardener. The big house, the superintendent's, had two gardeners. Phil said: 'It was very formal. They used to whitewash the rocks on the sides of the roads. From an eight-year-old's view it was like the Raj in India.'

As for the men: 'They were, in a way, hidden away. They had recidivist alcoholics on the streets, what did they do? They sent them here. Drunks, criminals, the suicidal and the sick, all packed into dormitories and made to get up early for work each day and go to church twice a week. They weren't really trying to fix them. It was more hard work and good food and fresh air and routine and good people around them so they would see the error of their ways and pop out the other end new men. And for some people it worked. Probably, half. They certainly had loads of return visitors. The record was twenty-seven times that someone came back. You have to assume that at that point he considered it home.'

Many of them were World War II veterans. He knew the Salisbury's gardener as Uncle Bill, whose war as a machine-gunner had scarred him permanently.

Later, when Phil was older and had left the island but returned sometimes to visit a friend, Uncle Bill was dying in hospital. He called Phil up for a chat, to get it off his chest. 'He had killed lots and lots of men. Part of the reason he was an alcoholic was this preying on his mind, remembering those men. Pretty heavy for a thirteen-year-old but I sat and listened. It was one of those moments when you grow up a bit. He died in hospital.'

Teapot Harry used to wear a tea cosy on his head with hair poking out of the holes. Back on the mainland he got drunk on a rail embankment and rolled onto the track and that was the end of him.

Above Phil and Gennene Salisbury

Opposite Salvation Army flag (right) still standing proud

Others hated the place. An ex-inmate, a journo working for the *NZ Truth*, dubbed it 'the Devil's Isle'.

For a boy this was home *and* paradise. 'The water's just there, and there were boats along the water's edge, and cows, and sheep, like being on a farm, and I'd always hankered for that. And beautiful beaches. It was a magical time for me.'

The Salvation Army was hierarchical. Children only went to the big house once, for the initial meet-the-boss.

Phil's dad was the housemaster. He'd meet the men at the wharf and escort them to the hospital block to be admitted.

They were kitted out in a kind of track suit, had their medication sorted out, mental health assessed. Too far gone and they were taken off the island and handed over to other institutions.

The men were given jobs and Salisbury senior's task was to make sure they turned up for work and went where they were supposed to be.

Most were obedient. Mount Eden prison was a dark threat. The island had two cells itself, still standing, each one bare as a fridge.

Being sentenced to Rotoroa was a privilege, although some didn't think so. Dinghies were sometimes stolen, perhaps not with conventional escape in mind. Pakatoa, the neighbouring island, was the women's equivalent of Rotoroa.

Might the women have stolen dinghies to row to Rotoroa? Phil didn't think so. 'I think they'd have put holes in the dinghies first.'

Women were accommodated on Rotoroa too from 1989, the island's population swelling to some 120 inmates.

Rotoroa closed to addicts in 2005. It was expensive to run, and the government had pulled subsidies, also closing Rotoroa's southern fellow institution at Hanmer Springs. The philosophy of treatment had changed, to day-patients and dealing with the family as a whole, rather than hiding them away on an island.

Patients were changing too. During Phil's childhood inmates were mainly older European men, alcoholics. Later a drug culture changed the clientele. They became younger, often Pacific Island and Maori with gang affiliations, Mongrel Mob and Black Power and Crips and Bloods, and in Phil's account they didn't get along, and they were intimidating.

Staff working with the men, all with degrees now, carried bleeper alarms. Drugs were being grown on the island, police came often. No one, staff or men, wanted to go to church.

It became hard to imagine those days in 1973 when the big dormitory block burned down. Then, every man had rallied to make 20,000 concrete blocks for a new one.

———

So. What of Gennene Salisbury? After all, she and the twins were in the same situation as Phil's mother had been: cutting ties, making a new life, even if she no longer had an island-full of addicts to cope with.

It wasn't quite a cold start for her. She and Phil knew a family on the island and had spent many weekends with them.

She'd grown up in Waiau, a small North Canterbury farming town, and enjoyed the country life, especially when it came with beaches.

She was working in a bank then and took six months' leave of absence.

Rotoroa would be great for six months, she thought. 'Both of us made the decision to come here,' she said, 'but he was really *really* keen.' Of course, they stayed. Now, she didn't much like leaving the island.

No palm tree with a hammock and a tall glass featured in their story. The island was hard work. It had to be knocked into shape, literally, for the Salvation Army had simply walked off the island and left everything behind, furnished houses and all. What to do with it? The Army looked at letting it out for camps, approached the council, unsuccessfully, about turning it into a regional park.

They could have sold it, of course. Having an island to yourself was a standard millionaire's prize. But what about the cemetery, the church, the history? The Sallies wanted Rotoroa open to the public.

John Gow, a former merchant banker, and his wife Jo who lived across the channel amid his sculpture park in Connells Bay, Waiheke, approached his friends Neal and Annette Plowman about buying the island. The Salvation Army didn't want to sell, but a 99-year lease was the best of both worlds: they got the money, still owned the island, and it was the Plowmans to do with as they wished. What they, and the Gows, wished was to renew the island as a refuge, for conservation, the arts, its own history, with unrestricted public access.

The Rotoroa Island Trust was formed to do the job, John the project manager, and the Salisburys their right-hand people.

They cleared the island, literally. They tore down many old buildings. Phil

demolished his old family house, put a digger through his bedroom, wrenched out the trees he once picked fruit from. Contractors cut down and chipped 25,000 pine trees.

At the end of it he was in despair.

He said: 'I knew it would be very hard to pull down the buildings because of my memories as a child but I knew this part of the island's journey had come to an end. We shut it for three years.

'Logging trucks, bulldozers, excavators, they just chewed the island. This beautiful place, with all my childhood memories, in a matter of months looked like the Somme. I thought, this island is *stuffed*. I don't think it will ever come right.

'But sometimes you have to go backwards to go forwards. We churned it up

Above Rotoroa noticeboard

Following Jail time (left); changing addictions

THE TWELVE TRADITIONS
OF NARCOTIC'S ANONYMOUS

1—Our common welfare should come first; personal recovery depends upon N.A. unity.

2—For our Group purpose there is but one ultimate authority—a loving God as He may express Himself in our group conscience. Our leaders are but trusted servants; they do not govern.

3—The only requirement for N.A. membership is a desire to stop using.

4—Each Group should be autonomous except in matters affecting other groups or N.A. as a whole.

5—Each Group has but one primary purpose—to carry its message to the addict who still suffers.

6—An N.A. Group ought never endorse, finance or lend the N.A. name to any related facility or outside enterprise, lest problems of money, property and prestige divert us from our primary purpose.

7—Every N.A. Group ought to be fully self-supporting, declining outside contributions.

8— Narcotic's Anonymous should remain forever nonprofessional, but our service centers may employ special workers.

9—N.A., as such, ought never be organized; but we may create service boards or committees directly responsible to those they serve.

10— Narcotic's Anonymous has no opinion on outside issues; hence the N.A. name ought never be drawn into public controversy.

11—Our public relations policy is based on attraction rather than promotion; we need always maintain personal anonymity at the level of press, radio and films.

12—Anonymity is the spiritual foundation of our traditions, ever reminding us to place principles before personalities.

and ripped it apart and had fires like you wouldn't believe and tore down the old buildings. Then we started planting and putting new tracks in. The diggers filled the holes, smoothed things over, root-raked the paddocks, and the grass started coming back, and the trees. We started in 2008. It opened to the public for the first time in over a hundred years on Sunday, 27 February 2011.

'Seven years ago this island was a wreck and look at it now.'

I looked. A new building sat at the end of the wharf, below an old pa, where Gennene met incoming ferries and explained the island. A newly planted pohutukawa forest flourished on the nearby hillside. Half a million new native trees were greening the island. Kiwi ran beneath them, and two of the world's remaining 270 takahe. A pathway lined with huge Norfolk pines and sheets of sculptured steel marking the alcoholics' 12 steps to redemption led to the wonderfully designed exhibition centre housing the island's history.

The brick chapel remained, now blasting out Army classics to the half-dozen people on the island, *Fire in the Blood*, or Phil's favourite hymn, *Climbing up the Golden Stairs of Glory*.

Once, you had 20 minutes to get to church from the time the music started. Several services a week, attendance compulsory, although most wanted to go: the services were a social event, people standing around chatting for half an hour afterwards. Above the church, stone steps led to the old superintendent's house, now available to rent and popular with the families who ran over its kauri floors, big enough for 18 people.

High on a nearby hill lay the cemetery, fenced, graves in neat lines. We could see most of the island, Ladies Bay and Mens Bay enticing in the blue, the Gulf comforting, fathomable.

They'd spotted kiwi up here briefly. The takahe kept to themselves. Saddlebacks and whitehead too. The island was renewing itself as a sanctuary, this time for endangered wildlife.

Here lay Phil's teacher, Beth Drummond. She'd married three alcoholics on the island. Husbands two and three were both named Harry. When they asked her where she wanted to be buried, she replied: 'Just bury me with Harry.' They didn't know which one so they put her in the cemetery with Harry three.

'This,' Phil said, 'is the most significant thing I will do on this earth.' I liked these two. They were good people doing good work.

Motuihe

'The Crown bought Motuihe
in 1872, and the island's
fortunes turned gloomy.'

Motuihe lay neatly, close to Auckland, a spot that
had served it well and badly in roughly equal
proportions.

Its beaches on either side had always been
favourite anchorages for yachts and launches and
you could take a dip in still water with the island
spread low above you.

Maori once lived there in two headland pa, and
battles were fought, but they were overshadowed
by European drama. The Crown bought Motuihe
in 1872, and the island's fortunes turned gloomy.
That same year a shipload of smallpox victims were
quarantined on the island.

During World War I the remarkable German
raider Count Felix von Luckner was imprisoned on
Motuihe along with Dr Erich Shultz, the governor
of German Samoa, and his senior officials. Von

Luckner, always a slippery customer, escaped of
course. He and his crew were eventually captured
at the Kermadec Islands.

The island was used as a wartime internment
camp for persons deemed suspicious, mainly
people from German settlements in Samoa and
New Guinea. According to one of the guards on
the island, they were 'a happy little camp', prisoners
shopping in Queen Street. Their barracks building
remained. The internees were cleared off it to make
way for victims of the 1918 influenza epidemic,
which in two months killed 8600 people in New
Zealand.

Motuihe's cemetery recorded the graves of a
soldier, a guard who died of influenza, three seamen
from the influenza-stricken steamer RMS *Makura*,
two anonymous souls and one woman who'd died

nursing patients there. The list was probably not
exhaustive.

Almost all the New Zealand passengers aboard
the *Makura* were taken to Auckland over the
protests of the city's mayor, who complained that
such a release was unheard of anywhere in the
world and was 'reprehensible in the extreme'.

The island became home to an animal
quarantine station until it moved to Matiu/Somes
Island in Wellington Harbour.

Motuihe became a public domain in 1963
and was now home to kiwi, geckos, tuatara,
saddlebacks, the rare and the endangered. Volunteers were restoring vegetation, and the only cries
of dismay to be heard came from yachties when
someone came into their anchorage too fast and
spilled their drinks.

THE
DRAMA
QUEENS

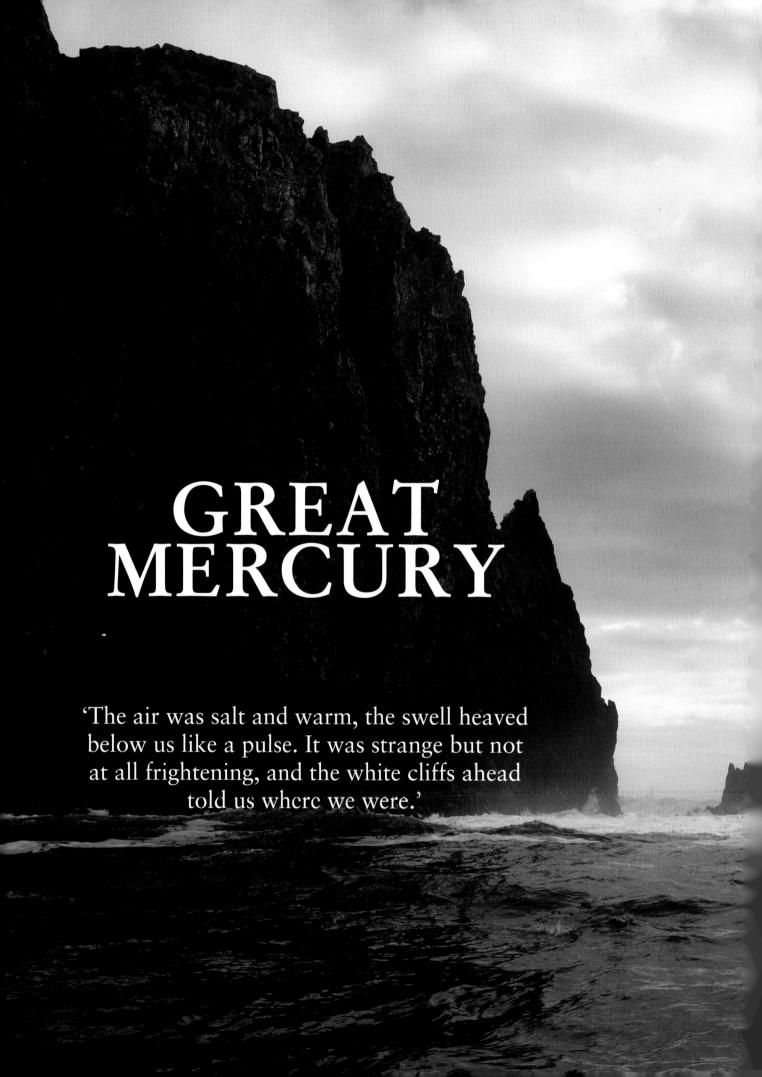

GREAT
MERCURY

'The air was salt and warm, the swell heaved
below us like a pulse. It was strange but not
at all frightening, and the white cliffs ahead
told us where we were.'

The rich and famous were drawn to islands. Larry Ellison owned one. So did Richard Branson and Johnny Depp and lots of others. Mostly they kept their islands to themselves.

Ahuahu, Great Mercury Island, was owned by Sir Michael Fay and David Richwhite, once the darlings of the bright new world ushered in by David Lange's Labour government in the 1980s. They'd become less popular with the public over the sale of state assets, allegations of insider trading, oh, and the winebox business, Fay cheerfully reminded me later when I was working down the list.

They had every reason to keep themselves to themselves.

Publicity had done these two no good at all but this book was as much about islanders as islands and Great Mercury needed its owners. I approached Sir Michael without much hope but found him so accommodating we visited the island twice.

We went there by boat the first time. It sailed from Whitianga, the nice little port town being assaulted by the overflow from expensive Auckland: to get into the place you passed a canal housing development and went through one of those dreary places full of cut-price shopping barns.

No one could develop its most outstanding feature however: the sea. We passed a scatter of islands, the Twins, Motukoranga, Motukoruenga, the Needle, Ohinau, Flat, Old Man Rocks, Black Rocks, and an archipelago opened in front of us. Korapuki, Atiu, Red Mercury, Double, Middle, some that were simply rocks sticking out of the sea and all of them aperitifs for the main course, Great Mercury, the biggest of the island group named by Captain James Cook busy observing the transit of Mercury there in 1769.

We nipped up the west coast of the island into the shelter of Huruhi, the island's enveloping harbour, and there, waiting at his jetty, was Sir Michael himself.

I had not seen him since the glory days of his America's Cup campaign in 1987 on behalf of the Mercury Bay Boating Club, when eventually he won the Cup in

Pages 192–3 The white cliffs of Ahuahu

Previous Great Mercury

Opposite Cliffs of Ahuahu at close range

a New York courtroom and held it for as long as it took his opponents to appeal.

He did not look hugely older, face more pointed, pixie-ish in a smile, still tall and straight, still a lot of hair. He wore high boots and clean jeans and a Great Mercury Island sweatshirt, like a station owner at his local A&P show. Fair enough: he thought of his island as a station, remote and self-contained, and his farm staff and his personal staff made quite a crowd. All the same, I thought we might be the fat lambs.

We went into his boatshed, although I saw it as a two-storeyed handsome hall-on-the-sea. We walked along a hallway with a group of sculpted, life-sized warriors lurking at its end, up a wide stairway and into a room running much of the building's length. A giant book of photographs by Helmut Newton, best known for sexually provocative fashion photography and portraits, lay open on a pedestal rather like a music stand: here was David Bowie, recently dead. A portrait of Fay's old black Labrador Marco on the wall. Heavy beams, a coffee table on an old aircraft engine, models of his yachts, a stag's head above the fireplace.

A collection of Maori artefacts, most from Great Mercury, lay on a shelf. Here was one made of rock from Tahanga, above Opito Bay, 'the best tool-masking basalt in the whole of New Zealand', that one from Great Barrier stone. He stroked a beautiful, tiny adze.

Sir Michael sat behind his desk, big enough for a brisk game of ping-pong, and I began to learn about the main thing in his life, Great Mercury Island. When I asked him, much later, which had been the most satisfying part of his life, his business, his America's Cup campaign, or living on his island, he said, 'Through lots of adventures, lots of ups and downs, this place has anchored me.'

Great Mercury Island, Ahuahu, was said by the Ngati Porou to be the place where their ancestor Paikea, the whale rider, landed at the end of his journey from Hawaiki. He covered himself with ahu, sand.

Fay believed that Auckland University research would prove that Ahuahu once had the oldest settlement in New Zealand so far discovered, wresting the honour from Marlborough's Wairau Bar which was thought to have been occupied around 1300.

He and Richwhite bought the island in the mid-1970s, when they were a couple of apprentice buccaneers with gold in their teeth.

It had been farmed since 1929 by the Mizen family, who had battled distance, isolation, fire, storm and fickle markets with courage and ingenuity, which came to an end one day in 1975. Pat Mizen, the head of the family, was attempting to head off a stampede by galloping his horse along a hillside so steep he had to hook up his inside boot to keep it free of the ground. If his horse had lost its footing he would not have had a chance. 'The two of us would have gone down two hundred feet in a rolling, flailing tangled heap,' he wrote later. He was 57. Time to go, he reasoned.

The government at the time was pushing an 'open spaces' policy, seeking to protect attractive coastal land for the public. He'd begun negotiations with

Matt Rata, the Minister of Maori Affairs and Lands, when Fay and Richwhite appeared. On Fay's very first walk, on the first day he set foot on the island, he picked up a tiny black stone adze, the same one that now lay in his office. It sat in the palm of his hand, warm and consoling.

The farm was run-down. 'It was derelict,' Fay said. He ran a hand through his hair. 'Buildings were barely habitable, it was covered in gorse, there were no roads that worked, a handful of sheep, and it was pretty much bankrupt.' A shame for Pat Mizen. A life's hard work.

The young men saw only beauty. 'Those days were full of ego, full of testosterone. If you're going to live on an island, I don't think I could cope with a little island, but this has a massive scale to it.' They were in love.

They flew in on Freddie Ladd's amphibian, landed on the middle of the island, walked through the back country, found the adze, walked on Peachgrove beach, looked at the rocks, the pohutukawa. It took Fay's breath away. He was captivated.

They leased the island in 1975 and two years later bought it outright. Wherever he went from that moment, Auckland or Sydney or Geneva, he always kept that smoothed piece of rock with him. His island proved the most enduring love affair of his life and that is why we made two journeys to Great Mercury Island.

On our first visit, 40 years to the month after he took over the farm, someone came in to say the boat was waiting to take us back to Whitianga whenever we were ready. Fay had been talking for quite a long time about the island but we hadn't seen it properly. How could we appreciate it without covering the ground? How would we understand it, value it, applaud it, delight in it as he

Above The markers

Right The young men saw only beauty

did? For he was an enthusiast, an island artist, a man enthralled by his place.

Now, here was his proposal. He'd fly us back out to Great Mercury on his helicopter whenever it suited. We would have dinner, stay the night. We could take a farm truck and drive wherever we wanted to.

That was how we came to be standing in the heliport at Onehunga, wondering which of these huge, gleaming black machines was ours. The pilot, Keith, directed us to one of them. There were five passengers including us: a couple of plumbers grinning ear to ear and the Richwhites' youngest son Christopher, who everyone called Topher.

Rangitoto passed below, and Motutapu, and all the others lying in their sleepy sea. As we flew over Pakatoa, where Kerridge Odeon's lost dream of paradise was preserved virtually intact, Topher said it reminded him of the television series *Lost*, as the place where the Others lived. I hadn't thought of that, but he was right.

The green Coromandel islands passed below like one of those panoramic travel films Kerridge Odeon were so fond of, and the Coromandel Peninsula and its bays which all looked different from above, then the archipelago with Great Mercury as its centrepiece.

We flew over the island's south end where runabouts clustered in bays whose sand was so white, water so translucent, they could have been travel posters for Fiji, except they were not, they were right here and despite the hot day in the middle of summer they were not crowded nor were there tourist hotels or bars or boat rentals or anything but sand and bush and water and New Zealanders doing what they'd always done so well, messing about on the beach.

Above Fangs

Then we flew along the white cliffs on the eastern side of the island which Paikea must have seen from afar, beacons in the mist. They rose sheer from the sea, high enough for a veil, a wisp of cloud, to lie over their brow.

I went to Peachgrove Bay later to see why Fay had fallen so instantly in love, and it was a paradise with its stream and kids playing in its lagoon, exactly as it seemed from above, ordinary average New Zealand families having a good old day by the sea.

Zane Grey, the wealthy American author and game fisherman, established a camp for his entourage near Whalers Bay here at the bottom of the island in the 1920s. The Press Association reported at the time that his camp 'is one of the prettiest ever seen'.

Now this was the curious thing. The rich liked islands, and one reason for that was privacy: they could keep the baying public away from their bays.

Fay and Richwhite actually *liked* people on their island. 'This is a big place and it can take a lot of people,' said Sir Michael. 'Now they're the best asset the island can have. They take care of it. They keep the beaches clean. It's self-policing in a sense.'

Only their own 2-hectare home blocks of Great Mercury's 1870 hectares were private. 'We'd like a bit of privacy and people respect it. There's only been a handful of incidents over the forty years, normally involving a bit too much drinking.

'My wife liked it here but you either get islands or you don't. It's a tough environment if you're not plugged into it or you're not busy. She lives in Auckland at the moment, my kids are overseas.'

Topher had told us that the Richwhites' houses, two grey concrete sculptures beset by glass and pools, were known as the James Bond place, while the Fay house was called the Flintstone house.

The Fays' house both grew from the earth and vanished into it, as much sculpture as home. Winding staircases, heavy doors, curving roofs, rocks, tiles, sea-wrought pohutukawa logs dragged from the beach. No symmetry, nothing the same. It would take a long time to become bored with it, I thought.

The house was designed by the French-born architect and sculptor Savin Couelle, who called himself a 'gypsy architect' and liked Sardinia where he spent time as a boy. For the Fays he designed and built two houses, the Up House (where Fay lived) and the Down House, which of course was further down the hill and used by his children.

———

Before dawn next morning we crept down the stairs. In mid-summer the harbour was full of sleeping boats. We climbed into an amphibious Sealegs, nosed into the open sea and went warily southwards, for rocks and reefs lay all around. One stuck from the sea like a fang.

The air was salt and warm, the swell heaved below us like a pulse. It was strange but not at all frightening and the white cliffs ahead told us where we were. They were patterned, lined, wrinkled, creased, carved by wind and sea. They shone through the yellow and grey dawn, the archipelago ghostly all around, Ahuahu vanishing to the north in shadows and suggestions, the slow swell ending suddenly in a crash of cream, erupting from a blowhole a little north. We could see the faint terraces of an old pa.

What must it be like to own all this? I expected Fay to say he was merely its steward, but he didn't, he said no one could own all of this, the island never talked to him in that sense. He seemed as overwhelmed as we were. The island was strange, mysterious, eerie, he said. He sensed its spirit.

We went on, around the top of the islands to a place where the Cathedral Rocks, Moturoa, jumped from the sea, sheer and dark. They looked like the three black fingers of a drowning person.

Some 30 people died here. Pat Mizen was an archaeologist, amateur but thorough, and he'd recorded a tale passed down from one of an attacking force.

Under the heading 'The Final Massacre' he told of a last party of 30 survivors taking refuge on top of Moturoa. Mizen said the rock was said to have a flat top and although almost perpendicular its volcanic creation had left footholds. They carried up food, and water in gourds, and soon enough the attackers arrived and laid siege. Only one man at a time could climb the so-called path; the stronghold was impossible to take. The attackers sat below for a week or so, grew impatient, devised a scheme.

'You've done very well, you're to be admired,' they called to their defenders. 'Come on down, we'll have a feast.'

The islanders were said to have fallen for it, although they might have had no option: with plenty of food and water the invaders could have camped below indefinitely. They were given seats of honour, and as the umu was opened, a signal was given and each attacking warrior turned and clubbed their guests to death.

Various versions of this tale existed; they were all probably of the Ngapuhi's last raid south, in search of utu, attacking Ahuahu then Tuhua or Mayor Island, and ending at Motiti where they were wiped out.

Mizen noted the man telling the tale, the last survivor of the attacking force, 'laughed at the cupidity of the fallen'. The old farmer climbed the rock himself to confirm the story. Sure enough, the rock *did* have a flat top, and people had been there for he found buried paua shells. Below, he discovered a human thigh bone in a crevice.

I looked at the ragged edges, cleaved, split, crenellated like battlements at the top, the surf cracking at their base and running white from black cracks. A wilder, more terrifying refuge could not be imagined. But I was not a desperate man with a taua on my heels.

Traces of old pa survived all over the island and Mizen mapped them all. We climbed one of the finest, Tamawera: 'Alone, magnificent, almost impregnable,' said Mizen, and almost certainly the most important pa on the island, 100 metres above the sea surrounding it on three sides. Underneath a mighty sea cave ran two-thirds of its girth, ending in a hidden boulder beach. A swamp on the landward side was once a lake, with stone jetties and a causeway.

It resembled a European fort; other pa terraces survived from an era of wooden palisades, but these terraces were faced with stone. Rock walls defended it, defined house pits, supported platforms. Even now, centuries past its peak, it was majestic, and we stood on its top and marvelled.

Later we crossed the tombolo, the low-lying spit dividing Great Mercury from the sea making it look like two islands.

Fay showed us tiny holes in a bank, burrows for kotare, tiny pieces of eggshell lying outside, a strange clattering coming from the chicks within while the parent kingfishers screeched dismay from the trees. He knew this island centimetre by centimetre.

———

Great Mercury was the biggest in an archipelago of seven islands. The next biggest was Red Mercury, where Count Felix von Luckner, the German raider captain, hid after escaping a prisoner-of-war camp on Motuihe in 1917.

The other six were now publicly owned nature reserves, guarded zealously by DOC.

New Zealand held the world record for the number of islands cleared of rats, but other records were not so good. The nation had the world's largest number of seabird species, for example, but also the greatest number of threatened seabird species.

The publicly owned islands had now become arks, sometimes for species on the absolute brink. The tiny Middle Island once held the world's population of giant tusked weta: four. They were now being bred in captivity and transferred to other islands.

Dr David Towns worked jointly for DOC and Auckland University of Technology on restoring the ecology of the islands. As he saw it, six islands were good, but including the seventh, Great Mercury, was critical. Each island's habitat had a spillover effect on the others, and Great Mercury had so much more to spill.

Kereru, for example, were efficient at spreading seeds and so regenerating native forest. The wood pigeons preferred Great Mercury and would spread outward from there, as long as the bigger island could provide them with a habitat.

Following Sir Michael Fay

Great Mercury's owners were willing. Libby Richwhite, David's wife, was keen on conservation and had approached DOC in the 1990s. That led to Great Mercury becoming, like its neighbours, free of rats. It was a long, expensive programme where Great Mercury and DOC shared the $1.5 million bill, and it worked.

Everyone agreed that it was better to look at the archipelago as a single land mass; after all, that was what it had been 6000 years ago. Great Mercury, it was hoped, would also become an ark, a much bigger, more diverse and eventually safer one.

Now there were 292 rat traps on the island and Sir Michael Fay knew them all. Today he spot-checked one, found it without its egg bait, took its number, vowed to check his records and talk to whoever was responsible.

New life was returning to the island. We walked through regenerating bush in cushioned silence broken by the distant squawk from one of the kaka finding a home here.

The huge tusked weta were appearing. Once they'd been a prime main course for rats. I hoped I would not meet one, although their long, curved tusks were used for pushing opponents, not biting. Fay thought its recovery an even bigger story than the more cuddly black robin's.

The big question for both David Towns and Michael Fay was succession: the island was in good hands now, but would it stay that way?

Fay was preoccupied with the island's future. How could he and Richwhite secure it?

'The big question for me,' he said, 'is, what happens to the island. What do you do, how do you manage this place in a more demanding environment with more people, more pressure, how do you preserve the archaeological sites, the habitat? You might well be preserving one of the oldest areas of settlement in the country, largely intact here because there has been no pressure of development.'

Who would own Great Mercury in the future? And how? I hoped he would resolve it. To me he seemed a man whose interest in his island had swamped all others and brought him some peace, at least.

He said: 'There's a lot of freedom in not having to care any more. Jobs don't seem that important. I don't read anything about business at all now other than Fonterra and dairy prices, because I've got some dairy farms.

'This for me now is a lovely time of watching. I don't have a sense of having to do anything except watch and sit still.

'This island has heaps and heaps of magic. To indulge yourself in it when you don't have to do anything else, you can just say no, and get into this thing, islands and rats and strange things, and trying to understand.'

We stood on top of the white cliffs we'd seen in the dawn. Walls of pure cream dropped to the sea. I felt at the end of the world, the end of everything. This was the most sensational island I'd been on. He'd made me fall in love with it, too.

Opposite Rough at the edges

Slipper

'From here Slipper and its near neighbours Penguin and Rabbit looked as happy as the children's storybook their names seemed to have come from.'

Slipper Island lay only 4 kilometres off the Coromandel coast, soft in the late afternoon, yet in the hard light of day it wasn't as cosy.

The family who once owned this island were still fighting over its fate. Insults were being traded.

None of this could be seen from my vantage point on a hill overlooking the island: a spot gouged in the hillside above an Ashram yoga community and occupied by the shell of a caravan with five bourbon-and-cola bottles (all empty) arranged on its roof. From here Slipper and its near neighbours Penguin and Rabbit and, of course, Shoe, looked as happy as the children's storybook their names seemed to have come from.

Except for a small area of reserve land the island was still privately owned. In 2013, 0.57 hectares of beach and dunes in one of the two main bays, Home Bay, was declared a public reserve, allowing public access for the first time.

The Needham family bought Slipper in the 1970s. There were 14 children in the family. Christina Needham was the youngest, living in Tairua, crossing to the island for weekends and holidays, an idyllic life she loved.

'I pretty much grew up on the island,' she said. Slipper was a working farm then, mainly sheep; some 217 hectares of paradise whose fine beaches today lay white in the sun. Smoothed hills ran back from the bays, the fickle light picked out a headland here, an islet there, all vanishing and reappearing like a conjuring trick.

The island was only 4 kilometres from the mainland and had in its own way directed the lives of many of the 14 Needham children. The easiest and fastest way of getting to the island was by air and 10 of the 14 had become pilots. Christina was an Air New Zealand pilot; others had also become commercial pilots.

But the family was riven by disputes over the island's sale to an Auckland woman. Some supported the sale, others did not. They posted their objections to it on a website, complaining that they learned of the sale and purchase agreement only through the media, that both the family's heritage and the island's Maori history had been misunderstood.

Sites in the island's two main bays, South Bay and Home Bay, were believed to be among the earliest places occupied in New Zealand. Very early stone adzes had been found, and pieces of fish hooks made from the bones of the biggest species of moa, the first species to become extinct.

Warren Gumbley, an archaeologist who examined ancient sites on Slipper, believed its human history went back to the very early Polynesian settlement of New Zealand in the late thirteenth or early fourteenth century. Seven, possibly eight, pa sites were found, indicating the importance of the island:

it was both productive and strategically located.

The most convincing single item of evidence was a trolling lure shank found by Christina's mother, Nora. It was one of only three objects found in New Zealand which had been made of pearl shell found solely in the tropics.

The island, Warren believed, represented a microcosm of the history of Polynesian settlement, from the very first arrivals until the European era: 'A cultural and historical landscape such as Slipper Island's is now very rare in New Zealand.'

Some sections around South Bay were subdivided for family members, but with the bulk of the island sold out of the family Christina Needham was now working to have significant archaeological sites recognised and protected. She was lobbying to save her island. 'It's deep in my heart,' she said. 'I love it.'

MOTITI

'The airfield separated the island into north and south. For some the fence running across the island beside it was Motiti's equivalent of the Berlin Wall.'

At Motiti we flew into a divided land. The airstrip was a de facto demarcation line, Maori on one side, Pakeha on the other. This was not so much an island as a political situation.

Our fellow passengers were a woman and her son. She lived there, he'd come to fish and dive on the Maori side of the line, or as he called it, 'the natives' end'. I thought he was joking until I heard the bitterness.

Don Wills met us in his 4WD. He was bitter too, unusually, for he was an even-tempered man. Things had been broken all over his car while it had been parked at the airfield, lights and mouldings, smashed and left beside the car.

Everyone knew who had done it although they weren't naming names. Young people, now returned to the mainland, for school had resumed. Whoever they were, the vandalism was racially balanced at least. A woman named Mere found her car damaged too. The vandals were eclectic.

The island was already at odds over the wreck of the *Rena*, the container ship which hit the nearby Astrolabe Reef at speed on 5 October 2011.

The French navigator Dumont d'Urville was caught in a storm in 1827 and narrowly escaped the reef. But he got away, with only primitive charts to guide him and sails to propel his ship. The *Rena* was manned by lesser sailors. It poured oil over the clean seascape, layering beaches in a thick layer of black scum, shedding cargo up and down the coast.

Claims overlapped hearings swamping settlements in their own oil slicks. The *Rena* owners wanted to leave part of the wreck on the reef. People on Motiti, the closest island, suffered most from the wreck. Te Patuwai, who owned the northern half of the island, saw the reef as their own, once an island itself, and were seeking customary title. Some wanted the wreck removed completely. Others, such as Nepia Ranapia, a Motiti elder, believed it best left where it was. Nepia wanted the money on offer from the *Rena*'s owners used to buy the airstrip, on Wills' land. 'And if they gave us enough, we'd like a wharf.'

Previous Motiti

Opposite Nepia Ranapia

Right The lifeline,
Paterson's Inlet

Others accused the ship owners of a divide-and-rule strategy.

The airfield separated the island into north and south. For some the fence running across the island beside it was Motiti's equivalent of the Berlin Wall. Motiti Pakeha said they were forbidden to cross to the north. 'Incorrect,' Nepia said. 'There are people here [on the Maori side] who are troublemakers, that's all.'

Were Maori likewise unwelcome in the south? That appeared uncertain. Don seemed flexible, more disappointed than worried by it.

He and his brother Vernon and their families had been on the island since 1979. They remembered when the two ends of the island were once a coherent community and shared social occasions. Now young people had no respect. Only the week before there'd been a police raid on paua poachers and the island was in uproar.

Nepia was eloquent on the subject.

Above Don Wills at Paterson's Inlet

'Traditional governance was the old people. But what happened was Christianity came aboard. They let their values go. They lost their way.

'By doing that you lost who you are. For example, in a democracy we have an open-door policy. Under Maori structures they are closed-door policies. Which is, anything that had to be done, any issues that needed addressing, the elders did it. So if you were naughty you came before the elders. If you could not explain yourself, off you go. And you went off the island for about a year and you came back and behaved yourself.

'That's a closed-door forum as opposed to an open-door forum. In an open-door forum everyone has their say, mokopunas and all. And that's why the respect for the elders has gone, *peeeeow*.

'The marae now becomes a debating chamber. It was never like that. Everyone screams and yells. You get yelled at, you get screamed at.'

I'd contacted one person said to be a community leader and asked permission to visit. She'd replied that the people had met and decided that it was not convenient. Maybe later.

She was at the airport as we flew in, greeting someone else. She looked awkward and I felt sorry for her. It was like having an unexpected visitor when your home was a mess; and we were not even invited guests.

The situation seemed so . . . sad.

A soft wind puffed the grass with the blue sea all around. On the Maori side of the line stood a neat marae with the village peeking from bush.

A simple white church once stood here, built with great pride and opened in May 1920. The *Bay of Plenty Times* of the day reported that 'a large attendance of Maoris and Europeans' from throughout the Bay of Plenty and beyond were present.

'After the service (in both Maori and English) a sumptuous dinner was served, to which all the visitors were invited by the Patuwai tribe of Motiti.'

It was a fine building, costing £400 ($800), a lot of money in the day. Mr H. Bateman gave a bell, Mr J. Ricketts the matting, the Tauranga Band the musical accompaniment, and the Patersons, who then farmed the southern half of the island, gave a bullock for the hangi. All was harmony then.

Much later, in 1955, the *New Zealand Herald* described an island idyll, a close Maori community of 100, a third of them schoolchildren, living in a paradise producing maize, kumara, watermelon.

In his history of Motiti published in 1979, A.H. Matheson recorded 'an almost deserted island'. Kumara crops had been ruined by the black rot fungus, maize was no longer economic. Young people saw no future for themselves and left. By 1967 the permanent Maori population was less than 10, although the Ranapia family persevered with a mixed farming venture.

Now the total population was perhaps 40 people.

Part of the blame, Nepia said, lay with bureaucrats.

A heavy-handed approach by the authorities, he said, had messed up what had been a good relationship between the two ends of the island. 'There was always a line in the sand here, across the board agreements. Here's an example. These are the values of our people, and these [he pointed to the respective sides with a stick] are the values of the general people. Now you have to get a building consent process. Never had one.

'On our side we've always had agreement with our people, you never build in the middle of a paddock. There's papakainga [a form of housing development on ancestral land] up there which our people partitioned out. So you build there. We had traditional rules. We can't insure our houses, we can't sell our houses. You need a building consent process to onsell your property. So two different values. Everyone says, one rule for all. It's very difficult. So what we propose is, you have your traditional basket here, and we have a mutual basket in the middle for the environmental health of the island. The planners don't want to know about it.'

I read the proposed plan for the island. It seemed the usual stuff, encased in environmental fluff and curtsies to the tangata whenua.

Nepia remained hopeful. 'I think it's going to work out okay.'

But I could see big complications on this small island.

———

Two tribes, Te Patuwai and Te Whanau a Tauwhao, fought over this fertile island for a century. A lot of blood was spilled.

In 1867 the Native Land Court settled their boundaries. The Patuwai then owned, roughly, the northern half of the island, and Te Whanau a Tauwhao the south.

The southern portion of the island was then leased to a Pakeha, George Alexander Douglas, who retired from his business as a storekeeper to farm cattle and horses on Motiti. Douglas later bought the entire southern part of Motiti, setting aside an 80-hectare reserve for the Whanau a Tauwhao, which he then leased back.

That established a pattern which more or less remained the same since.

———

Right Vernon Wills, riding his range

On the Pakeha side of the line, avocado groves lay plump and green.

The two brothers, Vernon and Don, both kiwifruit growers, were holidaying in Fiji when they got an idea: why not buy a property over there so they could go to Fiji for all of their holidays? But they could find nothing suitable. The third man in this triumvirate happened to be a real estate agent. If not Fiji, he suggested, why not try a lot closer to home, Motiti Island in fact?

The Patersons, who had farmed Motiti for 82 years, had finally decided to sell. It was 1979.

'We were lucky enough to be there when the crest of the kiwifruit wave came,' Vernon said. 'We were making big money and looking for alternatives. We came out, looked, fell in love with the place.'

They bought not just an island, but a life they never regretted.

Don had spent his childhood fishing, surfcasting, snorkelling in long underwear and a mask made from an old tyre tube. Motiti felt like home from the word go.

The land ran cattle then. They tried kiwifruit at first, found the growing too stressful, had a go at avocados. Fertile, ancient volcanic soil, frost-free climate with the sea contributing ambient temperatures a few degrees above the mainland's meant they got a head start on their competitors with early harvests. The fruit fitted the sea rather than fighting it.

Although the season was over, Don had picked a few plump avocados from the top of a tree as a present to us. He ate avocados every day, on toast for breakfast, avos for lunch. At 77 years old his cholesterol was very low. I blame the avocado, he said.

Ours ripened in a week and were delicious.

———

But now the Willses had sold, or were selling, most of their holdings, except for blocks of family land dotted with the holiday encampments, cottages and caravans of their six children and 13 grandchildren. Their home areas were in a trust for their children, so created as to make the land very difficult to sell. The idea was that Willses would be here forever.

Vernon loved the quietness. 'The island has a lot of mystique. Don and I both loved the sea, the diving and the fishing. Our families come out for holidays.' He'd play Mr Whippy, ringing an old school bell, taking ice-cream to the beach for the kids who lined up for it.

The wider family came too: Gail Wills, Don's wife, was one of 10 children, and many of her brothers and sisters and their children learned to swim, fish, dive here, learned an outdoor life. The island was a child's dream.

Above Home Bay

Above Avocado
groves, Motiti

Motiti broiled in the spring sun. We climbed into Don's wagon and he took us bumping over tracks to see the yellow pohutukawa first, of course.

A man known only as 'a Mr Potts' discovered two yellow pohutukawa on Motiti in 1840. Those two trees spawned the bright yellow cascades of today's northern summers, although the species was still rare enough to be remarkable.

On Motiti the trees stood proudly at the sea's edge turning yellow in the summer, often amid land being restored to native vegetation in partnership with DOC.

We went down to Home Bay, once Orongatea, where the generations of Pakeha farmers had built their homes and swam among the rocks in the clear water. It was one of the island's three good beaches, one of them Wairanaki in the northern half, the third Wairere Bay at the southern end. Three good beaches but no natural harbour.

Don wiped wet sand from a smooth, round rock. A line, a circle, koru marks like stars in a firmament, emerged from the dark. Carved in the stone, Nepia said later, by people 'way before Maori ever got here, even before the migrations from Hawaiki. Moriori people. Oh yes. There's evidence all over the place.'

This, he said, was a map of the Indian and Pacific oceans, a chart, each koru representing a country. 'We have the chart, the karakia, of that rock, what it represents, the migration path.' Part of an earlier migration, he insisted: 'The temples of rock they built are still here but never exposed.'

A mystery, coming and going on the tides.

A tiny bay, shown as Paterson's Inlet on my map, was the key to success on the island, for getting people, stock, produce, cargo on and off it was always its main economic stumbling block.

Once a railway and a punt to waiting ships served, in good weather. The first Patersons had a better idea. In 1913 they built a breakwater in a notch in the coast which became known as Paterson's Inlet. Large scows once poked into this small place, which their crews called 'the hole'. Although the original breakwater was smashed by storms, the little port of Motiti had served ever since, exporting everything from racehorses to cattle, maize to avocados. The Willses once shipped squash to Japan, loading it onto barges. The breakwater was still there, battered but unbowed.

We went down to the south where the island ended in a sharp point then stuttered over a reef laced yellow in the blue sea, ending in a small island, steep and bushy: Motu Taumaihi, a natural fortress. This was once the mighty Matarehua pa, sacred, where ancestors of Tupaea, a chief of Te Whanau a Tauwhao, and other Tauranga chiefs were buried.

Vernon had something else to show us. I'd seen a lot of books about the American West on his shelves and was curious: this was hardly home on the range.

He took us down to a spacious building behind his cottage. The sign said: 'Home Bay Saloon'.

Inside, the décor was back country: bush saws, horse collars, swords, old guns and shell cases. A wagon wheel hung from the ceiling, pictures of cowboys hung on the walls alongside holstered Colts, a cartridge belt, a World War I helmet, tomahawk, lance and a shell collection compiled by his son Andrew when he was studying marine biology. A billiard table shared the floor with a honky-tonk piano whose keys had been most recently pounded by his friend Ellie. Halved wagon wheels supported tables. Friends, all of them wearing cowboy hats, would sit at the bar on stools topped with saddles, gearing up for a weekend of huntin' and fishin'.

It seemed very odd. But then, Motiti was, wasn't it.

WHITE

'Anything seemed possible in this impossible
world with its cast of villains.'

first saw White Island very late at night. Smelled it, a reek from the bowels of the earth, rotting, smoking, eggy. You got that around Rotorua, or Hanmer Springs.

Now it was carried on the night breeze rolling over the salt and standing my nerves to full alert, for there was no disbelieving the supernatural on a small boat at night. My god, I thought, what on earth was *that*, if it was in fact earthly.

Of course it was, gas and rock and base elements boiling up from far below and popping on the surface like a boil.

The island appeared, bulking in the dark. From the other side, the southern side, something glowed, a deep dark colour seeping through cracks ebbing and flowing, glowing and dying, and thoroughly spooking the horses, those ghastly creatures of the dark.

I learned when at last I visited White Island, Whakaari, properly that I'd been watching Noisy Nellie, a fiery crater superheating the rock.

The island stood 48 kilometres offshore in the Bay of Islands, almost as high as Auckland's Sky Tower, a malevolent, smoking pile of hot rock, ash and sulphur.

From 1975 until 2001 it stoked into its most active period for hundreds of years in a long sequence of eruptions blowing lava bombs and rock and huge clouds of gas and ash 10 kilometres into the air. What would a massive eruption do to the Bay of Plenty? The question worried geoscientists and no one wanted to discover the answer.

On the island itself authorities warned, unnecessarily, that if you were caught in one of the eruptions which could occur without warning you should run like hell, watch out for fumaroles and craters, and find a large rock to hide behind.

Why would you want to visit this smoking, stinking pile? Well, where else in the world could you go right inside a live volcano? Nowhere handy, was the consensus among the passengers aboard the big PeeJay cruise launch skimming over the water between Whakatane and White Island. I could report that it was an experience not to be missed, especially when you came away uncharred.

You suspended judgment when you walked into a volcano. Anything seemed possible in this impossible world with its cast of villains. All around us were craters, toxic, bubbling things with such names as Donald Duck, which along with Noisy Nellie beat off the competition from Big John, Gilliver and Rudolf.

This new world had no connection with the old. It was in technicolour, mauve, and purple, and pink, and red, and violent yellow.

We walked beside mounds which appeared solid but were as fragile as eggs, albeit boiled ones, so an errant foot might break through one of them and burn to a stump. Guides escorting tourists through the heat got full marks for keeping cool.

An early worker here, Donald Pye, a fireman at the nearby sulphur works, disappeared one night. All they found of him were his boots. Some concluded he'd committed suicide, although that did not seem likely. Being scalded to death by mud was not a popular course to the next world, and why would he save his boots?

Mata Browne, our guide, had met the unfortunate man's descendants on the island. They'd been curious about his death. They'd concluded that he might have slipped into a pool and thrown his boots onto the edge to guide his workmates, until he lost his grip and slipped through the gates of hell.

That did not seem likely to me either, but it was easy to believe anything here. Dino the pink dinosaur first appeared on White Island web-cameras in 2004. When the camera moved, so did Dino. He became world-famous, one headline claiming that a dinosaur had been discovered on a Pacific Island. He was amazingly enduring in an atmosphere which destroyed shoes and clothing, for he was made of plastic.

We were not nearly as phlegmatic. We hugged the track, a black path leading through sulphuric rock.

———

At the time, White Island was at level one on the volcanic activity scale. Level one indicated minor volcanic unrest. People could go to the island up to level two, which indicated moderate to heightened volcanic unrest, but I was happy not to be among them. Level one was bizarre enough and besides, the 1980 Mt St Helen eruption in Washington State had killed many volcano-watchers.

Levels three to five described actual eruptions from minor upwards, when the island was off limits.

White Island had last erupted in 2012, the same time as Tongariro. The two volcanoes were connected by a long line of suppurating earthy boils. They started at Ruapehu, then Ngauruhoe and running across the North Island past

Taupo and Whakatane to White Island and ending far beyond the island in a string of undersea volcanoes as the Australian plate overtook the Pacific plate in the tectonic scuffle of the earth's crust.

Scoria lay all over the place, addled rock like solid froth but light as pumice.

Now the island seemed like one big crater, Nellie all but filled in and silent, lumps and pinnacles framed against the sea. I kept an eye out for big ones to hide behind.

If you held a chunk of rock up to the sky it glittered as grains of silica caught the sun. It was a complicated equation but simply, the more silica, the more explosive the eruption.

A stream crossed the path. I sipped a little water. It was sour, not lemon-like, just bitter. We walked across a lemon-streaked plain, little boils of water bubbling all around, the mud-pits hinting at what lay just below. The mud was 70 to 80 degrees Celsius, not boiling, but acidic. In one pool the bubbles pushed through water of bright yellow-green, beautiful as a viper. All the while the cracked cliffs hovered like spectres. Mata told me he knew of a man who'd proposed to his girlfriend on the edge of this venomous pool. She'd cast a nervous eye over her shoulder and quickly said yes. Maori once cooked titi, muttonbirds, in these pools. The vents hissed and shushed. Everyone coughed and wheezed and reached for the masks around their necks.

This was a beautiful, evil place, like Dali's vision of Hell. Steam billowed into the sky.

Vents hissed all around. Everyone coughed and sneezed.

Even the sea foam was streaked with a brown scum.

All around lay the bright yellow sulphur. I picked up a lump the size and colour of a grapefruit but pitted and scarred by incredible forces, forged in the fire.

Pure sulphur was said to be tasteless. I licked it. True. Then I licked a film of

Above Volcanic vista

Following Inside the volcano

sulphur powder. It was like putting my tongue over battery terminals, a shock which jerked back my head and set off a gale inside my nose.

It was said that 3 kilograms of gold a year went up in smoke here, around $16 million worth. Once, though, mining sulphur was as profitable.

Mining began here after J.A. Wilson, Judge of the Native Land Court and obviously a man unconcerned about conflicts of interest, bought a half share in the island in 1874. He also bought land at what became known as Sulphur Point in Tauranga, where his factory turned White Island sulphur into sulphuric acid. It didn't really work out for Wilson who managed to antagonise not just his workforce but the entire town of Tauranga. It didn't work out for his investors either. They saw none of the wealth he promised and the company went into liquidation in 1886.

After the White Island Sulphur Company of Vancouver acquired the island in 1913 mining resumed. The sulphur was to be extracted on the island by heating it in a retort and running off the pure product, but after only three months a retort burst and killed a fireman. Then Pye disappeared. Worse was to come. By September that year 10 men were working on the island, although historians speculated there may have been one or two more, who for their own reasons worked on the island incognito.

They were all well when the supply boat called on 8 September. A week later the same boat could not raise any response from the island. The skipper, Albert Mokomoko, returned to Opotiki, then (for no real fears were held for the men) made another trip to the island a few days later. This time, he found part of the crater wall blown away and no sign of the factory nor the men's accommodation. Men and buildings had simply disappeared under a lahar of boiling mud, ash and rock, forever.

All searchers found were paw prints. They followed the prints to the other side of the island, to a bay well away from the holocaust, and there they found a lonely cat, the only survivor of five, which they named Peter. An old photograph of him in the arms of his bowler-hatted rescuer shows a tabby striped like a tiger.

Peter went back to Opotiki with them, was dubbed Peter the Great and fathered scores of kittens which were given away as talismans. Peter the Great became a legend, even the hero of a children's book.

Mining was abandoned, but resumed as fertiliser production nine years later with a rather nervous workforce. Some had answered advertisements inviting them to live and work on a Pacific island, true as far as it went. They found no women in grass skirts. Instead their eyes were constantly streaming in the acid steam, they coughed incessantly and inside the crater endured noise like a modern jet engine, and had to clean their teeth three times a day to stop them turning black. A newcomer was said to have taken one look then climbed the mast and lashed himself on until the boat departed. The enterprise died forever in the Depression.

Now there wasn't much left, an old retort which once distilled the sulphur, cogs, splines, anonymous chunks of iron. I wondered whether I was standing on a mass grave.

An old scow anchor stood nearby like the end of Neptune's trident. Beams, chains, winches, a jumble of steel rusted in the poisonous air.

——————

Maori called the place Te Puia o Whakaari but Captain Cook settled on White Island 'for as such it always appear'd to us'. Maori were attracted by its good fishing and its muttonbirds, titi, but they probably had no trouble selling the place to two anonymous English officers for two hogsheads of rum. The story might be apocryphal and the pair were said to have been killed in the New Zealand wars.

Or the buyer might have been Phillip Tapsell, a flax trader from Maketu, who paid two hogsheads for the island in the 1830s. His claim was recognised by the Crown in 1868. Ownership passed on to his family then to Judge Wilson and W. Kelly and following them a succession of owners. The island simply beat off all attempts to profit from its sulphur, the last of them by White Island Products which went broke in 1933.

White Island was bought by George Raymond (Ray) Buttle in 1936. Its owners had gone into receivership, the island was put up for tender and the successful tenderer didn't come up with the cash. Ray put in a last-minute tender and the family story was that when he asked how long it would be before he was advised of the result, his lawyer went into the tender office and returned five minutes later: 'You own the island.' It cost around £240.

Above and opposite
More scenes from inside
the volcano

Ray later wrote: 'Strange as it may seem, the island is unbelievably beautiful . . . Surely it is one of the wonders of the world.' Yet according to his family Ray never went there. It was simply too difficult to get to, then.

Under pressure to sell their island to the government later, the family compromised. It became a private scenic reserve in 1953, even Maori customary muttonbirding rights eventually disappearing.

Ray's son John became the next owner in 1957. It was now owned by the

Whakaari Trust whose trustees were John's three sons, Andrew, James and Peter.

What was it like to own a volcano? 'It's just unreal,' James said. 'You can't really believe it.'

———

Peter and Jenny Tait, the Pee and Jay of their boats' names, former dairy farmers and commercial fisherpeople, became first charter boat operators, then White Island tour company. Curiously, most of their passengers were international. New Zealanders just took White Island for granted. I was one of them, until I went. It was splendid, spectacular, terrifying.

A few weeks later a disaster occurred which had nothing to do with eruptions. Sixty tourists and crew aboard the *PeeJay V* had to leap into the sea when their vessel caught fire while returning from White Island.

No one was seriously hurt, but it showed you took nothing about this island for granted. Ever.

THE
WILD
ONES

MATIU/
SOMES

'Everything here spoke of a frightened,
punitive, ignorant and intolerant society,
even in the grip of a war.'

This was a good day to visit Matiu/Somes Island. A grey wind blew. Rainclouds drooped over Wellington's hills. Squalls punched the harbour. Cold seeped into skin and bone.

The island hunched in the harbour, implacable. People had come and gone, Maori, prisoners, outcasts. They'd stripped the island and replanted, built fortresses and abandoned them, assembled prisons for humans and animals for reasons long lost. A sombre day suited it.

The tiny Mokopuna appeared at its far end. Matiu/Somes was a difficult place to live, but could anyone inhabit the rough rock of Mokopuna? No one, as it proved.

An old concrete jetty poked from the southern side of Matiu/Somes. We were greeted, checked for rats, seeds and bugs. This island was still carefully guarded; only the enemies had changed.

Traces of two pa had been found on the island. It had always been a fortress. The island was first named by Kupe. It entered the national archives as the place where Maori either seized the brig *Lord Rodney* or persuaded its captain to take an invading force to the Chatham Islands, to the great sorrow of the resident Moriori.

Under a 2009 Treaty settlement it was now owned by Taranaki Whanui ki Te Upoko o Te Ika, made up of Te Ati Awa and other Taranaki iwi and managed by the Department of Conservation. It had been free of predators since 1985. 'We try to keep it that way,' said the DOC ranger on the island, Diane Batchelor. 'It's very expensive to get rid of them again.'

A lean man called Malcolm McEwen took us in hand. He was a ranger, of the rather mysterious Eastbourne Forest Rangers, voluntary guardians of the public estate who had looked after parks and reserves since 1933.

He told us that most visitors to the island wanted to see tuatara, the lizard-like dinosaurs which had found another sanctuary there. We were more interested in its human history however.

Matiu/Somes was first a quarantine station in 1869. Its first occupants were

Pages 236–7 Mana prospect

Previous Matiu/Somes

Opposite World-beating quarantine station

Following Inside the station

from the ship *England*, carrying immigrants thought to have smallpox. So it began. In 1874 ten children were buried on the island, the next year another six. In 1876 island burials included a woman and her day-old baby. Typhoid took an awful toll.

On the edge of the island, above a cliff, sat a memorial surrounded by headstones. A couple of tuatara were often to be found sunning themselves on a rock below.

Here ended people who'd given away their lives in the old country for something they thought was going to be better. They'd come out in ships, the poorest crammed together so diseases spread quickly and here, in quarantine on this bleak place, some 40 died and were buried in graves scattered around the island.

Their graves had disappeared, names collected and recorded on this memorial, many poignant: Annie Smith, aged four, William Palmer, one, Elizabeth Butler, seven months, Winifred Lucy Moore, one month, baby Seodrowsky, died 30 January 1876, one day old.

Down at the bottom of the memorial lay poor Kim Lee, the worst story of all.

Accounts of Kim Lee's life and time in New Zealand varied but the most popular described him as a 56-year-old fruiterer who lived in Adelaide Road, Newtown.

He was living in New Zealand at a time when hatred of the Chinese gripped this narrow land. Doctors looked at his face and body covered in sores, his enlarged and suppurating glands. They diagnosed leprosy.

The Chinese were believed to be carriers of the disease. They were also thought to be drug addicts and generally unsavoury people, so the Health Department immediately burned his fruit and veg and all of his possessions and packed him off to quarantine on Matiu/Somes.

The quarantine barracks there were dismal but luxurious compared with Kim Lee's next quarters. Others on the island so objected to him that he was dumped on the neighbouring Mokopuna, which then became known as Leper Island.

He built some sort of hut there but lived in a cave just above the water where the historian and writer Elsdon Best later found a mug and some rough furniture he'd made. Food was sent to him by the lighthouse-keeper's dinghy when the weather was fine, by flying fox when it was not.

I could see three caves on Mokopuna from the memorial and circling the island later saw others boring in from the shoreline. Every every one of them looked damp and freezing cold. According to the Wellington *Evening Post* the regime of good food and exercise, and forced daily baths in the sea, were curing him of a disease then believed incurable. Health Department officers reported his condition as satisfactory.

He soon died, of course. He lasted less than three months. Newspapers reported that 'he was practically cured of leprosy but succumbed to internal complications'. His death certificate recorded heart, liver and kidney failure, which seemed to cover the field.

Malcolm McEwen had a different story, gleaned from a newspaper clipping.

'It says that he died after his mother heard that he'd been taken by the government. She committed suicide. When he got the news he died within days.'

Died 14 March 1904, aged 56, according to the memorial. Two further insults were laid upon him. First, in quarantine he was fined £23, or several thousand dollars in today's money, on a charge of opium possession; and second, a modern re-examination concluded that he probably did not have leprosy.

Tuberculosis was much more likely.

During World War I, Matiu/Somes housed internees and prisoners of war. The most famous were the crew of the German raider *Seeadler*, without their famous captain Count Felix von Luckner, who received better treatment elsewhere and was one of those who agitated for the 1918 Royal Commission which under Judge Frederick Chapman looked into allegations of beatings and abuse of prisoners on the island. The judge decided the complainants were troublemakers.

When World War II broke out Matiu/Somes was again in demand as a quarantine station.

Internees from Germany, Tonga, Samoa, Japan, Italy, Austria, Spain, Poland, Norway, Finland and Russia were held there. Some of the Germans were anti-Nazi, some were Jews, and some supported Hitler, which must have made for lively evenings.

One of them was George Dibbern, a notorious yachtsman who had also been interned on Matiu/Somes in World War I. He'd returned to Germany after the war, then left his family behind and sailed his home-built *Te Rapunga* back to New Zealand. He was popular, although he outraged many by taking up with a young, unmarried Napier woman, Eileen Morris, who became his crew. Despite his anti-Nazi views in World War II, back to the island he went.

Another was Oscar Coberger, who came to New Zealand from Germany in 1926, a skier and mountaineer who established a winter sports business that became synonymous with Arthur's Pass. He sold Sir Edmund Hillary and George Lowe their first ice axes, and his family were to become the pride of New Zealand in winter sports.

One Kiwi, John Klingenstein, was also locked up. He had a foreign name and communist views. That seemed to have been enough.

Thirty-eight Italians were imprisoned, to their great indignation. The best-known was Paolo Casa, who was in the fishing business in Greymouth; other Italians were from Island Bay. Paolo wrote a letter to the island's commander on behalf of fellow inmates complaining of miserable conditions and especially a lack of the privacy 'so well fit to their aged dignity'.

According to Malcolm McEwen they planted an olive tree, reasoning that as they were going to be there for years they might as well have something good to eat. The tree was still there but, said Malcolm, it never produced olives. As bitter and shrivelled as the internees, growing in the shadow of its past. I imagined the

Left Surviving barracks

Italians coming from their country of light, to this. Everything here spoke of a frightened, punitive, ignorant and intolerant society, even in the grip of a war.

Escape from the island, with its freezing water and nasty currents, was dangerous but in 1915 two young German internees swam to Petone and in 1918 four more made it to Ngauranga on a raft of kerosene tins.

In World War II three German prisoners, Karl Schroeder, Hans Finke and Odo Strewe, all anti-Nazi, broke jail in the lighthouse-keeper's dinghy, making oars out of planks.

They finished up near Petone and after six days on the lam were caught and returned to the island.

The three then plotted a second escape. They'd tunnel under the wire and make a raft from empty oil drums. Schroeder made a sextant from scrap wood to navigate with, a finely made instrument with a little box for the lens. They never used it because the camp commandant was tipped off by a letter whose stiff accents showed through the clumsy lettering. The sextant now rested in a glass case in the island's visitors' centre, so much despair on show.

Maurice Gee's novel *Live Bodies* began with an escape attempt from the island based on this episode, although in his book the escapees prefabricated a canoe and hid its parts.

I once knew one of the men interned on the island, an Austrian called John Braunias, and asked him what he thought about that part of the book. He didn't think much of it. He said he and a couple of mates had once hopped into a boat

Above A hut for 60 men

and rowed across to Petone for a beer. John liked a story. Perhaps it was true.

The guards were bored. Prisoners worked six hours a day, lounged around for the rest. For almost all of the time they were no trouble at all, just men looking to get this over with and go back to their families. But it was better than actually fighting.

Malcolm McEwen pointed out a big, perfectly round hole in a rock. Guards had passed the time shooting at it, sculpting the hole with bullets.

A single barracks building remained on the island, one-sixth of the total accommodation for prisoners. Malcolm and I worked it out; this hut must have held about 60 men. There was something very New Zealand about it: nicely painted, simple, wooden floors, once lined with wood. Its residents must have been cold as cadavers. It reminded me of the barracks at Burnham Military Camp where I'd once been interned myself, although the Army called it National Service.

Much later, the island returned to being a quarantine station for animals. It was reputed to be best in the world. Even humans had to pass through a lock like a space ship's, take off all their clothes and shower before they could get properly into the quarantine building.

Inside were pens and gates and a huge furnace where everything was burned, right down to the animals' urine. This was an era when New Zealand agriculture was expanding its gene pool with imported strains, different species. The quarantine station was a busy place for a decade, until technology passed it by: imported semen and ova were easier and more efficient.

Now the concrete-block buildings were painted a nice shade of turquoise and cream.

The naked island had been clothed with new bush and trees and now kakariki and robins and penguins and geckos and skinks were everywhere. It danced to a new tune. A wind turbine pounded out the beat, blades snapping in the gale.

MANA

'A largely vanished native forest with its trees, shrubs, plants, grasses, seeds and rich understorey was taking hold, getting a grip, rising literally from the ashes.'

We crossed to Mana Island from Porirua Harbour with a boat-full of people whose pleasure was planting. Plenty of that was going on over there. In the previous three decades the island had been converted from a drab, dry place to a green refuge.

These people called themselves the Friends of Mana Island, and so they were. One of them wanted to see a tree she'd helped plant five years ago. She might have been talking of a niece.

The island sat flat-topped and tilting, one end 30 metres lower than the other. It had been a marine terrace, lifted straight up from the sea slick as a whale. Maori legend said it was smoothed off by a taniwha attempting to join the birds and fly, hitting the island and skimming its top. The legendary Polynesian explorer Kupe named it Te Mana o Kupe ki Aotearoa.

Mana looked barren from a distance. Up close, the Friends insisted, lots of bush was growing in the valleys.

Sure enough the grey became green, then bright green with emerging species, as if lights had been switched on under the canopy. The back side of the island, which could only be seen by boat, looking simply ferocious, beaten-up cliffs, spikes of rock, a reef of needles at the north end, a shingle beach with the kind of high-tide jumble you itched to kick through.

The island looked entirely uninhabitable. But an eddy, a swirl in the sea as it ran down its sheltered east coast, created a calm where boats could beach. The ferry ran in, and we landed on the island's only piece of flat ground. The Friends of Mana hopped off. Alicia Hall, wife of ranger Jeff, and their three children, Finn, aged six, Brodie, four and Tara, seven months, hopped on. A good chance to get off the island and go shopping.

Mana was rather like a stage, with hills as its wings. The flat behind this beach was the centre of Mana theatre. It always had been, for both Maori and Pakeha.

Mana was once the stronghold of Te Rangihaeata, Te Rauparaha's nephew and fierce Ngati Toa leader. They drove out the resident iwi who'd occupied the island from the fourteenth century.

Te Rangihaeata was the terror of colonial settlers and enemy iwi alike. When he and his uncle sallied from their island bastions the rule for their opposition was, best duck fast. His answer was: 'If the Pakeha attacked a Maori village and killed some of our people, it is called a great victory. But if the Maori attacks and kills in time of war, it is called a blood-thirsty massacre.'

His finely carved whare puni sat there on the flat near the present-day boatshed.

Te Rangihaeata left after the so-called 'Wairau affray', when the New Zealand Company, intent on grabbing land for settlers, confronted the two chiefs near Blenheim. The British were routed, 22 of them and four Maori killed. An inquiry held Pakeha to blame, but Te Rangihaeata knew he hadn't heard the last of it and quit the island.

Under their Treaty of Waitangi settlement Ngati Toa now owned the pa site. The remainder of Mana was to be given back to the iwi, which would then return it to the Crown as a public reserve.

All that was left of their occupation were a watercourse, some kumara pits and a pou, for Ngati Toa sat more lightly on the land than the following waves of Pakeha did.

Following a dodgy sale of the island to three Europeans for goods worth £24, fraudulent even by the standards of the day, two of the new owners took over. One, John Bell, set up as a farmer, exporting the first Mana wool to Sydney in 1835. He also established a whaling station. In a period roughly between 1832 and 1850 as rascally a group of men as you'd find anywhere in those rough days caught whales around Mana, establishing a fine reputation for lying, cheating and drunkenness.

The government 'settled' disputes over Mana's sale in 1865 by buying the island itself and leasing it as a sheep farm for the next century. For 60 years from 1893 the Vella family farmed 212 hectares divided into two paddocks. Mariano Vella, the patriarch, travelled to Austria for another wife after his first died from a heart attack. The returning newlyweds were among the survivors of the SS *Wairarapa* which was wrecked on Great Barrier Island in 1894 with the loss of 121 lives, New Zealand's third-worst shipwreck.

Their old woolshed on the island survived too, now a miniature museum. It hunkered low to shelter from the wind, its kanuka rafters running over two ancient belt-driven shearing stands. It even seemed to have some leftover wool on the floor which turned out to be cast-off gecko skins lying in creamy drifts. Outside, a concrete pad, a drenching area.

Farming removed most of the remaining forest from the island. It became a quarantine and research station in 1973 until a suspected scrapie outbreak had the sheep slaughtered en masse in 1978. The last cattle left the island in 1986. It became a scientific reserve the following year.

Above Mana perspective:
restoring the ruin

What was left?

Almost all of the forest had gone. The biggest trees on the island were clumps of ancient macrocarpas. They were the farmers' most enduring monuments. Still, kakariki and robins liked them.

Many native species had disappeared too. The island was an ecological ruin. Without the stock, grass went to seed and the next disaster for poor Mana was a plague of mice.

Mice were so thick that a visitor described fierce competition for his lunch. Millions of the little rodents swarmed. A very basic trap was said to have caught 204 of them in a single night.

Three years were spent getting rid of the mice. They were gone by 1990. Not one had come ashore in the 25 years since. The wharf was removed to stop rats immigrating from boats. Predators and rodents were wiped out. People could still land on Mana but rangers ensured they followed quarantine rules.

Yet a single rat devastated the shore plover population in 2011. The plovers were disappearing, mysteriously, when one of the previous ranger's children found a stash of dead birds. Cameras picked up the rat. Two months and a huge effort went into catching that one animal.

The small, colourful shore plover was one of the world's rarest shore birds. The entire world population in 2013 was fewer than 200 adult birds, and Mana had about 30 of them before the rat got into its work. 'Like,' the island's ranger Jeff Hall said, 'sending a child into a street-full of ice-cream shops.'

When he came to the island only nine birds were left. The last two breeding pairs were caught and put into the captive breeding programme.

Opposite Jeff and Alicia Hall with Finn, Brodie and Tara

Above New life

Then, in February 2015, a group thought they saw a cat. An intensive search followed. Three certified cat-detecting dogs and their handler made two visits of three days combing all 217 hectares of the island. They didn't find a cat. Nor did 14 motion detector cameras specially deployed.

The search continued until the following spring. No cat was ever found.

It was a lot of fuss but the stakes were high.

Rare skinks were accommodated on the island. Geckos were everywhere. About 30 takahe sheltered on the island, the biggest colony outside Fiordland, all with names such as Tilly, Alec, Squeak, Selwyn.

Mana suited them. They bred well and their offspring were moved to boost other colonies on other islands.

Rowi, New Zealand's rarest kiwi, found refuge here, along with brown teal, the yellow-crowned kakariki, North Island robin, tuatara, carnivorous snail or *Powelliphanta*, the all-but-extinct Wellington speargrass weevil, the world's heaviest insect the giant weta, diving petrels, fairy prions. The island was a sanctuary for species which had just about disappeared from the face of this earth.

All the while their habitat was being restored. A largely vanished native forest with its trees, shrubs, plants, grasses, seeds and rich understorey was taking hold, getting a grip, rising literally from the ashes. Half a million trees and shrubs were planted and those Friends of Mana accounted for quite a few of them. Project Crimson funding allowed for 1200 young rata to be planted and no possums were left to eat them. A couple of kowhai trees were planted by Finn and Brodie.

'One day they'll come back and see how the trees are doing,' Jeff said. 'I'd love to come back in a hundred years and see how it had evolved.' Mahoe and ngaio quickly colonised the empty spaces, and manuka, and lots of taupata, seeds spread by the steadily rising numbers of birds.

The island became a world-renowned model of ecological restoration.

'I've always felt we're the piggy in the middle, between Matiu/Somes and Kapiti, the diamond in the rough,' Jeff said. 'But we're coming into our own now.'

Thirty years on, bush filled the gullies. The Friends of Mana hopped off the boat and disappeared into the trees they'd planted. I stood under the canopy,

green kakariki chattering, common as sparrows in a city backyard. Tui called across the valleys. They were established on the island only in 2010. Now they were everywhere. Jeff took the top off a wooden, box-like bait station. Geckos massed inside, looking stunned, a gecko ghetto.

Up close, the island did not look at all flat. Ridges and gullies roughed up the skyline. A few scarce wetlands had reappeared; so many had gone. Jeff opened another box. Voluptuous skinks glared. 'If we had rats here that would make a pretty good meal,' he said.

We tiptoed along a track. A pair of takahe was nesting nearby, helped out by last year's chick. The only sign of them was a grunt from behind some flax.

Down below, a boat, a runabout, was anchored just off the shore. Jeff watched the crew, three men. 'Hope they're aware of all the precautions,' he mused. 'They're allowed to be there, but not to come ashore. There's only one place they can do that.' Which was a few hundred metres away. 'You've got to have faith in people.' The three men messed about in their boat for a while then lifted the anchor and buzzed off through the chop in waves of spray.

Island rangers needed many skills, conservationist, minder, universal trades-person, public relations officer, diplomat. Alicia was studying for a counselling qualification which, it seemed to me, would be useful.

Jeff did a degree in parks and tourism management at Lincoln University, started work in the Department of Conservation as a hut warden and worked his way up. He'd worked with the kakapo team in Fiordland, 'out in the wild and getting around'. He'd do a month with a pack on his back, out in the bush every day. When he'd come out for his two weeks off he'd meet Alicia in Hokitika, she'd want to go tramping, and he'd go oh no, that's just what I've been doing, I just want to sit down for a while. But more often he'd put on his pack again and he might end up going back into the bush with some of the biodiversity staff and getting back amongst it. 'It becomes your way of life,' he said, unnecessarily. 'Body and knees willing I'd be in the field forever.'

He showed me a little opening beside the track, a bush cave. The boys' fort.

He and his family usually went off the island for their four days' block leave, catching up with the mainland business most took for granted in their daily routines: shopping, groceries, dentists, doctors, Plunket.

In his spare time on the island he helped with the boys' home-schooling, fixed the house, got into the water, caught sprats off the concrete landing with the kids, played with Lego, built huts, messed about on the beach.

When they lived on the mainland he'd work during the day and come home in the evenings and his family weren't involved with his job. On the island they were. Finn would go with him on his takahe checks. What a life for kids. You knew you were in the right job when your kids were fascinated by what you did, I mused. Fathers everywhere would envy him.

He said: 'The boys surprise me just about every day with some of the things they're absorbing. Last week someone asked the question, "what's the difference between manuka and kanuka?" and Finn squeezed the leaves of a couple of plants and said, "that one's manuka," squeezed another, "that one's kanuka," the difference in the feel. Little things like that. Another time when his cousin was out here he tried to break off a flax frond for a sword and Finn says, "those are important to feed the tui."

'He's becoming very environmentally aware.'

It was one of those blue days in Wellington which seemed more perfect than anywhere else, but the afternoon was growing cold.

The Friends were gathering on the beach ready to go home. I asked the woman I'd met coming over on the boat how her tree was doing. Very well, she said. She looked pleased. We took a last look at the old fortress. It had taken a century and a half but Te Rangihaeata would have felt at home.

Opposite The old
Mana woolshed

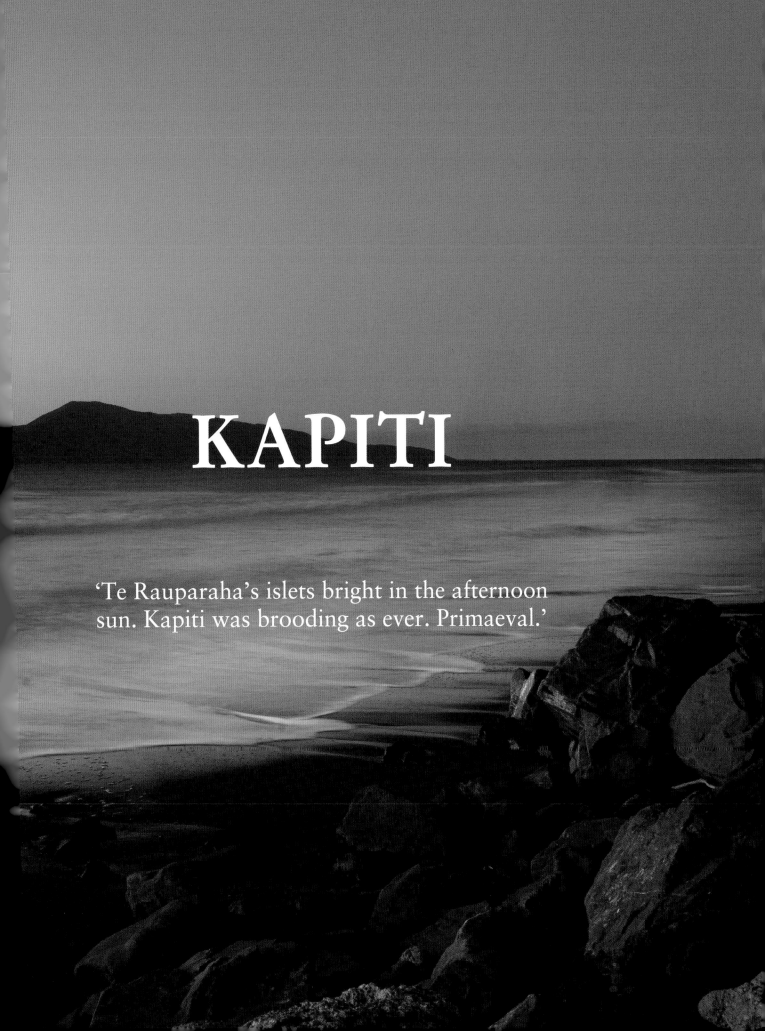

KAPITI

'Te Rauparaha's islets bright in the afternoon sun. Kapiti was brooding as ever. Primaeval.'

A very long time ago I read a poem by Alistair Te Ariki Campbell called 'Looking at Kapiti':

'Massive, remote, familiar, hung with spray,
You seem to guard our coast . . .'

Campbell lived at Pukerua Bay across the water from the island whose dark hump filled his view. He was tormented and fascinated by it. In 'Sanctuary of Spirits' he wrote:

'This island is alive with ghosts . . .'

And Kapiti's most famous resident, Te Rauparaha, haunted him:

'Madman, leave me alone!'

When I lived in Wellington I thought of those lines every time I drove along the coast. Kapiti sat black on the horizon. It *was* the horizon. It was everywhere.

I longed to go there, but never did. You needed a permit, you had to go by licensed ferry.

Now, much later, the island was still elusive.

We'd got the permits. We'd booked our passage across that tricky channel. Nothing could go wrong, could it? Well, yes.

The ferry operator rang to say the boat had been cancelled. For the next few days also. We were stranded in Paraparaumu, Kapiti tantalising across the water.

In the end we hitched a ride in a helicopter, floating in the air above the currents and chop that were so good at keeping intruders away. We arrived at the dark isle the easy way, no waka, no fighting the tide, no staring at the weather and hoping it would hold off, just for the day.

Te Rauparaha took a little longer.

The Ngati Toa chief battled his way down the coast from Kawhia. He finished up here, literally perhaps, for some believed that his body had been taken from its grave at Otaki and reburied on Kapiti.

Te Rauparaha established his new Kapiti address permanently in the battle of Waiorua, a rare flat area at the north of the island. Several enemy tribes combined

into a huge force of some 2000 warriors who packed an armada of canoes and attacked his Kapiti fortress.

They landed at Waiorua, whose defenders held them off while messengers rushed to alert Te Rauparaha at his pa to the south.

Te Rauparaha and his nephew, the great fighting chief Te Rangihaeata, roared into battle. Far fewer than the invaders, perhaps only two hundred of them, they won the fight in hours. The epic victory cemented the great chief's mana, and that of Ngati Toa.

Whanganui's museum now housed the huge waka *Te Mata o Hoturoa*, one of the invading fleet. Its hull, which could carry 70 paddlers, was carved from a single totara log which still carried bullets and scars from the battle.

An underwater bridge linked Kapiti and the mainland. The same fierce winds which made the Rau o Te Rangi channel between the two such a fearsome place carried silt and sediment from the sea cliffs around the island and dropped it neatly on the opposite coast.

Meanwhile, debris was being washed down the Waikanae River and creating a bump at its front. Probably the two would meet, eventually, and Kapiti would be an island no more.

Right now though it was definitely an island.

Wind, sea and earthquakes had taken a giant bite of its west, so that the island rose from its gentler east then dropped abruptly into a sea which stretched unbroken all the way to Australia.

Kapiti might once have been connected to the South Island.

It looked a little like a miniature South Island, in fact, the watery Waiorua at the top, the Rangatira foreland bulging like Banks Peninsula, the rugged south dissolving into rocks and islets.

Two of those islets, Tahoramaurea and Tokomapuna, were Te Rauparaha's favoured homes. They offered sheltered water and were more easily defended than the main island. I looked at them from the beach at Rangatira. They

Above Mana perspective

Following The new forest

seemed inhospitable, desolate. The pa must have been a cold and dreary place in a gale. Even not in a gale. But it offered a prime waterfront site and extensive views. Te Rauparaha was as interested in good real estate as the next chief.

When the Ngati Toa leader moved out, whalers moved in, and remnants of their stone walls could still be seen on Tahoramaurea.

Maori, whalers, farmers, all gone now, their marks covered in regenerating forest. 'Nothing beside remains'. Visitors more interested in tuatara than anything those vanished people had done or left behind.

The government took much of Kapiti in 1897, except for a small block in the north which was still owned by Maori who offered nature tours and accommodation. The aggrieved Ngati Toa only got their island back this century, the Waitangi Tribunal giving ownership of most of it to the iwi for 10 days, after which it would be given back to the Crown and managed by DOC as a nature reserve.

At Rangatira now there was a boatshed and a sea-battered slipway with a trolley on rails and old names scratched into the concrete. I picked a bright green tennis ball from the tide debris on the shingle beach, so foreign it looked as if it needed a permit.

I sat in an old farm homestead, built in the early 1880s, talking to Genevieve (Gen) Spargo and Nick Fisentzidis, rangers.

They were talking about Richard Henry's time on Kapiti.

I was startled. Richard Henry was one of New Zealand's conservation heroes but I didn't know he'd lived on Kapiti. 'He could have sat exactly where you are,' Gen said. I was sitting at a polished wooden table, definitely twentieth century, perhaps even twenty-first, but the house was right. It had been built in the 1880s.

Richard Henry immigrated to New Zealand from Australia around 1874 and became a staunch conservationist, appalled by the damage being done by such introduced pests as stoats and ferrets. Soon the kakapo would vanish, he predicted, and although no one took any notice he was almost right. He spent a couple of years searching for the takahe, thought extinct after 1898 and not rediscovered until 1948.

He became king of his own domain in 1894, placed on the state payroll as caretaker of Resolution Island in Dusky Sound. There he became the pioneer of the modern way, capturing threatened birds and moving them to Resolution and other island arks. In 1901 he found a stoat or weasel on Resolution and sure enough, the kakapo *did* disappear.

His birds doomed, his life's work ruined, Henry went slightly mad, moved to Kapiti Island for three years, and died in the Auckland Mental Hospital in 1929.

Much later, after the takahe was found alive if not well, one of the more stalwart birds was named Richard Henry in his honour. As for kakapo, three of them were released on Kapiti in 1912 and one ancient stalwart named Jimmy survived until the mid-1930s.

I tried to imagine him sitting glumly in my place at the table, wearing his cardy.

Perhaps he was now a spectral figure on Kapiti; after all, the island seemed full of them. If so, he would be a happy ghost. The island was full of threatened birds, kaka, kokako, hihi, kiwi, saddlebacks. Flocks of kereru astonished visitors. And, at last, he would have found the takahe, stalking the island paths and what was left of the open country.

Five takahe at that moment, essentially birds that weren't needed for breeding and had been retired. Duds and studs, Gen said.

The truth was that the more successful the reforestation of Kapiti, the less suitable it became for open country birds such as the takahe. Other islands were taking over.

And now, here were Henry's philosophical descendants, Gen and Nick, sitting where he might have sat.

I looked at them more closely. Conservationists, certainly. But was there a certain . . . sparkle in their dull-green DOC shirts?

Oh yes there was. They had a relationship made, if not in heaven, then in the Department of Conservation's head office.

They met, fell in love. First with each other, then with islands. They became a kind of two-for-one deal.

They worked up the island-keepers' hierarchy, going on field trips first, then promising not to get in the way if they were taken to other islands. Nick listed Gen as the person who inspired him most.

It was a kind of apprenticeship. Gen, who'd once wanted to be a police dog handler, spent four months on Hauturu/Little Barrier on her hands and knees searching for climbing asparagus, a wiry weed that smothered the forest floor. In the island business, evidently, you started at the bottom. Worth it? You bet.

'I just love islands,' she said. 'I think it's the remoteness.'

Before I started this book I had an image of people who lived on islands, Robinson Crusoe-ish, unkempt, wild. Instead, I found a disciplined profession. Living on islands demanded order, attention to detail.

Department of Conservation islands had an extra dimension: a curious public.

Any notion of a couple of modern hermits went out the old villa's ancient sash window.

Departmental policy, said Gen, was not to have a person on an island for more than about six years negotiable. 'So you don't have the situation that you had in the past where people had some crazy ownership stuff creeping in, reluctant to share the place.'

'This island is so accessible, there's nowhere you can just sit and be a hermit,' said Nick.

'You can't be a hermit any more on a DOC island,' said Gen. 'So many awesome people visit . . . it's quite cool because you get to share these special things.'

Nick said: 'In the past there's been an idea of what an island ranger, an island caretaker has been. A person who can fix everything, spend lots of time by themselves, be isolated. With communications now, being able to email from your phone, and having visitors, the kind of staff who are suited to these places are quite different.'

True. It did not take long with Gen and Nick to frame a mental recruitment description: young, eager, alert, interested, articulate, committed . . . the kind of qualities a management consultant would drool over, although I suspected these two wouldn't think much of that.

Nick said: 'The reason I wanted to work in a place like this is that it's a throwback to what the mainland used to be. No other place has the sweep of species we have here and the history and is still only five and a half kilometres from the mainland. You get to walk around in this jaw-dropping place all day.'

Later, he confided that starting a family was on his to-do list. After all, he offered, look at the ranger family on Mana Island next door. A happy family with three kids.

Next? Hopefully another island.

'I'm curious about Hauturu/Little Barrier,' Gen said. 'Who knows? We're not missing out over here. We have everything we need. It is a huge privilege and a huge responsibility at the same time to be helping to care for these places. It is an honour. It gives me goosebumps when I talk about it.' (Yes, she had goosebumps right now, she confessed.)

'Islands do take it out of you. If you don't remain strong and support each other then . . . it's a beautiful massive role you take on and you can give your whole life to it.'

Nick: 'You don't switch off. It's not a nine to fiver . . . it doesn't stop raining after five pm. A boat that hits the island or a fire that starts somewhere doesn't know whether you're working or not.'

Gen: 'You might sit down for your G and T at seven o'clock and then a kayaker comes and it's all on for the next three hours and you're laying bait stations in case he's brought something with him.'

(Everyone needed a permit to land on Kapiti, but there was always someone . . .)

Gen and Nick were going off the island for a long weekend.

We waited on the beach at Rangatira, beside the old boatshed that had served the island for decades. It looked very much like one Richard Henry was photographed beside, hands in pockets, looking rather wistfully out to sea.

Te Rauparaha's islets bright in the afternoon sun. Kapiti was brooding as ever. Primaeval. With that, we hopped into the helicopter and flitted off.

Motuopuhi

'Cloud streaked off the mountaintop like smoke from fires deep within its crater. It looked forbidding, and secretive.'

Motuopuhi lay deep in the nation's heart, yet few New Zealanders knew of it.

It was not even an island when Te Rauparaha sought refuge there.

It was a pa on a peninsula, the stronghold of Te Wharerangi, chief of the district where Lake Rotoaira lay south of Taupo.

Te Rauparaha, the Ngati Toa chief then based in Kawhia, had detoured to Lake Rotoaira in search of food on a journey from Whanganui. According to Patricia Burns' book *Te Rauparaha: A new perspective*, he'd sighted a group of Ngati Te Aho travellers and, when one of the chiefs in his group suggested 'why go to Rotoaira when food is here?' attacked the Ngati Te Aho and eaten some of them.

Later he'd revisited Lake Rotoaira and found the Ngati Te Aho none too pleased. They were anxious to have him to dinner, and Te Rauparaha could guess the main course.

He sought refuge in Te Wharerangi's Motuopuhi pa with the Ngati Te Aho on his heels. Desperate, he hid in a kumara pit while the chief's wife Te Rangikoaea sat over its entrance.

Sitting under a woman's genitalia would have been seen by most chiefs as a fate worse than death, but Te Rauparaha was more practical, reasoning it was the last place his enemies would look. Or, in an alternative version, a woman's sexual organs were said to have protective powers. Either way, he cowered there muttering to himself *'Ka mate, ka mate'*, 'I die, I die', while his pursuers searched for him everywhere except the place they knew he could not be.

They left empty-handed.

Te Rauparaha popped out of his pit chanting

'*Ka ora, ka ora! Tenei te tangata puhuruhuru nana nei I tiki mai whakawhiti te ra.*' 'I live, I live, for this is the hairy man who has fetched the sun and caused it to shine again.' '*Hupane kaupane! Whiti te ra!*' 'The sun shines again!'

This, of course, became part of Te Rauparaha's famous haka, once heralding every All Black game. Every New Zealander knows at least part of it.

A sketch by George Angus around 1846 showed a heavily fortified pa defended by three rings of palisades, a fierce and snowy Tongariro behind.

It was a wahi tapu, a sacred place now, for Te Wharerangi and many of his people had died there when the pa was sacked in the 1820s after a battle thought to be the first in the region where firearms were used. Access was strictly forbidden.

The lake below it, Rotoaira, lay on a well-used path between Whanganui and Taupo. It was an important stopping place, a pataka kai, a food storehouse for the Ngati Tuwharetoa.

When the Tongariro power scheme raised the level of Lake Rotoaira, Motuopuhi became an island, even more difficult to get to, dark against Tongariro's exploded top. Cloud streaked off the mountaintop like smoke from fires deep within its crater. It looked forbidding, and secretive.

I spoke to a man who had the right to go there, although he'd only been twice in his life. He knew the spot where Te Rauparaha had hidden. That was one of the reasons he'd gone there, so that the knowledge would be passed on and not lost. 'You don't see it, until you're told,' he said. 'Then, it's quite obvious. If you didn't know where it was, and you went out to the island, you'd never find it. We've tried to keep it to ourselves.'

CROWNS
OF THE
SOUTH

ARAPAOA/
ARAPAWA

'The Peranos had been replaced by a family
of modern adventurers.'

The Cook Strait ferry aimed for a snarl of rocks spiking from sheer cliffs. At the last minute the ship turned and headed for what I hoped was a gap, although could a ship *really* squeeze through that?

Rocks scraped by, looking close enough to rub your bones. In a trice we were in calm water, a lake, a refuge. The ship wheeled to the left. Houses and fishing boats lazed in the nearby bay. A couple of weird white structures sat in a paddock like wigwams. The windows of an old house high on a hill frowned. Could anyone have lived up there? So close to the edge?

A gaunt structure rose beside the water like an apparition, a skeleton of concrete and steel.

Welcome to Arapaoa Island, 75 square kilometres lying beside the Tory Channel, the mainland needle-thin on the other side. Until 2014 it was known as Arapawa, a spelling mistake; the pronunciation remained the same after the change.

Whekenui, the bay just inside the Tory entrance, once sheltered a whaling community.

Whalers hunted humpbacks passing through the strait on their invisible pathways to the north. The huge mammals were dragged back to Fishing Bay next to Whekenui and stripped to their bones in the factory whose dark remains still hovered beside the water.

The whalers' children sat at desks in the tiny Whekenui school while their fathers searched for whales from high on the cliffs. The school rang with the chatter of whalers' children, Peranos, Heberleys, Guards. They were just workaday names then, nothing special.

When a Union Jack went up on the whalers' lookout, the factory boiler would be fired up, the mothership *Tuatea* would get under way and all the kids would rush out of school, for usually the whale would be driven into the Tory entrance and killed right in front of the bay. ('It saved the towing.')

The Perano whaling station in Fishing Bay only closed in 1964, for lack of

Pages 274–5 French Pass rapids

Previous Arapaoa/Arapawa

Opposite The markers

whales. The school shut when the whaling did, the same year.

The whales were coming back but no one would think of hunting them now, in New Zealand at least. Saving whales had become a worldwide crusade.

Yet surviving whalers became celebrated. Joe Heberley was one of them. He and a clutch of other old whale-hunters still manned a lookout on the cliffs high above Cook Strait, but they weren't interesting in killing whales any longer, only in preserving them.

Joe Heberley's whaling pedigree was immaculate. He had five generations of whalers in his blood. His mother was a Guard. Heberleys were whalers to the core.

Joe was once the youngest whale gunner in the southern hemisphere, 17 years old, earning £70 a week straight out of school, big money then.

Joe and Heather Heberley now lived in a wide house in Okukari Bay next to Whekenui. Address: 'First house on the right, South Island.'

From the sea Okukari seemed to be the same bay as Whekenui, but on shore it was quite distinct. It had its own geography and its own history.

This was the Heberley family enclave. Joe and his sons were farmers and fishermen. Their handsome fishing boats were moored in the waters below. Merinos shuffled in the woolshed yards, ready for shearing the next day.

In their garden lay whale rib bones, vertebrae, a whole head. Inside, a whale's shoulder blade and vertebra stood next to the fire. Harpoons and hooks. A picture of Uncle John, a whale-chaser gunner until he was drowned. A photograph of James (Worser) Heberley and his Ngati Awa wife known as Te Wai, he stern, she puzzled, hung in the hallway.

Worser started it, really. Whaling brought him to New Zealand in 1827. According to Heather's book *Flood Tide* he was saved by the Ngati Toa chief Te Rauparaha from being tomahawked to death, became the first Pakeha to climb Mt Taranaki, and was Wellington's first pilot (Worser Bay was named after him). He built his first house at Te Awaiti, next to Fishing Bay.

He died in 1899 aged 90, stuck in the mud in Picton as the tide came in, clutching his carved walking stick. He was buried with its head still in his hand. His stick now lay in a stand in the Heberleys' living room, with a newer carved piece at its head.

———

At the end of Joe's fourth-form year at St Bede's College in Christchurch his dad Charlie called to say he was going whaling on Great Barrier Island in the north, and that Joe was going with him. The two were close. Charlie drove the whale-chaser and Joe worked the gun. Half a century later he could still feel the speed, excitement, the danger.

They were successful for three years then the numbers crashed. The last whale was caught in the Hauraki Gulf in 1962. Joe gave a downward whistle. The Japanese, the Russians, the Norwegians. They were as much loathed by New Zealand whalers as they were by the anti-whaling lobby.

His real catch up there was Heather. She and her parents cruised the Hauraki Gulf on the family yacht *Mangawai*. One day she sailed into Joe's bay on Great Barrier. He liked what he saw. He invited Heather and her girlfriend ashore to

Right Joe Heberley; Joe's ancestors Worser and Te Wai

have a look at the whaling factory. She liked what she saw. Joe was young, tanned, handsome, dashing and a gunner on a speedy whaleboat.

'I thought he was the coolest hunk.'

So, she married him in 1961. They went home to the farm on Arapaoa.

The Peranos' whaling factory there was looking for a gunner. But in a year, they killed only a few humpback whales. The industry was dying.

They switched to sperm whales, and Joe worked in the factory that year, its last. The sperm whales were caught in the deep water off Kaikoura and towed back to the Tory Channel. They were days old when they arrived, blasted with explosives, blown up and stinking like dead sheep, and Joe was driving a winch then, hoisting blubber as it was flensed. He said: 'I hated every minute of it. You were covered in blood and guts.'

Heather said: 'I had an old agitator washing machine and the fat would float right up to the top of the machine, oh, it was terrible.

'I was an Aucklander. I used to go dancing on Saturday night at Saint Sep's (Sepulchre's) in Khyber Pass, everyone used to go there, but then I met someone called Joe Heberley and he didn't know which was his right foot, so . . . they used to have dances in the Sounds, everyone would go, and they used to have one at Curious Cove, and we went there a couple of times and there was an older generation, the Fishburns, and Alby Fishburn he was a big man and his wife was this littlest wee lady, and could they dance, he was fabulous, and occasionally he would ask me to twirl around the floor with him and it was just lovely.'

Joe: 'I'd sit and watch. I was brought up down here, we'd never done things like that.'

Heather: 'We'd go up to my parents' in Auckland twice a year and they'd come down once a year. I used to do my Christmas shopping in Auckland because it was so hard to get Christmas shopping done here, two hours in the boat, two hours back, because we didn't have the faster boats we have now. I went up there, saw the Christmas parade with the kids every year until they grew up. Then home on the train to Wellington, on the ferry.'

————

Now, instead of whalers, boatloads of tourists waited for the whales' misty spouting as they surfaced. More than half a century had passed since Joe Heberley killed a whale.

Yet Joe was still whaling, after a fashion.

He was one of the old whalers who sat in a hut with a long window opening out into the strait, counting whales for conservation. A Heberley, three Peranos, two Nortons and Basil Jones, who used to be a flenser at the whaling factory.

Each had his own seat. In the old days they got 10 shillings and a notch when they spotted a whale and now it was just the notches. Each seat had notches in its supports, one for each whale spotted, so many that the seats looked like the tribal artefacts they were.

'Unbelievable the competition,' said Joe. 'It always was.'

They yarned to each other about the old days.

'Once we were coming back from Arid Island near the Barrier, we'd caught a couple of whales up there, Dad was driving the chaser, the other two chasers were in front of us, and we saw this thing in the water, a whale, asleep. Dad said, "load the gun" and we just snuck in. There was always competition. The other two boats called us up. What were we doing? We said we saw something there, we were just going to check it out . . . we snuck right up to him, he wasn't showing too much meat above the water, Dad yelled out, "make sure you don't take too much water with the harpoon", all hell broke loose when the harpoon hit it, the others saw the cloud of smoke go up, what are you buggers up to? We're fast! Tommy Norton still reminds me of that. The whale went mad, just took off. We had a hundred fathom of rope out in about ten minutes.'

Once a whale charged a chaser, an old Fairmile, and put its head right through the planking at the bow into the crew's quarters, coming out with blankets and clothes in its jaws.

Now, Joe said, watching them was almost as exciting as catching them. 'You notice your mate sitting beside you looking in the same place for quarter of an hour and you think "mmmm, wonder why he's looking in that direction". There's a severe fine if you say "thar she blows" (that's what you say when you spot a whale) and it's not a whale.'

Heather: 'Usually a cake of chocolate and if it's a severe fine it's two cakes of chocolate.'

Joe: 'As soon as we spot a whale the scientists take off through the heads and we give them directions where the whales are. They take photos. Every whale's got a different pattern under its tail. Then they DNA them, fire a little dart into them and get a skin sample.

'This year was special, we saw a white one. I'd never seen one before. Kaikoura saw it, then we did, then a month or so later it was reported off Australia.'

Now I put the obvious question: the irony. The killing had stopped, saving the whales had become an international campaign. But the whalers were celebrated and now, instead of killing whales they were saving them.

Joe had heard it before. 'We've all got the same attitude because we all know it wasn't us who done it.

'It's just great now. Great to see one. And the numbers are building up.'

Did he ever wish he had a good boat underneath him and a harpoon? 'No. No longer. We know they're threatened and we're lucky to see them. That's the way we see it. Now we're conservationists to the hilt.'

In rather the same way, the old whaling station at Fishing Bay had been cleaned up, tidied, sanitised with notices, walkways, fences. The station caught 4200 whales between 1911 and 1964. Now it looked as if no whale had ever been harmed in the making of this place.

———

In the middle of the bay stood the two tall white beacons that had guided ships through the Tory entrance since 1881. They were filled with stones to stop them blowing away. Each evening until 1930, when the lights were changed first to gas then to electricity, a beacon-keeper would row over from Okukari Bay, light the kerosene lamps, and in the morning turn them off again. The steps inside were worn down by his feet.

Once, authorities were planning to build new beacons and let the old ones rot away. Heather spent five years getting them listed by the Historic Places Trust.

The beacons still had vents for the oil lamps, although now they were powered by electricity, one long flash, one shorter, so they were known as Winky and Blinky.

They looked like something between a tower and a teepee. The water-taxi driver once brought guests who mistook them for accommodation, thought they'd be a cool place to stay.

———

The old Whekenui school still sat behind the Arapaoa homestead. It was long closed, now holiday accommodation. The Peranos had been replaced by a family of modern adventurers.

Mike and Antonia Radon bought the Perano farm in 1993. He was from California, she from Porirua. Their three children were from right there on Arapaoa Island.

When you tracked through their lives, Whekenui Bay had an irresistible logic to it. Neither of them could have been squeezed into a suburb. They were pioneers, pathfinders. They made their money through imagination and hard work. They lived on their wits. They'd lived on the sea, or under it, and now they lived beside it. They grew their food and home-schooled their children. This was the most settled they'd been.

Mike was diving for abalone and building boats in the family business in the United States when a friend suggested he take a look at New Zealand. So he did, and the next year he came back, to the Chatham Islands, then travelled around New Zealand.

Antonia meanwhile had moved to America. She'd gone to her sister's wedding in Alaska, fell in love with *that* place. Her life took a new turn, or rather a

Following The Radon family: Mike and Antonia with James, Jacob and Sara

whirl. She went to Mexico, learned Spanish, worked illegally, was caught in the States, given a choice, next plane out or jail. She drifted around the world and eventually returned to America, this time legally. Worked in a kina (sea urchin) factory, illegally.

The sea urchin industry was booming. Fortunes were being made. She learned to dive, moved to another boat, married its owner. 'It was kind of quick. I was only twenty-one. After a couple of years I realised I'd married the wrong person.' Returned to New Zealand to find herself. Found Mike also. He was trying to patch up marriage number two. Antonia married him.

They saw the Perano farm advertised for sale. They went to Arapaoa and looked at it.

'I offered five hundred thousand dollars for it,' Mike said. 'His wife started crying right on the spot. The farm wasn't big enough to run economically. Interest rates had gone sky-high. Who could afford a five hundred thousand property and pay twenty-four per cent interest?'

They could, because they were earning a *lot* of money, diving. 'We used to make four to five thousand dollars a day. It was really good money. Between the two of us. There's good money in diving. Even now we could make two to three thousand a day, gross. But everything costs a lot more now.'

They bought a boat they could live on in California, called it home, dived for most of the year, sent money to New Zealand, rebuilt the house and the small village of houses and outbuildings that made up the farm. 'We did, oh, so much work,' Antonia said.

Mike recited an axiom which seemed to have governed his life. 'The more you work the more you make.' He didn't mind chancing his arm either. Once his accountant in California told him of some fishermen in Bristol Bay, Alaska, who

Above Jacob and Antonia

had made a lot of money. So, on the eve of his return to New Zealand, Mike got onto the internet and looked up Bristol Bay boats and permits, found one that would cost him US$100,000 to buy into, and with no time for the full journey arranged to meet the seller halfway between their two houses. He thought it looked like a good investment and stumped up the money.

That kind of story usually ended in woe, but not for Mike and Antonia. 'One of the best things we ever did. We've built it up, another permit, a better boat. Everybody wants to go to Alaska. This year we all went. Summer it's nice but winter oh my god you don't want to be there.'

Now they'd bought a worn-out farm in the Marlborough Sounds, but they weren't farmers anyway, not of sheep or cattle. They had a paua farm in mind.

They produced tiny paua for re-seeding depleted paua beds, selling them to quota-holders. They owned their own paua quota. They produced paua pearls too. Antonia was wearing a few of them, set in gold. This one, she said, touching one at her throat, was worth about $4000.

Mike said: 'We're paua people. It's our life. Paua for people like us is a religion. It's been my life for fifty years now. I want my kids to be able to do it.'

The kids wanted to do it.

Here was Jacob, with papers tidily stacked all over the floor of the schoolroom. He was said to have a photographic memory. His father said: 'He reads books and *remembers* them.' Jacob, his twin, Sara, and younger brother James all saw careers on the farm in their future.

In large sheds dozens of buckets circulated seawater, imitating the paua habitat. They filled, tipped, ducked, bowed, glissaded in a plastic ballet, like the Cuba Street water sculpture in Wellington, or the children's playground in Hanmer Springs where Mike got the idea. Antonia bred Jack Russell terriers and the place seemed full of them, little brown and white, bright-eyed dogs everywhere.

———

That house high on the cliff was called Gunyah. Joe Perano, founder of the Perano whaling enterprise, built it for his wife Pattie in 1945. It featured a fine art deco marble fireplace and hand basins, a splendid old walnut bedroom suite. Nearby a World War II gun emplacement was dug into the hillside. I spent the night there. Close up, it didn't seem anywhere near the edge.

A wind razored in from the strait. The ebbing tide kicked up a fuss in the channel entrance, creating rapids over the rocks. Seabirds crowded the turmoil. It was early spring, and cold.

The tiny rounded fin of a single Hector's dolphin, unique and very rare, worked across the sound and disappeared into one of the island's bays. It looked awfully lonely.

MOTUARA

'Then a more attractive form of technology took over: Rein, fully certified kiwi dog.'

We went to Motuara in an eco-tour boat with some young Australian women who had studied marine biology and were ready for a season of showing off the Marlborough Sounds to tourists.

We passed a seal sleeping in the shallows, a flipper waving. Dusky dolphins nipped by. The water was shiny and rippled and our two giant outboards shushed over the wavelets.

Queen Charlotte's island markers whizzed by, Allports, Blumine, Pickersgill, all of them pest-free sanctuaries. We sidled along Long Island and passed an unusual low terrace jutting from its side, said to be the site of Captain James Cook's vegetable garden.

And there it was, Motuara, last stop before Queen Charlotte Sound dissolved into Cook Strait.

Motuara lay near Ship Cove, Captain Cook's first anchorage in the South Island and a place he returned to during his next two Pacific voyages, not always happily: the island was not far from Wharehunga Bay where, on Cook's second visit, 10 men from the *Resolution*'s sister ship *Adventure* were killed, cooked and eaten.

Here on the frontier of the unknown amid nature red in tooth and claw, Cook raised the British flag on 31 January 1770 and took possession of the South Island in the presence of the chief of the island, who he called Topa. He claimed the island for the mad King George III, named the sound for his unhappy queen, Charlotte, and gave the wine bottle they emptied to Topa. The spot was now marked by a beehive-shaped memorial.

Almost 250 years later a sign on the Motuara wharf warned visiting boats not to stay too long. The island was free of predators and no one wanted stowaway rats leaping ashore. For the tiny Motuara was still playing a big role in the nation's affairs as one of the island lifeboats that were dragging birds from the edge of extinction.

Previous Motuara

Opposite Island markers

Of all the endangered New Zealand birds the kiwi, as the national icon, had to be the firm favourite. This island was one of the saviours of the rowi, the large brown Okarito kiwi.

Once, rowi were common in middle New Zealand, in the top half of the South and bottom half of the North Islands.

Now it was New Zealand's rarest kiwi.

Only 160 of them were left in 1995. Stoats were chewing the kiwi's young to extinction.

The Department of Conservation hatched their own plan. They would take chicks, either by pulling them out of their burrows or by hatching eggs, and put them somewhere safe. Then, when they were big enough to beat off the stoats, return them to their habitat around Franz Josef.

The epicentre of this adventure, termed Operation Nest Egg, was a tiny hut with a blue tarpaulin stretched over a platform as a verandah. The hut had just enough room for two narrow bunks and some gear.

In this hut, for the present, lived Rob Graham, Anya Kruszewski, and Rob's dog Rein. Rein was a true star, handsome, indulgent, gracious to her many fans, with her own Instagram page.

A farm homestead once stood here. All that was left of that venture, apart from bush slowly recovering from devastation, was an old brick fireplace and some gnarly macrocarpas.

Above Anya Kruszewski and Rob Graham with Rob's dog Rein; rowi

This spring Motuara accommodated 51 kiwi chicks. All carried transponders, or electronic tags, telling their human minders roughly where they were.

Then a more attractive form of technology took over: Rein, fully certified kiwi dog. She did the rest, sniffing out each bird.

It had taken four days to capture all 51, check them over, and release them. Two birds had been kept. One had a growth on its leg and the other a worm problem. They were to be taken off the island, flown to Massey University, fixed up, and returned with the rest. They'd be on Motuara for just a few weeks before the whole 51 would be returned to Franz Josef.

By the new millennium the technique had increased the number of birds to 200, by 2012 to 375, by the end of 2015 to some 450. By 2018 their population should have reached 600. A remarkable achievement. What then?

Without human intervention, Rob said, the young kiwi would have a survival rate of only five per cent, not enough. Trapping predators would increase the rate to 25 per cent. Removing the young kiwi to a sanctuary raised the rate to about 80 per cent. But it was costly. 'Ideally we want to increase the population to six hundred to eight hundred birds then scale back and use less intensive monitoring techniques. We can go back to trapping and know that with a twenty-five per cent survival rate we have a self-sustaining population.

'We're spending all that money on just kiwi. Nothing else benefits. Kiwi are cute and fluffy. They are our national icon. We'd be laughing stocks if we let them disappear. But there's a whole lot of other stuff out there that matters.'

He and Anya were carrying a kiwi apiece, down to the waiting boat.

The birds were not gracious about it. They gave little annoyed moans, rather like disturbed babies, and a sound like a plastic zip fastener. But they lay quietly enough in their carers' arms. They had pale greyish feathers, and little whitish legs.

They looked soft but felt coarse. I know that because I touched them, although they made clear that they didn't appreciate it.

I'd been a New Zealander all my life without ever getting close to our national symbol. The only kiwi I'd ever seen were just little bundles in darkened cages. Now here were not just two kiwi, but the world's rarest.

The Australian women were delighted. They gooed and crooned. The kiwi looked resigned. Rein watched solemnly.

And we all cruised back up the sound, conservationists, Australians, kiwi, dog and all. Glossy water and blackening bush, the sky streaked dove grey and primrose.

D'URVILLE

'He said: "Tractor be buggered. I'll be hiring
a helicopter to look for the bodies."'

The explorer Dumont d'Urville tried French Pass early in 1827. His journey around the world almost ended there and then.

It took him five days to get through. He left his nationality on the pass, his name on D'Urville Island, and bits of his ship on the rocks.

The pass ran between Tasman Bay (named for one explorer, Abel Tasman) on one side and Admiralty Bay (named by another explorer, Captain James Cook) on the other. It was a nautical shortcut, saving a long journey into Cook Strait around the top of D'Urville Island with the rocky Stephens Island at its tip.

The difficulty with the pass was that the sea took a shortcut too, squeezing one vast body of water into another through a thin gap, racing one way with the flood and the other with the ebb.

The pass then looked like a river rapid, except much more dangerous. Ships fought watery jet-streams and whirlpools, the most dangerous of them the notorious Jacobs Hole which could suck in a whole vessel.

Olive Baldwin in her book *New Zealand's French Pass and d'Urville Island* gave page after page of strandings, collisions, wrecks and drownings, and noted that even her own meticulous records were not conclusive: she'd talked to an old man who was a boy on Stephens Island in the late 1890s and who remembered a ship in distress struggling towards Admiralty Bay one foul day, his mother crying out, 'My God! She's going down!' She found no record of the ship's name.

No wonder that D'Urville was one of the biggest but least-known islands, strange and wild.

To negotiate French Pass the modern explorer had first to cope with the French Pass road. It started off easy, ended up hard. A beautiful drive through bush and bays finished in a shingle string of a road atop a high sharp ridge with the blue sky above and the blue sea below, both of them alarmingly close.

There wasn't enough room for the car and a tiny lamb that ran before it for so long that I stopped, picked it up and put if off the road. That was usually regarded as a dumb thing to do, and here lay a note about island life. There'd been a car in front, and by the time I arrived at the island, almost everyone I spoke to knew about the lamb.

So. My first encounter with D'Urville Island came when I telephoned to rent a bach from Sue Savage. It was early spring, wet. 'You've got a four-wheel drive haven't you?' she asked.

I hadn't. I'd rented something old. I thought it would suit. 'You'll need one,' she said. Back to the rental car company. They had a new-ish 4WD. But . . . no insurance on the ferry ride over to D'Urville. And wait a minute . . . no insurance on D'Urville roads either. The car was expensive. Christine Aston, who ran the ferry with her husband Craig, told me they'd never lost a car overboard. That was reassuring. The roads . . . well, no one was sanguine. We simply drove slowly and kept our fingers crossed.

When we wanted to get up to the northern tip of the island — not a great distance, but a one-and-a-half-hour journey — we had to call the two farmers who owned the roads. One was relaxed. The other asked what sort of car we were driving, then:

'Have you *seen* the road?'

'No.'

'It's steep, and it's slippery.'

'Yes, I know you're thinking you'll have to get the tractor and tow us out of trouble but . . .'

'Tractor be buggered. I'll be hiring a helicopter to look for the bodies.'

Everyone agreed this was a road in name only, to be tackled by novices on a good day in dry weather and then on a quad bike. Not today, in the wet.

———

It was raining. Hard. We slithered up the spiny back of D'Urville and slid down the other side, turning off onto a road which became a track then disappeared altogether. We were in Kupe Bay, which locals called Cuppy.

At the bottom was a little blue cottage. The sea shushed on the beach. Lemons, oranges, tangelos, guavas grew around. Could this be paradise? Oh yes, its residents insisted.

At last count D'Urville was the eighth most populated island in New Zealand, although it was a hard one to compute. Terry Savage, who was once chair of the residents' association and should have known, reckoned on a permanent population of 32, although he conceded others argued for 52. Craig Aston, the mailman, calculated 17 families in full-time residence. As well as many baches and holiday homes.

Jeanette and Pip Aplin lived there. They met when she was 18 and Pip

Above D'Urville skies

was 20. She said: 'We believed we didn't need people. We were into tramping, the bush, the great outdoors.'

They became lighthouse-keepers, of course. Pip's first posting was to Stephens Island, 150 hectares of rock off the northern tip of D'Urville bought from Maori for a lighthouse and famous for its tuatara.

They stayed on that island for a year, until Pip was transferred to Dog Island, a truly bleak slab in Foveaux Strait. They lived there, in the eye of the westerly gales, for two years, then went back to Stephens for another five.

Which was odd, because they agreed the landing at Stephens was both terrible and frightening, the sea journey to Picton horrible, and even picking up the mail seemed perilous.

Yet they liked the island. 'And living in dinosaur country was pretty special,' said Jeanette, 'all these tiny dinosaurs [tuatara] running around, all the seabirds coming in, insects galore, to live there is very special.'

After almost nine years on these tiny islands they went to Arthur's Pass where Pip became a park ranger and they found themselves surrounded by young people skiing, tramping, having fun.

'We found it quite puzzling,' said Jeanette. 'It was as if we'd had nine years

Above Pip and
Jeanette Aplin

out of our lives, up in a cloud or something. Nine years outside normal society. So we had plenty of catching up to do.'

All of that was quite easy to follow. Nine years marooned on rocks deemed dangerous to shipping *did* seem likely to remove you from normal society. Cafés and bars and cinemas and street lights *would* seem worth catching up on.

Yet they became nostalgic for the Dog. That island, Pip said, was his favourite. 'Were it possible I'd have gone back there to live.'

Jeanette said: 'At one stage we thought, "Wouldn't it be good to go back there and spend the rest of our lives revegetating the island."'

Pip looked nostalgic. 'Imagine doing homestays. People could fly out.'

But why, I wondered, would they want to go and live on one of the coldest islands in New Zealand, in one of the roughest straits in the world?

Simple, said the Aplins. Pip: 'It was a lovely island and you could see the boundaries. I like islands for that reason. The edge isn't over the horizon, it's right *there*.'

Jeanette: 'I know islands have a romantic appeal for a lot of people, I guess we just take it one step further.'

They'd decided they needed a bach, which, as they described what they wanted, seemed to me to be somewhere lonely to escape from somewhere even lonelier.

They found 10.5 hectares on D'Urville in a bay known locally as Iron Pot. They bought it sight unseen. It was, of course, remote and by most standards lonely, even for the Aplins.

As she caught her first sight of their island paradise Jeanette thought, 'Oh no, what have we done? It looked so . . . empty. [This from someone who'd lived on the Dog?] Then as soon as we landed it was wonderful. Birds were singing, snapper were cruising along. We thought it was heaven. And it was so civilised after living in lighthouses. There were two farmhouses here and they both had three children.'

'Somewhere along the line,' said Jeanette, 'I've realised I'm a real people person. Probably when I was forty-something. We'd left the lighthouses then.'

There might have been a light on the other side of the bay, but I couldn't be sure. Their access over adjacent properties was tenuous. Their way in, and out, was by dinghy. Their sociability seemed, well, a qualified success, although I took their point: getting along with others in a small place took more effort, not less.

Dusk was falling around their tiny, beautifully built cottage and the big workshop with three wooden boats beside it. The last light played on varnished wood. A wood-range warmed the room, books, some written by Jeanette, were comforting. She gave us soup, roast chicken, little buns stuffed with fruit.

Islands had been their lives, so the question had to be asked:

What was their appeal?

'For example,' said Pip, 'people go to islands to escape from the rat-race, from the collapse of society.'

'But not necessarily,' said Jeanette, 'because it's a dream, a magic dream to live on an island. It's not just getting away, it's going to this magical land.'

Yet once she'd been anxious about what the isolation was doing to her children. 'I really felt the children needed to learn how to live in the world and not be isolated.'

Now, their daughter Helen was living on D'Urville with them too, with her husband and three children. Their son Fred was living in Reefton, the West Coast town.

Helen, Jeanette said, felt that she'd come home. She seemed startled that I might think Fred had taken himself off to an isolated place too. 'I don't think living in Reefton . . .'

Pip popped us into his little boat and rowed across the bay, still as a lake, the sky clearing and the moon peeping, and we slid across the water to the blue cottage in the soft evening air, the bush smelling of rain. The last I saw of Pip was his small figure fading into the blackness. Living here didn't seem to be too much of a stretch, not really.

———

Our cottage belonged to Sue and Terry Savage, who lived in a much bigger house built by one of the three Hope brothers who once farmed the bay.

They'd bought the house and four hectares of land in 1989, 'rundown but pretty cool'.

Those were the good old days and they were working for the New Zealand Motor Corporation, later Honda, at the motor assembly plant in Nelson. In the shadows of 1992 they took voluntary severance. He was 47, she 39.

They decided to live on D'Urville. 'We'd made some good investments.' Pip and Jeanette lived across the bay, and a fisherman lived next door, and they made up the permanent population there.

They were self-sufficient. They had a big garden, and an orchard, and the bay's micro-climate allowed them to grow much of their food year-round. There were plenty of fish in the sea then, and still were now. The two of them could get their bag limit of six blue cod just like *that* — a snap of the fingers — while the rest of the country paid a fortune for a fillet.

Well yes, they had to adjust. In the rain that day the island had seemed brooding but they leapt to its defence. 'We've never felt like that. We come on the island after we've been away, through the bush, it's so beautiful, the sun coming through, we've never looked at it like that.'

The island was changing, slowly. The old farmers were disappearing.

Opposite Sue and Terry Savage

Following Pip Aplin, commuting

The big money had already arrived in the north of the island. Well-known names. Rumours. The stories common on islands.

Sue sat in the still morning. Drizzling. No wind. 'I don't miss anything. We don't buy many clothes. Why have stuff you're never going to wear? We eat what's in the garden. We go to town [Nelson] with a list of shopping, a couple of appointments, and back again. We may not use a car for months on end. We don't need a new car.'

Well, hardly ever. Sue was driving to Nelson, went to sleep at the wheel, crashed. She produced the news clipping. The irony of it, apart from going into town to get a warrant of fitness, was that she crashed at Hira, on a wide paved highway, having negotiated the tricky track from her house, the road across the island, and the demanding French Pass road safely. 'It was such a good ute too,' she said. 'I was so wild.'

———

Three generations of Craig Aston's family had lived around the island.

His great-grandfather had the first shop in French Pass. His other great-grandparents lived and farmed in Deep Bay in Admiralty Bay.

His father delivered the mail around D'Urville, and would meet the freighters going through French Pass with freight, mail and passengers. He was a fisherman.

Craig was a fisherman too, catching cod and butterfish and perch and shipping them off to Sydney where the money was. He was a mailman as well,

delivering mail along D'Urville's east side. He and his wife Christine operated the ferry. Typical islanders, making money where they could.

They owned the house next door to his parents' place in Ngamuka Bay on the island, and when his father died and his mother went to a retirement home they moved into the parents' house and used their own as a holiday let. So now he lived in the house he was born in.

His parents were remembered in a plaque on Fishermans Point on the D'Urville side of the pass, where a narrow passage let small boats squeeze through. He and Christine hoped for a plaque there too, although as they talked, robust, cheery, full of life, the memorial seemed a long way off.

We loaded the car onto the Astons' ferry and set off across the water. We wanted a closer look at French Pass for a photograph. I was happy to view it from a distance but Craig obliged. He swung the big ferry towards the maelstrom.

The pass had changed in the last couple of hours. It looked like soup that had been on the stove too long. It bubbled and boiled, bulged and swirled. Gouts of water came from somewhere far below the surface. Waves formed and crashed. Tasman Bay was making for Cook Strait at around 8 knots. It picked up the ferry and twizzled. I thought of the insurance company and frizzled.

Craig and Christine looked not the slightest bit worried. They manoeuvred the ferry through the rapids with the confidence of whitewater champions.

We reached the ramp at French Pass and I blew a kiss at terra firma. We drove onto sealed road half an hour or so later. The mud tracks of D'Urville, the wild road to the pass, were a safe distance behind. Out to Rai Valley and a mussel pie. Civilisation.

Hautai

'The wind moaned, rocks became spectres
in the dark.'

The *Queen Bee*, a three-masted barque, was on her twelfth voyage bringing immigrants and cargo to New Zealand and was bound for Nelson when she struck Farewell Spit on the night of 6 August 1877. The incompetent captain sent off a dinghy to the mainland for help but the following day, with the ship breaking up, the remaining passengers and crew abandoned the *Queen Bee*.

The ship's cutter, heavily overloaded and constantly taking water, was swept right across Golden Bay then Tasman Bay and washed up in Te Puna Bay on the southern tip of D'Urville Island. There they encountered their first Maori, who came rushing toward them over the hill, and by all accounts the survivors were thoroughly terrified. Joy Hope, born 1922, of the Ngati Toa/ Ngati Koata people living on D'Urville Island,

remembered the story like this: 'They were a bit worried. But they didn't get eaten.'

In fact, local Maori warmed and fed the survivors until help arrived, then provided a boat to take some of them back to Nelson where they received a heroes' welcome.

Much of the southern tip of D'Urville Island, some 400 hectares, was still owned by the Kawharu family. Joy Hope was one of them, growing up in the Kawharu farmhouse standing in Ohana Bay near Savage Point where the west wind howled. She remembered some of the *Queen Bee* wreckage washed up on family land.

A gold ring belonging to the master of the *Queen Bee*, Captain John Davies, was given to the Kawharus and passed down the generations. Margaret Kawharu, who lived in Nelson, kept it safe.

Just across the water lay a tiny island, Hautai. The island was named for one of the sailors crewing the *Tainui* waka to New Zealand.

Some said Hautai was spooky. It should have been.

In *Angelina,* the story of his grandparents' lives on D'Urville Island, Gerard Hindmarsh's grandfather Vincenzo Moleta told of a Maori man arriving in their bay in a canoe, to borrow some tools. The man had his two young sons with him. While he was picking up the tools the younger boy threw stones at the older, the two screaming abuse at each other. Their father picked up a manuka stick from the beach and dashed out the younger boy's brains. The remorseful father wailed, the surviving son screamed.

The boy was buried on Hautai. The man was beaten up and banished. Police were informed but no action was taken. Who could read a story like that and look at the island without a shiver?

On the bright morning I went there, with the Kawharus' permission, it was bright as a button. It looked like a tuatara, spiny and scaly, lying still in the sun.

Stock wading across from D'Urville had left animal tracks up the hill, and I followed them to where two graves huddled at the top looking back to ancestral land on D'Urville. On one, the name Wetini Parata, Joy's great-grandfather. Another headstone, worn to the shape of a ghost, lay in front.

Centuries of family history lay beneath my feet, some of it more recent: Eva Rickard of Tainui, the renowned land rights activist, was related to the Kawharus and some of her ashes were sprinkled on the island.

This was the place where the Kawharus' ancestors were buried, most of them without headstones or markers. They were buried sitting up, and Joy remembered skeletons exposed by a storm, sitting in a row. Her father, very upset, crossed to the island and covered them.

On another occasion she and her brother Ross, who now owned the land, found human bones exposed. They took some home. Ross remembered a skull. Their father, a superstitious man or perhaps just sensitive, made them take them back, immediately. It was growing dark. The wind moaned, rocks became spectres in the dark. 'We were terrified. But I never took any bones again.'

Craig Aston, the ferryman and Joy's cousin by marriage, told of rugby games, people rowing to the Kawharus' bay and walking over the hill to Te Puna Bay. Joy remembered them too: 'Walking over the hill for the rugby and back for a feast and a dance in the shed.

'Life was lovely,' Joy said. 'I had a lovely childhood.' She would go over to the island often. Sometimes she played there with other children, but not often: 'It was not a very attractive place. Very wild.'

She liked looking at the graves, sitting quietly in the sun, the terraces of the old pa at Ohana still clear in the light.

Opposite Ross Kawharu and Joy Hope

HARBOUR
HAVENS

PUKERAUARUHE/ BROWNE'S

'First he had to convince the government that there was an island. The department was not at all certain of the matter.'

Pukerauaruhe Island was said to mean a heap of ferns but it did not look like one and was so barren it would struggle to grow very much at all.

Local people called it Browne's Island because a man called Wally Browne had built a cottage, a bach, on this islet in Port Levy on the northern side of Banks Peninsula. I used to set a net for moki and butterfish off the island and marvel that there was room for anything, let alone a bach. It was just a rock.

Wally loved it.

He and his family spent many happy years on the island/islet/rock. Eventually, he was said to have grown so angry with the government he set fire to his bach and burned everything on the island, and in Port Levy, a community not much given to liking the government, they said good on him. But that was much later.

Wally's island was just a memory when I picked up a *House & Garden* magazine one day and read an article about a Waiheke Island woman. It wasn't her house that caught my eye, admirable as it was. On the wall she had old sepia photographs of, yes, Browne's Island. She'd spent summers there as a child.

So, it was true. People *had* lived on that rock. Wally could hardly have been the crusty old hermit of legend. He had had grandchildren, and one of them was Kate Hastings, the woman on Waiheke Island.

I went to see her. She had photographs, documents. Best of all, she had two works of art. One was Wally's diary, handwritten in pencil, sometimes in ink, on yellowing pages inside shiny black cloth covers. A square of cardboard on the front carried its title, *Island Episodes*.

The second was a typescript, carefully preserved, interspersed with photographs. It was titled *The Story of an Island: Our Island Home*, by Cora A. M. Browne, Kate's grandmother.

The young Wally Browne was sailing his little 6-metre yacht *Senorita* around Banks Peninsula in the 1930s when he saw his island. It was love at first sight.

Pages 312–3 Quail Island jetty

Previous Browne's Island

Opposite Work of art

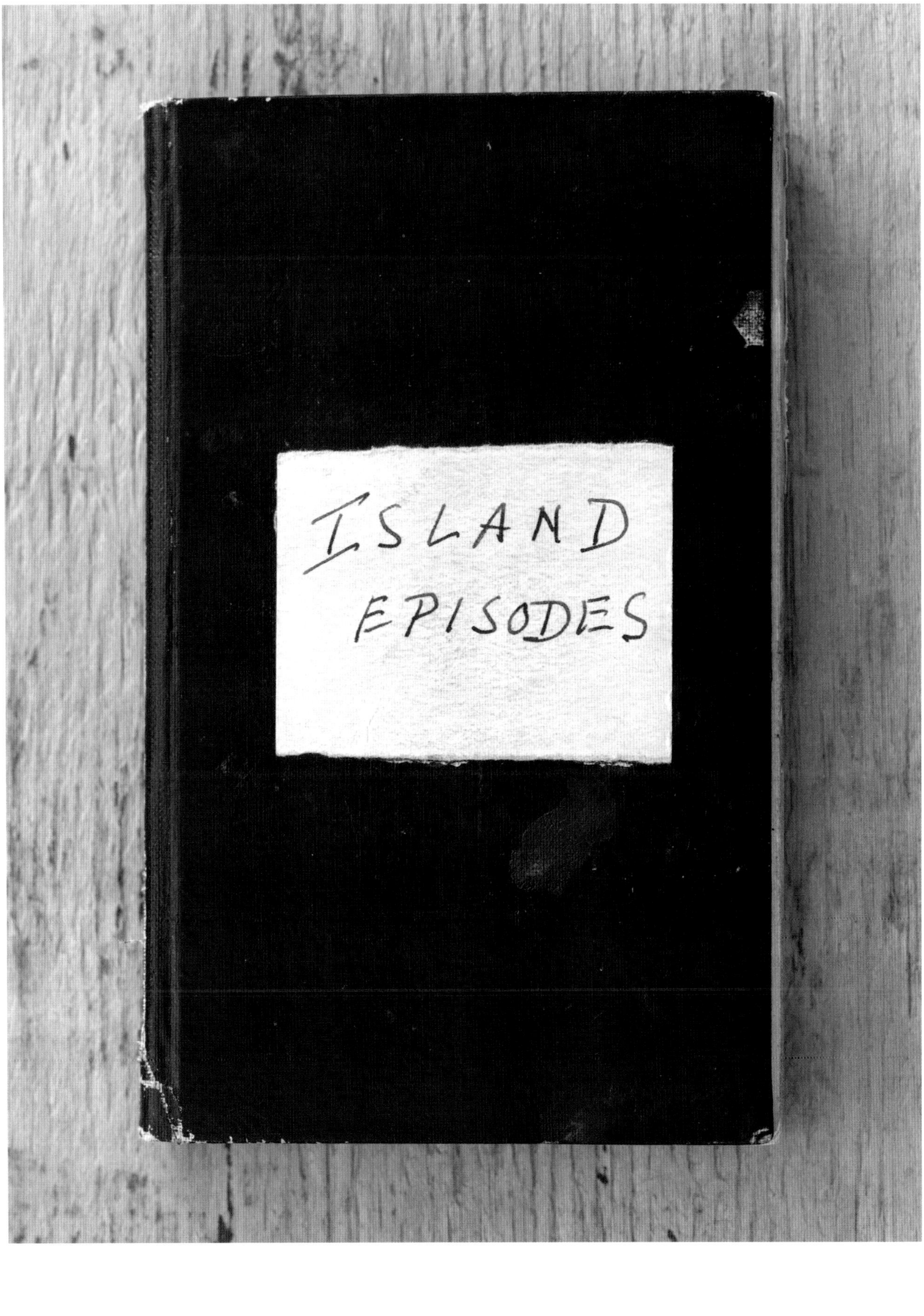
ISLAND
EPISODES

The very next week he went to see the Lands and Survey Department and asked to lease it. First he had to convince the department that there *was* an island. The department was not at all certain of the matter. The only island in Port Levy, they thought, was the much bigger Horomaka, the island of treacherous rock.

The dialogue went something like this:

Clerk: Can't be done.

Wally: Why not?

Clerk: The island is not on our Lands and Survey map therefore it doesn't exist.

Wally: Now hang on a minute, mate. I was standing on it two days ago. An island is an island, it just doesn't up anchor and sail away you know.

With the basics out of the way, they came to an agreement. The government would lease the island.

For £1 a year, payable in advance, Wally had his own island kingdom. He would have to keep it clear of noxious weeds, of course. And, oh, rabbits. While the department was now reasonably certain it owned a hitherto unknown island, obviously it was still unclear about its size and composition, for a rabbit could hardly survive there.

The year was 1932, and Banks Peninsula was still a remote and foreign land. There were few roads. A small fleet of steamers serviced the bays.

There was no vegetation on the island at all except very coarse grass, two spindly trees — an apple and a lilac — and a few clumps of matagouri.

Early photographs of Browne's occupation showed the island with a wig of stunted trees, the 20 or so pines and macrocarpas planted by Wally who built his cottage among them, carting everything from Lyttelton in his little boat. It was a basic place: baches were, then. It was built partly of driftwood, bits of a wrecked trawler. Bunks, some basic furniture, walls papered with newspapers. A roof, held against the gales by rocks. Slowly the pines and macrocarpas and even a pohutukawa grew until the house was all but hidden.

There was so much of himself in his island that his grand-daughter Kate thought of one as growing out of the other. 'He built this little hut and just kept adding to it. He built jetties that got swept away, until finally he built this drawbridge affair. He'd take us to the boat then he'd take the dinghy back — he sculled, standing up, he was a great big tall man, then he'd go back and wind the jetty up and that kept it safe. Huge storms would sweep up the harbour. For me it was always a big adventure.'

His bach was the castle in his kingdom. Everything had to be brought in, water, firewood, food, although there were plenty of fish. Later he added a few luxuries. A windmill charged batteries for lights.

'My father was Bernie, his brother Doug. That's what they did as kids, go to the island. Later they'd pick me up from boarding school and we'd all go to the island. They had an incredible grapevine at home so we'd have a big tea box full of grapes and off we'd go. For my father and his brother, what an adventure.'

Photographs showed them as boys, happy, bronzed, confident, rowing, fishing, either on the sea or in it.

This was a friend's testimony:

'I loved old Wally's house. It had a little attic, very comfortable and shipshape, small and warm and cosy just like a yacht's cabin. On the back of the section was the quintessential bloke's shed, laden with tools, timber, dinghies, masts, old sails, boating gear and paraphernalia of such abundance that it all hung like grapes on a vine in a bumper year — the roof sagged with it all.'

'When we are asked how we fill in our time at the island,' Cora wrote, 'it is rather difficult to answer as each day is different. Most mornings we power or row down to the Heads to set the nets . . . if the weather is fine and seas smooth

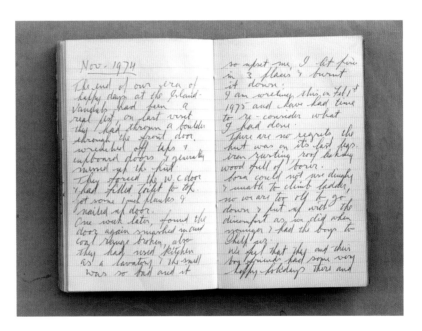

we go for picnics in the *Murare* [the Brownes' later yacht] often going outside the Heads to some of the eastern bays, Pigeon Bay and Little Akaloa . . . I must confess however a lot of our time is spent talking. We have many visitors. What could be pleasanter than sitting over a cup of tea or a glass of beer talking about old times . . .'

Wally's own log was more prosaic. This is an entry from 31 October 1939, a few weeks after New Zealand declared war on Germany: '. . . the mooring was gone and at dinner time the sickle fell from the roof and broke four saucers and one plate. We were dragging for the mooring chain when suddenly the grapnel caught in the chain and snapped . . .'

On 11 August 1945: 'Japan offers surrender. Fitted new chimney on Shacklock stove. Great success.'

Sou'west busters, great hot days, 'sea like glass, glorious sunshine', boatloads of friends, wonderful Christmas holidays, a little concreting around the house,

Above Wally's diary

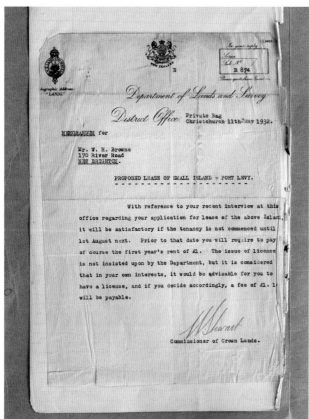

beers with cod for breakfast, moki for lunch, Cora delighted with the geraniums, 'Very pleased to find twenty-two years' effort rewarded with the flowering of the pohutukawa', visiting their neighbours, the Helps, on the farm still owned by the Helps family next to the island.

Around Christmas 1954, the idyll began to cloud. They arrived at the island to find the house ransacked, tools, gear, fishing nets, even two of Cora's tablecloths stolen. They tracked down the thief, a fisherman, who was fined £5 in court.

It proved to be the beginning of the end.

In 1968 the government decided it wanted its island back. It wanted Browne's returned to its natural state. First the Lands and Survey Department said the family would be given a final two-year tenancy. Then it changed its mind: Wally Browne would be given a lifetime licence to occupy his island.

Wally protested. He'd always encouraged people to use the island, he'd spent most of his life on his bach and his jetty and everything else. He wanted his sons' families to carry on. 'We very much regret,' the department replied.

Local legend held that Wally, saddened and sick of the fight, ended it by burning down his place.

Wally had the last word, a slightly different one.

In November 1974 he wrote the second-to-last entry in his log:

Above Island lease dated 1932; memento from a cook-up on the beach

'The end of our era of happy days at the island.'

Vandals had thrown a boulder through the front door, wrenched off taps and cupboard doors, wrecked the lavatory. A week later they'd returned, broken the prized coal range, defecated in the kitchen. 'The smell was so bad and it so upset me I lit fires in three places and burned it down.'

I could imagine him, 75 years old, remembering the latest typed letter from the Lands and Survey people, 'I am sorry etc', looking at the ruin of his beloved cottage, feeling all of his years.

The last entry: 'I am writing this on February 1st 1975 and have had time to reconsider what I had done. I have no regrets. The hut was on its last legs, iron rusting, roof leaking, wood full of borer. Cora could not use the dinghy and was unable to climb the ladder. We are too old to go down and put up with the discomfort as we did when younger and had the boys to help us. The memories of those times will always be with us . . .' He simply stopped writing. No full stop.

Now called Pukerauaruhe, the island stands much as it did when Wally Browne first saw it, narrow at one end and bulbous at the other like a teardrop, barren and rocky which, I suppose, was its natural state.

Cora died in 1981. She was 82. Wally died in 1995 aged 96. 'I wish I knew what he thought about life,' Kate said. 'He didn't say much.'

But who knew what men and women of that era thought? They seemed so certain, comfortable, reassuring. They got on with things.

Wally's log said it for him. He was a do-er. He was a man of his age. Perhaps he was a romantic, for he delighted in an island of his own. He was a Kiwi bloke who made something out of nothing. He certainly was not a wealthy yachtsman: a newspaper article recorded his retirement after 40 years as a debt collector with Christchurch's Municipal Electricity Department. An old piece of New Zealand, or a piece of old New Zealand. Gone now.

The *Senorita* lived on, and was still to be seen in Lyttelton Harbour.

As a footnote, the Lands and Survey Department's successors, the Department of Conservation, even in 1995 seemed uncertain whether the island existed. In response to someone who, like Wally Browne, sought to lease the island, they still confused it with its bigger neighbour, Horomaka.

Ripapa

'It was a fairytale castle complete with crenellations and what seemed to be arrow-slits.'

When we were young we used to get into Ripapa Island by scaling its stony walls. A reef joining it to the mainland was exposed at low tide and there, irresistible to small boys, was a perfect Victorian fort for the taking. Up its walls we'd go, and over the top, and there, in emplacements set into the rock, were *guns*, giant things with unimaginable power; tunnels disappearing into the rock, guarded by iron-bar doors. All of the impenetrable was so easily penetrated by children!

This tiny island in Lyttelton Harbour was always a fortress. Taununu, a Ngai Tahu chief in Kaikoura, came south and built a strong pa there. A map of its defences, built to withstand muskets, showed palisades running around the edge of the island almost exactly where later Europeans built their stone walls.

Taununu was killed during Ngai Tahu's kai huanga (eat-relation) war. He attacked a pa at Taumutu near what is now Lake Ellesmere and his Ripapa stronghold was defeated in retaliation by Ngai Tahu from the south, alerted by a seer called Hine-Haaka whose song prophesied:

Weep for yourself
On the morning
Your bones will be transformed into fishhooks.

So it was. Taununu escaped but was killed later at Wairewa, or Little River.

Ngai Tahu occupied the island until about 1832, when Te Rauparaha came marauding from the north. Ripapa was one of the pa he took, then abandoned, and that might have been the last of Maori on the island, had it not been for Te Whiti and his passive resistance at Parihaka.

This disgraceful episode saw his people imprisoned in 1881, without trial, and one of their jails was Ripapa Island. In the meantime the island had become a quarantine station for colonial immigrants and re-named, ironically, Humanity Island.

Only a few years later, colonial authorities recognised its worth as a fort. New Zealand had been worried about the Russians for much of the second half of the nineteenth century, once terrorised even by a fake story in the *Daily Southern Cross*, which reported the Russian cruiser *Kaskowski* (whisky cask) storming Auckland and taking the mayor hostage.

In 1885 a full-blown Russian scare swept New Zealand and fortifications were thrown up. Ripapa Island was one of them. Its stone walls and tunnels were built by the unlucky prisoners of Lyttelton jail, whose contribution to Christchurch's built history was remarkable: the city owed a lot to its criminals. They scraped off the top of the island and built subterranean tunnels.

Now called Fort Jervois, it was used as a harbour defence in World War I, its huge guns pointing fiercely out to sea. They never fired a shot in anger which was just as well, for this was a truly Kiwi affair. Billed as the most modern fort in the British Empire, Lord Kitchener, then Secretary of State for War, declared it useless: if all four of its guns were fired at once, the fort would collapse.

When a single gun was fired, in fact, cracks appeared. Baden Norris, the renowned Christchurch historian and conservationist, told me the last shot was fired in World War II, when the fort was again commissioned. The gun recoiled so badly it cracked its mountings. The shot had ricocheted off the harbour entrance and, he believed, into the nearby popular beach resort of Taylors Mistake.

After the war, scrap metal rights were sold to a Christchurch merchant. Fortunately, the guns, two of them hydro-pneumatic disappearing guns, defeated him. Two remained intact on the island, both now extremely rare prizes. Parts of the other two lay around.

Ripapa's most famous prisoners were not, unfortunately, the Parihaka Maori, nor the hunger-striking conscientious objectors jailed there in 1913.

The honour went instead to Count Felix von Luckner, captain of the German raider *Seeadler*, whose crew was captured in Fiji in 1917 and brought to New Zealand to be interned. Von Luckner was placed on what had been the battery hut on Ripapa Island and spent 109 days on the island in 1918. He was not impressed.

When he returned on a triumphal tour of New Zealand before World War II, he wanted to revisit the island. Permission was denied: it was a military installation, no Germans allowed. 'By Joe what a pleasure it was to see that old weary Ripa island again,' he wrote in the visitors' book of the launch *Awatea* which had taken him to the island. 'But there certain fools wouldn't let me land for fear I didn't know it well enough!'

Later the place was opened to visitors and small boys. It turned into an historic reserve. It was a fairytale castle complete with crenellations and what seemed to us to be arrow-slits. We ran through its underground gallery and along its tunnels to the four concrete gun pits, peered into the old torpedo store and mines stores. It was a perfect place.

Ripapa was closed after the 2010–2011 earthquakes. CERA, the Christchurch Earthquake Recovery Authority, thought it earthquake-prone. Two years later Baden Norris, who was one of the island's guides, asked when it might reopen. He was told that engineers had determined that the island was not, in fact, earthquake-prone. But it was said to have suffered some unspecified damage suggesting it should remained closed in the meantime.

Well, no one could accuse the Christchurch authorities of acting hastily. Another three years on, the island was still closed except, of course, to enterprising children.

Opposite Ripapa, guarding the Lyttelton heads

QUAIL

'A fortunate exile, although one of the men
certainly died and two others probably did.
One escaped.'

was not allowed onto Quail Island as a child. When I asked to go, once, there were frowns and shaken heads. Reputations were hard to get rid of, and Quail Island had one. Within my parents' memory the island had obeyed the biblical injunction on lepers: 'He is unclean. He shall live alone. His dwelling shall be outside the camp.' Fear of leprosy lay deep.

Quail Island was well outside the camp, over the volcanic rim from Christchurch and tucked away in Lyttelton Harbour. There lepers lived together but alone, each in his tiny hut, cast out of society to deal with the shadow of ages yet still a great deal better off than poor Kim Lee, the suspected Chinese leper cast into a bleak cave in Wellington Harbour and left to die.

Otamahua, Quail Island, was not at all bleak. From the terraces where the lepers' huts once stood in a natural amphitheatre you could see two nice beaches, the sea inviting. A fortunate exile, perhaps, although one of the men certainly died and two others probably did. One escaped.

Quail Island was other things too. A quarantine island for immigrants suspected of harbouring disease, and after World War I for influenza patients.

Animals were impounded there also. The island was used as a quarantine and training ground for four Antarctic expeditions. Both Robert Falcon Scott and Ernest Shackleton kept their horses and dogs there before setting off for the ice. Now, it was a fine place for a summer picnic.

Today we were with Ian McLennan and Lindsay Daniel, two of those people whose volunteer groups kept so many New Zealand islands alive. They belonged to the Quail Island Ecological Restoration Trust, whose interests went further than the history of the place. Quail Island, always dry, had been left largely barren by farming. The trust was replanting, restoring forest and shrub land.

'It's not all about kiwis and bellbirds and saddlebacks and all those trophy species,' Ian said. 'It's about building an ecosystem from scratch, getting the insects, the invertebrates there.'

The trust had cleared the island of predators, rats, rabbits, even hedgehogs, and were seeing wildlife return: insects, lizards, birds such as the korora, the white-flippered penguin. They'd even introduced the Californian quail, for the island was named after the native quail, koreke, once abundant but extinct since the late nineteenth century. (The Maori name Otamahua meant 'the place where children collected seabirds' eggs.')

It was a wet day. No matter, the two put on parkas and gaiters and showed us their island anyway.

This was once a big settlement, built for 200 people in a dress circle above Lyttelton Harbour. Christchurch's cold easterly funnelled from one direction and the bitter sou'wester blitzed over Gebbies Pass from the other. Hot in summer but in winter cold enough for inmates to complain to authorities, who grew trees for the wind to whine through. Angelic on a good day.

At its height the island population lived in 19 buildings, some of them huge. A few remained: a restored barracks, an old caretaker's cottage.

The barracks could have been welcoming only to people who'd been jammed into an immigrant ship for months on end.

A replica of a leper hut stood on its original terrace. I stood inside. It was tiny, but early last century these huts were 'plainly but comfortably' fitted out. The Christchurch *Press* in 1906 described the life of the first leper on the island, being slowly blinded by his disease: 'For the poor unfortunate who is compelled to live his lonely life . . . the pretty surroundings of the bay and the island must become terribly monotonous, if not hateful.' The *Press* asked readers to donate gramophone records.

Numbers slowly grew to nine, each in his own little hut. The *Lyttelton Times* visited in 1924 and found the huts well furnished, with books and family photographs and even wireless receivers. They kept pets: canaries, a cockatoo, a magpie ('a better speaker than the cockatoo'), even a parrot, which could shout 'allo dearie' from the trees.

It was a very New Zealand leper colony, but the awful solitude did not suit George Philips. He was a World War I soldier thought to have contracted the disease in Samoa in 1916. His leprosy was only suspected and after nine years on the island he was thought to be clear of it. He needed three tests showing negative results, and he would have been free in another 18 months. Too long for George, who appeared in one photograph taken on the island in suit, bow tie and watch chain, a tall handsome man. He took off.

There were two theories about what happened to him. In the first he turned up dressed as a priest at the Orton Bradley estate near Charteris Bay over on the mainland. He called a taxi and went off towards Christchurch. In the second, he joined one of the cocksfoot gangs then common on the peninsula and just melted away. Either way, George vanished. The nurse who'd been attending him disappeared at the same time. Neither was ever seen again; nor was any outbreak of leprosy reported from any part of the country.

Back on Quail Island, Ivon Skelton died of his disease. Ivon was born in Apia in Samoa. He had family on the West Coast and was visiting them when he was diagnosed with leprosy. He was just 20 years old.

Off he went into exile and died at 25. He was buried on the island — or so everyone thought. Today, his was supposedly the only grave. A little information plaque stood beside it, with a photograph of Ivon. It showed a bright-eyed young man with luxuriant hair nicely done, a self-assured lift to his chin, wearing a suit and a waistcoat and a buttonhole rose and a ring on his finger, leaning against a fireplace. He looked like a bright up-and-coming young man confident of success. He also looked as far from a leper colony as it was possible to be. That is where the mystery began.

Group photographs of the Quail Island lepers showed Ivon looking disfigured but clearly Samoan. The young man in the photograph was just as clearly not Samoan. There was no similarity between the two.

The mystery deepened. The previous year Ian McLennan had been contacted by a man, Ray, whose mother had lived in Blackball on the West Coast and had had some sort of relationship with Ivon. Ray had a postcard to his mother written by Ivon with a photograph of him taken in Dunedin. It showed yet another man, although he had a slight resemblance to the man in the graveside photograph. Now there were three photographs, all of them allegedly of Ivon, all of them different. 'You cannot really relate the three photographs to decide who's who,' Ian said.

When the grave was examined the plot grew even murkier. The Department of Conservation had moved Ivon's headstone a short distance from the original

Above and opposite
Inside the barracks

gravesite, which was being damaged by slips and storms.

The first grave was exhumed the year before I visited. No bones nor any kind of remains were found. 'Possibly,' Ian speculated, 'Ivon was not even buried on the old gravesite.'

The story that only one man died there might not be true either. Lindsay suspected two others had died. He was working on his theory.

He had information suggesting not only that another patient, Quail's first leper patient Will Villane, had died on Quail but a third man too, a 52-year-old Maori. Were they all in one grave? There'd have been some reluctance to handle their bodies. But Ian pointed out that Ivon's burial had been presided over by the Rev A.J. Petrie from Holy Trinity Church in Lyttelton, a solid citizen who everyone was sure would have brooked nothing untoward.

The researchers were seeking two files held in the National Archives which might shed some light. The first was a file on the lepers on the island, the second the diary of Nurse Margaret Corston, the first nurse to work with the men. The Ministry of Health would not release them because of the sensitive information they contained. Ian and Lindsay were taking their Official Information Act request to the Ombudsman.

Quail Island held another secret, much more recent.

A man called Graeme White was known as an amiable eccentric in Christchurch. He'd served time in jail for tunnelling into an abortion clinic, had been fined for attacking a statue of the war hero Charles Upham VC and Bar, for riding a bicycle without a helmet and for indecently exposing himself to a woman 'while tending a goat'. He was wearing only a money pouch over

Above From Quail to the
mainland, with King Billy
at left

his crotch, and a sackcloth, and while he was defending the charge he earned himself a further conviction when court staff saw his bare backside.

On the other hand, he was known as a compassionate man who helped people with mental illness and he'd won high praise from doctors for becoming only the second living person in New Zealand to donate a kidney to a stranger. They'd described him as likeable and intelligent.

He worked with the trust replanting Quail Island and when he was on the island he often dispensed with his usual sackcloth and wore nothing at all. 'It was a bit alarming,' said Ian, 'especially when you were working below him and you looked up.'

One day he'd joined the workers on Quail Island by leaving his car at Charteris Bay and walking across the mudflats to the island while everyone else took the ferry.

When it was time to go, the tide was in and the water was freezing. He'd have to swim part of the way but although he was offered a lift he'd wanted to get to his car the same way he'd come. Using a child's blow-up dinghy to float his wallet, car keys and what clothes he had, he set off. He was last seen on the nearby King Billy Island. Then he disappeared and his body was never found. The coroner concluded he'd accidentally drowned in water of just six degrees.

Above Where lepers once lived

Very little was left of all the enterprises, great, small and hidden from public view, that had once run their course on Quail Island.

Apart from the two surviving buildings the most enduring artefacts had been left ironically enough by convicts from the notorious Lyttelton jail.

Hard labour it was for them. Their job was to cut rock from a quarry above a place called Walker's Beach — where Bernie Walker had once mined shell for grit — then shape it with cold chisels and use it to build the stone walls and terraces on the island. Their work was superb. I looked closely at a wall, the rocks beautifully fitted together so tightly they could last another century.

Around them lay few other remains. The iron bins riveted together to hold immigrants' possessions. A crumbling bath from the bath house. Odd piles of brick, a few pieces of iron, even some old macrocarpas and pines planted for shelter, which DOC wanted to keep as part of the island's farming history.

When I'd finally broken the embargo and gone over to the island in my sailing dinghy long ago the remains of Scott's dog kennels survived well enough to work out their shape and layout. I thought I remembered a remaining leper cottage. Now, a replica kennel and cottage served as reminders.

The Crown took the island from Maori in 1849, paying its owners peanuts. The Maori owners objected and got nowhere. For 55 years Quail Island was leper colony and quarantine station. All of that ended in 1931. The island was made a reserve, at last, in 1975, after farming ended.

———

We were sitting high on a hill above the water looking over to King Billy Island whose sandstone was used by Maori for sharpening tools and by Pakeha for fine houses and public buildings. Nearby jutted a peninsula bought by the writer of children's books, Margaret Mahy.

A ships' graveyard lay below, the skeletons sinking into mud. Thirteen ships were said to lie here, the biggest of them the 58-metre *Darra*. She had been a huge barque, launched in 1865, a fast ship built for the Indian tea trade and used later as an immigrant ship. Even in 1950 she was good enough to be dressed up and used to represent the *Charlotte Jane* in a re-enactment of Canterbury's revered first four ships for centennial celebrations.

We sat up there looking down at the *Darra*'s bones and I asked Ian and Lindsay if they could live on this island where once hundreds of people had been brought against their will. Both said they'd grab the chance. Why? For the island's rich past, its intrigue, their pride in its restoration? Yes, but there was more.

'I mean,' Lindsay said, 'who wouldn't want to live on an island?' Put aside the history and the mystery. An island was an island.

QUARANTINE

'When a farmer friend told her to cut the lamb's throat or the ewe would die, she resorted to traditional methods: she cried her eyes out.'

338

Local knowledge was useful for getting to Quarantine Island. It sat roughly halfway up Otago Harbour, Port Chalmers on one side, Portobello on the other.

We reached it by the pretty, winding road running along the harbour's edge to Portobello, which looked as good as it sounded, then getting lost and foolishly asking a woman the way to St Martin Island. '*Quarantine* Island,' she snapped, 'is that way.'

The island was leased by the St Martin Island Community but many locals took exception to its new name. They preferred the more prosaic name bestowed on it by the early European settlers: Quarantine Island.

Its Maori name was more picturesque: Kamau Taurua, a place where nets were set. It was also called Midway or Halfway Island, and Rabbit Island.

When the St Martin community bought the lease they tried to name it St Martin, thinking it better than one suggesting hardship and disease. But locals preferred the grimmer one and it bounced back to Quarantine Island/ Kamau Taurua.

This, according to my guide, was down the road to the Portobello Aquarium — proper name the Portobello Marine Laboratory, but by then I'd had enough of names. The aquarium it was and it lay at the end of a narrow dusty road sidling along a small peninsula.

We walked down steps, zigzagged past a yellow submarine, detoured around laboratories, took a narrow walkway past concrete pools, navigated the fences and gates, and emerged onto a jetty. On the other side of a channel we could see another jetty, this one on Quarantine Island, where a woman was climbing into a graceful blue-and-white dory.

She manoeuvred it skilfully across the water and introduced herself as Kathy Morrison. We hopped in for the ride back to a jetty anchored by two wrecks, one of them the old harbour ferry *Waikana*. Kathy had fallen through its steel plating and cracked her ribs.

We climbed up to an old cottage and found a warm kitchen and, in no particular order, her husband Douglas Black, freshly made scones, and jam.

Kathy and Douglas were the island-keepers. I don't know what I'd expected, piety perhaps, a robe or two (hopefully), but these two were down-to-earth practical people and in the only religious phrase that came to mind, the salvation of this island.

The community sprang from a day's fishing. According to Lyndall Hancock's history of the island two Presbyterian ministers, the Revs James Matheson and George Knight, were fishing in the harbour one Monday in the 1950s, and stopped for a swim and lunch at an inviting beach on Quarantine Island. What a place for a community, they thought. One like Iona, on the tiny Isle of Iona in the Hebrides, an ecumenical community devoted to peace and justice. The St Martin Community was named after the fourth-century Bishop of Tours in France and, backed by the Presbyterian and Anglican churches, it set out to meld work and worship.

Quarantine then was essentially a ruin, a clutter of derelict quarantine buildings designed to prevent outbreaks of pestilence and disease such as smallpox and typhoid by keeping immigrants (usually the poorest) in isolation; a dismal welcome to their new country after being jammed into sailing ships for months on end in quarters where disease spread rapidly, heaving their dead overboard. There were accommodation buildings, kitchens, staff quarters, dining hall, hospitals.

The island was used up to World War I when soldiers were quarantined there. The sicknesses had changed although smallpox was still rampant: venereal diseases won lots of attention.

The island's use for quarantine formally ended only in 1924.

It was leased, on and off, and farmed rather despairingly, and by the time the two clergymen had their wonderful idea the last leaseholders were in debt and anxious to sell.

The fledgling St Martin Island Community bought it. Theme: 'Work and Worship.' Membership requirement: seven days' work on the island a year.

There was plenty of work. The jetty had to be repaired, buildings fixed up, ruins dismantled. As a farm it was, to say the least, run-down.

First of all, they had to build a chapel, designed by the architect Bob Oakley. It was a small, fin-shaped affair, walls of packed earth, its sail-like roof soaring up and framing a view down the harbour.

The keeper's house remained, the original now enclosed in an envelope of extensions, and was rented for income. The cottage, the old nurse's quarters, was now home to the island's managers, Kathy and Douglas and, earlier, their daughter Bryony.

Locals were not suspicious just of the name change: it was rumoured that the island was run by hippies.

I'd thought several things about Kathy Morrison and Douglas Black, and

not one of them included the word hippy. They were hard-working, for they had to be: they had ageing buildings to maintain, a farm to run, a whole island to maintain. They'd brought up Bryony there. They were the backbone of the enterprise. But . . . hippies?

Probably, Kathy said, Dave Wilson had given that impression. He'd been a minister who'd worked with unemployed people and he'd volunteered to be the island's first resident caretaker. He put out welcome signs, and he made soup for visitors.

Visitors to the island were sometimes much less attractive: thefts and vandalism were troubling the community. Even the fine old porthole window in the cottage, framing Harbour Cone, had been cut out and stolen.

Dave's presence on the island put a stop to that. But he was, perhaps, wild-looking. He had long hair and a long beard. In this quiet corner of Dunedin, where nearby Aramoana boasted the odd real hippy, some might have thought him hippy-ish, and in any event New Zealand had a long history of suspicion of communities, and love of rumour.

Dave Wilson died on the island. He'd made soup for a visiting group, scrubbed the bird poo off the jetty, then died quietly, in an armchair by the fire. His ashes were scattered on his island. Quarantine had been inhabited ever since.

Kathy, Douglas and Bryony were asked to fill in. Clever, Kathy said. If they'd been asked to go there and live they'd have said no. Instead, they discovered they loved it. Besides, Kathy had fallen in love with the donkey, Dudley.

Dudley was a stubborn beast. He gave Douglas a hard time. Douglas was a teacher, and his other love was singing in the City of Dunedin Choir.

Above and opposite Quarantine jetty

Following Kathy Morrison and Douglas Black, island-keepers

'I'm from Glasgow,' he said, 'and the only animals I knew about were Celtic supporters. I was left alone on the island one night. All I had to do was to get Dudley into the yards for the night. So I was nice, I cajoled him, patted him, but no way would he come in. It went on for hours and I was getting more and more frustrated. We lit candles in the chapel at dusk so I went across there and he followed me. I told him, I'm going to go in and light the candle and sit for ten minutes and when I come out you bloody better be in the yards. I sat for ten minutes and I came out and he was just standing there looking at me. Then he turned around and trotted into the yards.'

So Kathy said she'd look after the island for Dudley, and when they were on their way, they got a letter: sadly, Dudley had died.

They returned to the island anyway, and stayed for 12 years; now, they were back again. 'We were here for a year and we asked Bryony (then a teenager) what she thought and she said, stay for another year, so we did, and she was okay for another one, and in the end, we stayed all that time.'

Bryony and Douglas would go off to school together in the mornings, weather permitting: the journey to the mainland was short, but could be exceedingly wild.

Back on Quarantine Kathy had none of the skills an island-keeper needed: she knew nothing about boats, or building, or fencing, or sheep. When she found a lamb stuck during birth and a farmer friend told her to cut the lamb's throat or the ewe would die, she resorted to traditional methods: she cried her eyes out, until someone else suggested an alternative, and it worked.

'I was fencing up there in a howling southerly gale and I was thinking, this is me at fifty-five. I never dreamt I'd be fencing. But the fences are still there.'

They took off bargeloads of rubbish, demolished old buildings but saved one of them: the old married quarters for quarantined passengers, built in 1873 and one of only two island dormitory buildings remaining in New Zealand. Some 70 people died in quarantine on this island and this was their memorial. It was also Kathy Morrison's, for she saved it.

The building had had a varied career since its quarantine days. It had even been converted to a dance hall by one of the island's first leaseholders, Bob

Miller, a founder of the famed Port Chalmers boatbuilding firm Miller and Tunnage.

The building was leaning over and about to fall down when Kathy went to the Historic Places Trust, got some money and set about fixing it up. She was the project manager on a job which daunted even the builders. At one stage they said the work was too dangerous and went on strike until their boss sorted it out.

Once she painted the whole place, a huge job, and was photographed beside it wearing a huge, happy grin. That night a storm stripped off the new paint.

Now the building stood four-square but bare, awaiting more money to finish. She'd recreated one room, a tiny space where a whole family once lived. The poor had to be determined to achieve what the immigration posters promised, a new life in New Zealand.

Kathy was paid for the 60 hours or more per week she worked on the island, but so badly no one would count it as paid work. She was essentially a volunteer. 'It works for a couple, one works off the island and gets the money, and you get a house.'

Once, the community was strictly religious. But it was down to some 10 people, and seemed to be a religious community that was no longer religious. Now, they said, there were perhaps two churchgoers in the community, and neither of them was Kathy or Douglas.

'There was a stand-up time,' Kathy said, 'when some people marched to the chapel and some people went swimming, and I chose to swim that day. I thought, it's got to change. The kids were going nah, we're not going to chapel.'

So she was an architect of the change? 'People think of me more as the rot.'

She told the story of the small boy who came regularly with his father, the boatman. 'He'd ask what I was doing. I said that day I was chopping wood. He said he'd stack it for me. He loved the feel of it, the smell of it. Work was worship for that little boy. That's what it's about for me, the working, and the worship is in the process.'

Living on this island was her form of worship. She swam naked in the sea and a sea-lion fell in love with her. She was Douglas's own form of worship. 'She's the best thing that ever happened to me by a country mile,' he said.

———

I sat in the tiny white chapel, whose roof sailed towards the harbour entrance. Its candles were lit every evening. Wooden forms built of timbers from the wrecks below stood on the earth floor and its simplicity and silence soothed my soul. It was a welcoming place, a gathering place. Tibetan Buddhists came there every year.

Conservation groups came to the island to plant. Community groups, schools and others used the island. Today a language school from the university were to stay in the old keeper's house. Students were French, Japanese, Thai, Saudi Arabian, Kuwaiti.

The hospital sites where so many had lived and died were now marked by a few stones, or a piece of concrete, or a pile of old bricks.

I went through a gap in a hedge and sat under the trees around the cemetery. It was very quiet. The harbour below made no noise.

The last quarantined child to die on the island, on 3 June 1894, might lie in the cemetery. A plaque said the children's graves were marked by the little mounds arranged like corrugations on the earth. This, according to Lyndall Hancock, was wrong, but 72 people were said to lie here, only 45 of them officially recorded.

The Dougall family were the first island-keepers, John and Elizabeth Dougall and their family. Three generations of the family worked on the island over 61 years. Theirs was the only concrete grave in the cemetery, where John Dougall and three of his six children lay. John died after a stroke when he was 63. Elizabeth took over as keeper.

Nearby, a headstone marked the grave of an unnamed Italian baby Azzereti. A keen little southerly nipped up the harbour. Above the graves the trees leaned over.

ROARING
FORTIES

DOG

'He'd loved this place. Cold, lonely, desolate, to him it was magical, his paradise. They'd just about had to frog-march him off it.'

Aday of rain and gales had faded into light breeze and calm. A lucky day. Foveaux Strait was not best known for stillness. Sailors always feared it no matter what their craft, waka, square-riggers, fishing vessels, steamships.

The strait's shallow water was crowded with shoals, rocks and islets. Rips and storms gave this place an evil reputation among salts.

Yet it was a busy passage. It funnelled ships around the South Island past Stewart Island, and right at its narrowest point lay a long low rock, as much reef as island. This was Dog Island.

A graceful lighthouse stood in its middle, tallest in New Zealand. Once, it was rated the most important in the country, guiding mariners not just through the strait but into the busy port of Bluff.

You could stand at the Bluff lookout and look at the harbour entrance and wonder if it was an entrance at all. On a rough day, and there were plenty of those, it was a mass of breaking water. Even on a fine day waves broke mysteriously over hidden rocks.

Ships came around the western side of the Dog and approached the entrance obliquely. You could see the lighthouse had been critical once and was still important even in an age of electronic navigation.

People had been living on this island until 1989. That year New Zealand lighthouse-keepers ended a long, proud tradition and became historical artefacts.

From the lookout the island seemed only a long throw away. We flew over and as we approached the island I could see that it was just big enough for an airstrip. The Stewart Island Flights Cessna had fat tyres. They squished onto a roughly cut grass airstrip and I was delighted to see the toetoe stumps which once marked the middle of it had been shaven to the ground.

Today the sky was cleared by a scurrying west wind. We climbed onto terra firma, or as close to it as Dog Island offered, for its top was a bog in the wet.

Pages 348–9
Approaching a titi island with muttonbirders' gear

Previous Dog Island

Opposite For relieving lighthouse-keepers

We had a passenger. His name was Warren Russell and he was Dog Island's last principal lighthouse-keeper.

I'd met Warren this way. He lived in what seemed to be the closest house to the Bluff lookout, an eyrie looking down on the harbour entrance.

I'd knocked on his door several times during the previous day and the neighbour's dog had identified me as a person of interest.

Around 9 pm that evening I gave it one last go. His door was open, as it had been all day. I called into his empty living room. A shuffle from the back of the house. Warren appeared, smiling, as if he'd been expecting someone to come out of the night. This was Bluff, after all.

Look, I said, I'm a writer, I'm writing a book about islands, I'm flying over to the Dog first thing tomorrow, want to come?

Warren didn't even pause. 'Love to,' he said.

As the plane taxied back along the airstrip I could almost feel him vibrating in the front seat. It was the first time he'd set foot on the island for 20 years. He'd been back only once since he left it in 1989.

Warren climbed down from the aircraft and stood still. He was weeping quietly. He'd loved this place. Cold, lonely, desolate, to him it was magical, his paradise. He'd been happy here. They'd just about had to frogmarch him off it.

His house still stood, its windows now shuttered against the gales. He'd moved into it in 1980, when it was new.

The relieving lighthouse-keeper's cottage, more than a century old, sat on the other side on the main track dividing the island and running up to the lighthouse. It was a place of peeling wallpaper and tiled fireplaces, a museum of last-century living falling to pieces.

Behind it stood a shed that was once the box room. It was full of rubbish and lying in the midst of it were the tea-chests that had brought his family's gear to the Dog. They had rope handles and they were painted a pinky-beige. Everything was covered in bird poop.

A little further on lay the old stone lighthouse-keeper's house. It had stood there four-square for a century and a half, no small triumph in this place. Even in Warren's time it had been much as it was now, a machinery shed and workshop. A tractor and mower sat in one end of it. Ah yes, the airstrip.

Beyond everything else stood the lighthouse, on the highest point of the island, although that wasn't saying much because it was only 15 metres above the sea, or, as one early harbour official put it, 'very low and not seen 'till close upon it'.

From here you could see Warren's whole domain, 11 hectares.

The lighthouse was black-and-white striped. It seemed to touch the low grey sky.

Everyone thought it leaned slightly, but Warren had been around it with a plum-bob. 'I can tell you it's no more than a quarter of an inch out.'

The tower had been designed in 1863 by James Balfour, the marine engineer for Otago, lighthouse architect and one of those doughty colonists whose name jangled through the centuries.

It was two lighthouses really. The first had been built partly from stone quarried on the island, one of the reasons for locating the light there.

The height of the tower, the depth of its foundations, the dreadful weather, the cost of freight, made it the century's most expensive project for the fledgling Marine Department, costing double the average.

Worse, it trembled so badly in gales that engineers worried it would shake out its mortar, already weakened by lightning strikes. Cracks started appearing when it was less than a decade old.

It was repaired, and crumbled again. Something had to be done. So they encased the old tower in concrete, inside and out.

Now it was a lighthouse with another lighthouse inside it, both the tallest in New Zealand and the lowest at the same time. A spiral staircase climbed inside it. Warren said it was 125 steps to the top. He said he knew every one of them, especially on the night the light failed. 'The only time that happened was when a ship was coming. Do you think I could find the fault? I'd been up and down it three times when I found it. God, I was stuffed.'

He wanted to show me something. We walked around the curve of the lighthouse to its western side, where the wind should have been strongest. Instead, we were in a little pocket of calm. We stood marvelling over the aerodynamics of lighthouses.

Once, he said, someone rang up in a big storm and asked if he was all right. Yes, said Warren, why? 'And he said, all I can see is the top of the lighthouse.'

That was not unusual. The spray hit the rocks and flew right over the island.

'And just over here is where the cat's buried,' Warren said. The cat? Surely cats were forbidden here, where rare seabirds and penguins sheltered?

Well, yes, and that was the problem.

'The Department of Conservation wouldn't let me have the cat. But we'd had him a long time and the kids loved him. We decided he'd go when he died.

'So whenever they came out I'd stick him in a cage and hide him in a secret cave nobody knew about and cover him up with a sack so he didn't miaow.'

He showed me an overgrown track to an unexpectedly nice beach. He'd been walking there once when a seal shot out in front of him. He saw a tiny entrance, got down on hands and knees, found it widened into a cavern and that was where he hid the cat.

'He got hepatitis in the end and we had to put him down.

'We dug a hole, put the cat in and poured concrete in, wrote "Fred a faithful friend" in it.' A puzzle for some future archaeologist. No sign of the grave now.

That was not the end of Warren's lighthouse cat stories. He'd arrived on the island to find the previous keepers' cat. They asked him to look after it because it had been born on the island and would get run over if they took it to town.

Warren swore the cat was mad. It would sit in your lap one moment, hiss and claw you the next. Once it had a go at him and he put it outside.

The cat went feral. Russell searched for it. The island was only 11 hectares. 'But do you think I could find him?'

One night the alarms went off. 'I came running up here into the engine room and it must have been sitting here on the mat. He latched onto my leg, *aaargh!*, I thought, I'll get you, you bastard.

'The Ministry of Works were out here one day working in the engine room. They were walking down this path here and there was the black cat, following behind them. I raced into the bedroom, got the shotgun, shoved one up the spout, walked out and said to the guys, "Don't move!" *Boom!* Bowled the cat over. Some time later I was on holiday and stopped in Waikouaiti for an ice cream. One of the MoW guys was in the shop. He said, "I was on Dog Island when you shot the cat. I thought you were going to shoot *us!*"'

———

Strangely, for such a fierce place, there was not the usual litany of shipwrecks on Dog Island.

The most remarkable was the Union Steamship Company's *Waikouaiti*, which hit a reef off the island in thick fog on the evening of 28 November 1939. The crew were all saved but the ship broke up.

The ship was loaded with Christmas stuff, which according to Bluff legend was intended for the famous Invercargill department store, H&J Smith. Toys, dolls, fire engines, pedal cars, dolls' houses, bats and racquets washed off the ship along with fabrics, kitchen gear such as bowls and pots, even spices.

The lighthouse-keepers were allowed to keep anything they found and according to Bluff people there was plenty left over for them too. The beaches were covered with flotsam and jetsam.

'Everyone in Bluff had pedal cars and expensive dolls' prams,' according to Peter Ridsdale, whose Bluff house stared over the harbour.

Peter had an odd idea for a stormy island in cold climes, one whose usual traffic took great care to steer clear of.

He imagined it as a tourist resort, its ecology restored and flourishing, native species such as tuatara and titi reintroduced, walkways created.

He saw the keepers' houses renovated, the original stone house restored, perhaps as a museum. It might display artefacts such as the old lenses from the lighthouse, from the days when it housed an oil lamp. He envisaged a lighthouse-keeper back on the island, someone who could tell a good tale to visitors. Have recorded programmes triggered by barcodes, telling stories such as the one about Kiwa, the ancestor who tired of walking the isthmus between Rakiura, Stewart Island, and the mainland, and asked the whale Kewa to chew a channel so he could cross by waka.

The island was supposed to resemble a dog in shape, hence the European name, the reef jutting from a corner known as the Dog's Tongue.

Peter talked of stretching No. 8 wire between buildings and asking visitors to clip onto it. Lighthouse-keepers once crawled between buildings, he said, because

Right Dog Island's
lighthouse

of the wind. 'Two months ago we had a hundred and seventy-six kilometres per hour winds out there, you couldn't stand up.'

Back on the island Warren showed me the route he used to take between his house and the lighthouse in gales, dodging behind the other buildings for shelter.

'I never wore a jacket, just a seaman's jersey. Because once you went out the back door and the wind got you it would fill a jacket like a sail.' Blow him right off the island, perhaps. 'You have to live with these things. But when I look back now it was fun.'

Fun was what Peter imagined his guests having. The last flight of the day might bring half a dozen couples who could stay on the island overnight, sleeping in a lighthouse-keeper's house. 'I think there are few lighthouses in the world which offer the potential to stay on the island. This would become unique.

'And if people started in Dunedin they could come down via the southern scenic route and there are lighthouses all down the coast, all from around the 1870 period. A good lighthouse adventure.'

Sure, on a bad day the island was a godforsaken place. But on a good one, an idyll.

Some, he said, had called it a crank project. But he wrote to Maritime New Zealand anyway. He was then executive manager of Ascot Park Hotel, Invercargill's leading hotel. He formed the Dog Island Motu Piu Charitable Trust and a board of trustees began shaping the ideas into a firm proposal.

It took seven years or so, but at last they got a lease on the island.

The nation's least likely tourist resort was on the go, but Peter was suddenly struck down with motor neurone disease. His prognosis was terminal. He could see the Dog from his home, but he'd made his last visit to the island.

———

Warren grumbled and grieved over the island's condition. The houses were ramshackle, paths overgrown. Nature revelled in these conditions as much as Warren and Peter Ridsdale did. It was busily shoving out all traces of the intruders.

'I'm disappointed in the way they've let it go. It's disgusting.' He'd been warned about it by Raymond Hector, manager of the airline we flew on, and a member of the Dog Island board. 'But I didn't think it would be as bad as this.'

Warren arrived on the Dog with his wife Mary and two of his three children in 1980. The lighthouse service preferred families, believing they kept keepers sane. Wives worked hard, and just as the era of manned lighthouses was ending, the service decided to pay them a small annual allowance.

When Warren told me this story I thought they earned every cent of it.

'Once my youngest daughter cut her hand to the tendon. I got an old toothbrush, heated it, bent it around to keep her hand together and bandaged it up. My wife wanted me to take her to hospital but I said, she'll be right. I was talking to her a while ago and I said how's your finger and she said, nothing wrong with it.'

A secret garden hid under a cloak of greenery. Rows of trees had been planted to divide some flat land into three gardens, one for each keeper's family. Over the years they'd arched over and other growth had joined them at the top so they were now green tunnels filtering a strange submarine light. Much ingenuity had gone into making a garden in this wild place.

Fruit and vegetables once flourished here. Mary's aviary still stood in a corner, near the strawberry patch. An old fowl house and remnants of a glasshouse. A fish smoker, a killing shed for the sheep they once ran, a milking shed for the cows doubling as a shearing shed. In this arcadia keepers' families had been gardeners, shearers, dairy farmers, butchers.

They left it all behind in 1989. That was the year the island was fully mechanised and de-manned, although as I listened to Warren I thought unmanned might have been a better description.

He did not want to go. He fought all the way.

He saw the fight as personal. Permanent lighthouse-keepers could be sacked for two things: dereliction of duties, and insanity. 'Boy, they tried, on the grounds of insanity. Well, what they said was, it was not good for people to be living on their own on an isolated island. They implied I was going crazy.'

He'd had plenty of places to go crazy in. He'd served on Burgess Island, at the Mokohinau Islands lighthouse in the far north, Tiritiri Matangi, Farewell Spit, Puysegur Point and Cape Saunders, where he got a letter saying that his job was no longer available.

He went to his union. Told them he'd been given the sack. Couldn't do that, said the union man and went in fighting.

They reached an agreement. Warren would stay at Cape Saunders until they found another station for him. They gave him a choice.

One was Cape Reinga. But, 'Thirty thousand, forty thousand tourists, wasn't me.'

The other was Dog Island. 'They thought I wouldn't take either but what they didn't know was, I was quite happy to take Dog Island.'

So he took the job. Lived on the Dog while all over the country the lighthouse-keepers slowly went, one by one.

'Everyone fought tooth and nail for the lighthouse-keepers to stay and I was the last one. I said okay, just let me live in the house. It was a new house then. I'll stay there and look after things, just let me stay here. They said no, and that was that.'

He was the last permanent lighthouse-keeper in all New Zealand.

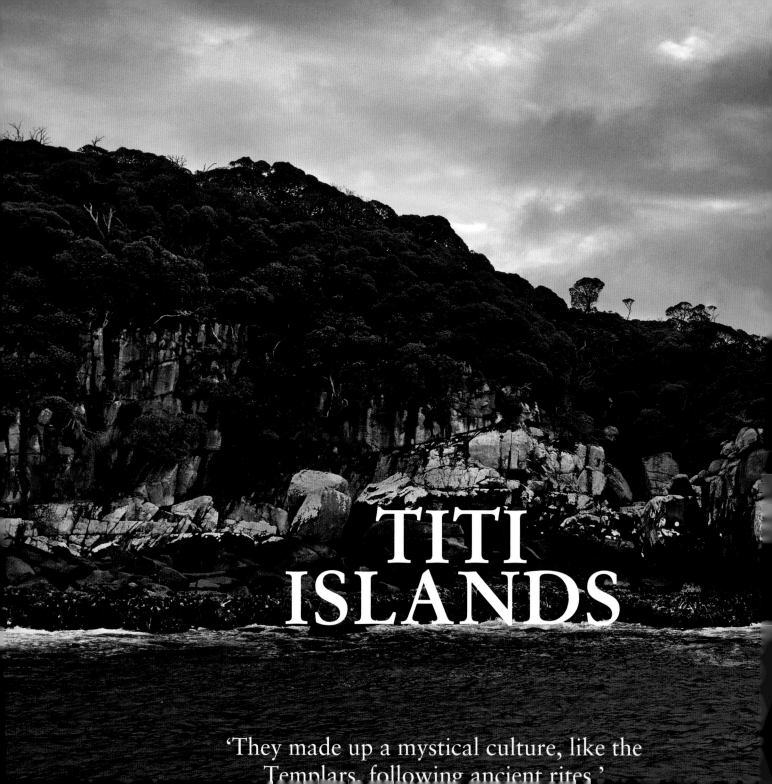

TITI
ISLANDS

'They made up a mystical culture, like the
Templars, following ancient rites.'

Bluff was a town of old houses and new utes, a modest place at the bottom of the South Island sheltering a towering ratio of millionaires per capita.

At midnight Bluff was a dark cold thing. Nothing moved. The place was as asleep as any small town could be at the witching hour.

Then came a rumble, a light. The *Awesome*'s crew was up and away. Their sleek boat slid through the water. Its decks were crammed with tanks, timber, roofing iron, plastic crates, buckets, pipes wallboards drums ladders food shovels petrol cans gas tanks kitchen sinks and bags that looked like wool bales and possibly were. Half a dozen passengers shambled aboard, sleepily. Hopefully. They were muttonbirders.

Captain Jack Topi stood at the wheel. I expected a mariner from the far south, a man who daily braved the cruellest of seas belting Stewart Island smack dab, to be a colossus with muscles like bollards and an iron gaze. That was more his crew, Pete Boyce. Pete was married to Jack's third cousin.

Jack was a svelte character with smooth skin and good hair and rather cuddly although I wouldn't have tried that one on. Pete reckoned Jack accounted for half a tonne of crayfish every year all on his own.

He eased the *Awesome* away from the wharf, piled the coal onto its huge V12 engine, glided along the short harbour, swung a right under Bluff Hill to avoid the reefs and rocks that lurked everywhere, and pointed south.

The night was dark but not stormy, by southern standards at least.

A modest gale nipped along Foveaux Strait, peaking the seas into steep points. Down in the fo'c'sl you were knocked from one side of your bunk to the other and every now and then, when you were getting complacent, the bow would jut upwards like a leaping marlin, hang in the air then crash, so that you were left weightless long enough to fear the landing.

Behind, the lights of the *Owenga 3* moved eerily through the night. The boat was skippered by Jack's father, Colin.

Previous Titi Islands

Following Writhing kelp and daubed cliffs

He looked young enough to be taken for Jack's brother, and sometimes was.

Families stayed tight here. You couldn't get onto any one of the Titi Islands, where we were heading, unless you belonged to the right family. Jack came from a long line of rangatira. His family links went back through so many centuries he had the rights to harvest muttonbirds, titi, on a dozen islands.

Muttonbird. Pronounced here, *birrrd*.

Some of the islands we headed for that night were called 'beneficial'. That was, they'd been owned by the families, whanau of Ngai Tahu, Ngati Mamoe and Waitaha, through the ages.

They made up a mystical culture, like the Templars, following ancient rites.

Others were islands that had been returned to Rakiura Maori by the Crown under the Treaty settlement with Ngai Tahu. They were all controlled by as tight a set of rules as you'd find anywhere. The ultimate sanction was eviction, a fate considerably worse than death.

One messy family had been told to clean up their manu, the area they were allowed to take titi from, or leave their island. Another broke one of the rules and lost their place on the island for a year.

My own favourite was the discovery of a woman who was not married to the man she lived with on their island. The man had the right to be there, she did not. Here, you *had* to be family. He was given an ultimatum: marry her or leave. For better or for worse, he rushed back and tied the knot. The happy couple promptly returned to their birding.

The honeymoon suite might not have been the usual affair. Muttonbirders' houses went from ordinary to bizarre.

Some were conventional enough, the kind you might find in some distant holiday settlement. Some had all the home comforts. Tane Davis's whare had a woodburner and a television set and a gas stove.

More were eccentric. Those lamenting the disappearance of the traditional Kiwi bach would take heart in the Titi Islands. Many houses, at least those visible from the sea, seemed to have grown to fit, a room here, a lean-to there. The nearest building inspector twaddled his papers far over the horizon.

Traditional thatched whare, small and rounded, were made from inaka, the scrub that looked like a Dr Seuss tree, its flax-like leaves growing in clumps from its branches. Floors were earthen.

Houses were made for spending two months of the year in. People began arriving some time in mid-March and everyone was off the islands by the end of May.

For the rest of the year they were empty, knocked around by rain driven by the westerly gales of the southern seas. First things first, that autumn. Mend your roof, fix your leaks, check your floors and walls. Get the generator going, make a cup of tea. See to the rainwater tanks.

At least they didn't have to clean up after the rats. One of the first things

Rakiura Maori did when they got all their islands back was to rid them of the rats that plagued birdlife and vegetation. They were proud of that. Now saddlebacks sang, kakariki fed on the forest floor.

Waka, canoes, took muttonbirders to their islands once. Then came big, old, slow boats like the *Brittannia*, some depending on sail, which took Morry Trow down to his family's island in 1938 when he was five years old.

The boats would return at half-time to drop off fresh bread. Weather depending. One year the Trow family couldn't get off the island until 15 June.

Later the Stewart Island ferry *Wairua* delivered families to their islands and picked them up at season's end.

Morry said: 'Most of the birders in those days, if they weren't fishermen they were oystermen. It was part of your employment. Oh I'm going muttonbirding. Okay. Today there's not the jobs. If you have got a job and you leave it they replace you. And now it's very expensive to go down.'

Some still went by boat, but many more by helicopter. Morry mused: 'It's so *easy*.'

———

Very early, Pete launched the *Awesome*'s dinghy and began delivering his passengers to their islands.

Which looked impenetrable in the grey light.

A ring of kelp writhed in a dawn-grey sea turning translucent green as it foamed onto shore.

The rock above was first black then startling cream as if daubed, lying in great blocks above the ocean and rising in cliffs. Bush celadon as the sea climbed away from the edge, singed bald and reddish on the ridge-tops.

Some of the birders talked of beaches but I never saw one, certainly not one you'd go to with a sun umbrella. Instead, the idea was to wait until the dinghy stopped bucking like a steer and merely hopped like a toad, choose a moment when the water shot above the kelp, and leap for the rocks.

A helicopter would later lift the bags and bundles from the deck of the *Awesome* and fly them to your house.

In the old days you'd be landed on the island by boat and your gear chucked after you to be lugged up the hill by a chain-gang.

Tane Davis's mother Jane first went to her island, Putauhinu, when she was a baby in a bundle. 'They'd finished unloading the dinghy and the men on the rocks called out, "Anything else?" And the guy in the boat said, "Oh yeah, there's this," and he picked up the bundle and threw it. And it was mum and that's how she arrived,' said Tane, who first went to his island himself when he was two and a half. 'In those days nothing was thought of it.'

Muttonbirds were once a rare delicacy. You had to know someone to get them.

The children in my own family hoped they would stay that way. Sometimes our father would return from a trip south bearing muttonbirds like prizes. My mother would cook them. They brought her a rare peace from her large brood, for the smell would drive us out of the house, gagging.

Telling that story brought pity in Bluff. Everyone there loved them. Trish Birch would cook up seven birds at a go, some left over for the next day. Others marvelled at her restraint.

During World War I, soldiers of the Maori Pioneer Battalion fighting overseas were not forgotten. According to a newspaper report in 1918 the Maori Soldiers' Fund had sent in the past year 4050 muttonbirds with another 6000 ready to go.

In World War II, men of the Maori Battalion were cheered by quantities of muttonbirds from the Titi Islands.

The birds taken last season by Trish and her family on Taukihepa, Big South Cape Island, had lasted all year, although she was usually well out of them by now.

As the new season opened, she had one bag of five birds left in her freezer. 'I don't go out birding myself. I stay in the workshop, plucking, waxing. I'm getting soft. I don't like the thought of killing them.'

She liked eating them though. 'We'll probably cook up half a dozen a day, at least. Also a heart stew. I save the hearts. Sometimes they don't quite get to the stew. Yum yum.'

Above A muttonbirders' whare; Tane Davis

'When you first come back from the island you've been eating eating eating so you want a bit of a break. Probably a month or two later you'll start eating them again. With roast pumpkin and potatoes. Fresh birds I usually stuff and roast.'

She was slightly apologetic. 'The breasts are very small. Not a lot of meat on them.'

But look, she went to the coldest, most remote part of New Zealand and rummaged in a burrow for her dinner, which in my book meant she could eat however many she liked. She was curator of Bluff Maritime Museum, immaculate, hard to imagine in her other life.

The muttonbirds were once packed into kelp bags, or poha. They were preserved in their own fat, the fat balls carried in their gut saved and rendered. After Pakeha arrived, they were also preserved in salt.

Most used galvanised buckets now, but the traditional kelp bags were still made by Graham 'Tiny' Metzger in Bluff.

He used only the best kelp and it was getting hard to get.

Pollution was taking its toll. One favourite place had been ruined when farmland beside the stream running onto the beach was converted for dairying.

The kelp was pumped up like a balloon, dried then encased in totara bark, just as carefully chosen, gathered at the top. The bag was fitted into a basket made of the finest flax, stripped, scraped, scalded, softened into a blonde pliancy. As it worked up the bag the basket loosened to a net-like lacing, each knot perfect.

The finished bags were shaped rather like an old-fashioned naval shell, and just as heavy.

A plaited-flax carrying strap ran from top to bottom with handles at each end so the full bag could be thrown into a waiting dinghy. Padding in the bottom of the basket cushioned its fall. They were beautiful, poetic.

———

Now, early April, all eyes were on the coming season. Would it be better? Tiny Metzger thought it would, because if the kelp was good, the season would be good, and the kelp that year was fine.

But truth be told, he said, in the previous year the kelp was good too, and he'd predicted the birds would be big and fat, and they were not.

No one knew quite why the titi were not thriving as they once did.

Certainly the sea was more polluted, and titi were far-ranging.

One oil spill in 1998 from the tanker *Command* on the far-off Californian coast killed an estimated 32,000 titi. One dead bird was found to have been banded on Whenua Hou, Codfish Island. That allowed Rakiura Maori to win compensation from a body set up to mitigate the effects of the *Command* oil spill. They used the money to both study the sustainability of the titi harvest, and to rid their islands of rats.

Muttonbirds were one of the world's most abundant seabird species but their numbers were declining. The study found that migration patterns were affecting the titi most. The little birds followed the summer, flying 64,000 kilometres around the Pacific each year.

At the same time food sources were dwindling.

The parent birds were battling climate change to feed their chicks. The previous season had been disastrous. The parent birds stopped bringing in the feed, the chicks died in their burrows.

Other factors could have contributed. For example, the krill the birds fed on was now being commercially harvested.

But, said Tane Davis, 'In saying all that, the harvest has changed; fewer birds are being taken. Areas of islands are not harvested, we have safekeeping areas, we can control the numbers.'

———

My word, all these islands, their names.

Kundy, where Morry Trow and his family had their manu, or muttonbirding area. In Maori, the island's name was Kani, meaning 'to saw'. 'We're not sure whether it was sawing wood, or (because there's a nice little bay there) sawing at the moorings. I guess the whalers or sealers found it easier to say Kundy.'

Big Moggy was said to have been named after a woman, an escaped Australian convict who found herself on the island with a Scotsman. One version of the story, the most colourful, had the Scotsman captured, cooked and eaten while she hid in a cave. Later a group of muttonbirders arrived. She cowered in her cave, emerging only at night for food. But the Maori were coming out at night too, for it was the torching season. They saw her, decided she was a ghost, and kept their distance. Later she was rescued by sealers.

Big, Betsy, Rat. All of the others. Putauhinu where the Davis family had their manu, the island's Nuggets lying close by. Poutama, where Jane Bradshaw returned from her job in Ethiopia to spend the season. Many others, with the huge Taukihepa, Big South Cape Island, blocking the ocean reaching far down into Antarctic waters.

And this was only one of the three chains making up the Titi Islands.

Trish Birch's family birded on Taukihepa. She'd first been there when she was two years old.

'We whakapapa right back to the original canoes coming out to New Zealand. We don't take things for granted. We treasure the treasure. When you get down there you can smell the island, you can really smell it, and you think, can't wait to get ashore, then you grizzle and groan because you've fallen down a hole or something, but you love it, it's a beautiful feeling. You can feel all the whanau around you, you feel safe.'

That autumn, I was pleased to be on a dry boat and not dicing with the kelp and the rock from a blow-up dinghy. The water was cold.

Huge waves had claimed two boats carrying muttonbirders to and from the Titi Islands.

Six people died when the *Kotuku* sank in 2006, and eight drowned when the *Easy Rider* rolled in 2012. One man survived the last tragedy by clinging to a petrol can for 18 hours. I imagined his desperation, his determination as he lay in those lonely seas, his body slowly freezing. It was almost exactly this time of the year.

Today, though, there was no sign of a rogue wave. The wind was easing, the seas routinely rowdy but too rough for Tane Davis to get off on his island, Putauhinu.

Instead, he got off at Taukihepa and flew to his manu in the helicopter which was to lift his gear from the *Awesome* in two huge bags.

He'd be on his own for 10 days, settling in, clearing tracks, getting the generator going, fixing things up.

Later he might go out and start a harvest, hooking deep into the burrows

Right and opposite
Titi Islands

carved by generations of birds into the bald earth under the rata and tupari, feeling for chicks. This was the first stage, nanao, lying on the ground, seeking out the chicks in their burrows.

The next stage of the season was when the chicks came out of their burrows at night, feeling for the strength in their wings, slowly growing the dark feathers of the adult birds. This stage of the harvest was called rama, or torching.

Each family made their own decision on how many chicks to take. The harvest was centuries old, and the muttonbirders wanted centuries more. Sustainability had been borne upon them from childhood.

Tane felt the breath of those centuries. 'It's a big part of my life and it goes through history. Once you arrive you feel that stronger. Particularly those who have passed on. My father, my younger brother, Mum's sister, you think of them. When you arrive there you walk back in time. So many things remind you.'

I was talking to him then in his spreading home in a leafy part of Invercargill, a long way from Putauhinu but only in distance. His island was lodged in his soul.

He was proud of what had been achieved there since the Treaty settlement returned ownership and management in 1998.

Rats had been eradicated. The rare Snares Island snipe had been translocated

to Putauhinu in 2005 to replace the extinct South Island snipe and were more numerous now than ever before.

The Stewart Island robin, the fernbird (transferred from Whenua Hou, Codfish Island), the saddleback were flourishing.

The greater short-tailed bat was thought to be extinct but Tane believed it had managed to survive the years of the rat on his island. Later they'd mount an expedition to find it. 'One of the Crown's stipulations was that the islands be retained and treated as if they were a nature reserve. This is one way of saying we're doing it. It's a good thing.'

———————

Muttonbirding ran through Bluff like blood.

One of the restaurateurs in a smart Bluff restaurant, Ross Wilhelmsen, an urbane fellow, had the right to take birds, finding his way into the closed circle through his equally sleek wife Linda, Morry Trow's daughter. Their son Jay, a cool young man with an All Black haircut who was a waiter in their restaurant, was right into it. They were hard to imagine lying under the tough scrub far to the south with their arms in burrows, but that's what they did, and they loved it.

Ann Trow told of her and Morry's son Jason standing very still on his island as a small boy feeling his family's traditions, the weight of centuries seeping into his bones.

For some this was their *raison d'etre*, but as a mere holiday it seemed to an outsider to have flaws. Certainly it was as expensive as a Fijian island sojourn. Most went down in a helicopter costing an arm and probably a leg. Then there was all your gear, boat, whare upkeep, buckets, wax, all the tools of the trade. A month or two off work.

Yet the lure was far stronger than palm trees and mai tais. An aneurysm kept Morry Trow at home. Even at 86 he mourned. He'd been down once, since, to finish a season and say hello to his island. But now he was in a wheelchair.

Ann had been down there with their son. She'd only returned the day before, leaving him on his own.

'Good for him,' Morry said. Ann said: 'I wanted to go and share it with him. I loved it. Although I don't know how long I'd want to stay there for. Two months seems a long time.'

'Oh, beautiful,' Morry said.

But why?

Ann said: 'It's very hard work. Plucking with your hands. My first year my hands were so sore. And my back was just aching. I didn't get the feeling back in my hands until two or three weeks later. Torching? It should be called torturing.

'You get up at five in the morning to gut the birds, get them ready and salt them and put them in the buckets. Then you go out getting the birds at eight o'clock and come back about two. Then I was plucking them. Then waxing them, then de-waxing them, and by that time it's about five o'clock. You have your dinner, go to bed at half past eight because you've got to get up and start again at five.'

Morry said: 'And that's a good day.'

———

The *Awesome*'s dinghy carried a passenger to his island. A wave crashed on the rocks shooting a curtain of spray into the air and when it parted, the man was scrambling up like an acrobat. The next wave flung the dinghy onto the rocks almost beside him. It slid back into the water and backed away. No one so much as gasped.

Patches of blue were being chased around the sky by grey clouds. A biblical shaft of light flowed onto the cliffs of Stewart Island with the granite dome of Gog shining behind. Birds followed the boat hopefully, sculptured mollymawks, Mother Carey's chickens, a couple of birds identified by Pete as very rare storm petrels. All the while the grey swell boomed and banged on rocks and the brown kelp danced. A helicopter daubed in pink appeared above the boat trailing a cable. In a flash it was hooked up to a bundle of timber and thudding upwards to an unseen house, reappearing a moment later for a load of shingle which, shipped south and flown to its owner's whare, must have been the most expensive gravel in the country. Time here was not just money, it was a lot of money. This was a highly mechanised efficient operation.

The *Awesome* put into Murderers Cove on Taukihepa, with its white-capped rocks and its dark history. Long ago, in 1810, Maori took revenge for the savagery of sealers by killing five of them. James Caddell, 16, was saved when Tokitoki, the chief's niece, threw her cloak over him. Caddell married her and became the first Pakeha chief.

The cove looked safe enough now, sheltering from the westerly, a little settlement of muttonbirders' houses sitting happily above.

The first reports of the season began sneaking onto the boat. The season was only as good as last year's, which was not a good year, but the birds were in better condition.

People shrugged. So. A long, expensive journey, a basic life up in the huts, and not all that many birds at the end of it all. No one looked disappointed. Still plenty for a feed.

We went round South Cape, a lump of grey rock in the grey sea, the very end of this long thin island nation. Then we ate cold crayfish patties and headed for home.

Following Traditional kelp bag (left); poha

NORTH
ISLAND

THE CAVALLIS

BAY OF
ISLANDS

HAUTURU/
LITTLE BARRIER

RAKITU/
ARID

GREAT BARRIER

KAWAU

GREAT MERCURY

THE NOISES

RAKINO

WAIHEKE

RANGITOTO

PAKATOA
ROTOROA

MOTUIHE

PUKETUTU

SLIPPER

KAPITI

WHITE

MANA

MOTITI

MATIU/
SOMES

MOTUOPUHI

SOUTH
ISLAND

D'URVILLE

HAUTAI

MOTUARA

RABBIT

ARAPOA/
ARAPAWA

PUKERAUARUHE/
BROWNE'S

RIPAPA

QUAIL

QUARANTINE

DOG

TITI ISLANDS

N

Acknowledgements

This book depended heavily on the kindness of strangers. Many people helped us in many ways. We thank them all, in particular: Hohepa Epiha, Richard, Vanessa and Millie Owen, Richard, Mahina and Liam Walle, Leigh Joyce, Michael and Gabrielle Marris, Norma and Maurice Brown, Nigel Atkin, Fiona Powell, Rod Neureuter, Sir Michael Fay, Don Wills, the Buttle family, Peter and Jenny Tait, Anneke Mace, Mike and Antonia Radon, Joe Heberley, Destination Marlborough, Philip and Jane Helps, Kate Hastings, Ian McLennan, Lindsay Daniel, Kathy Morrison, Douglas Black, Raymond Hector, Peter Ridsdale, Tane Davis, Trish Birch, Meri Leask and the Department of Conservation.

Thanks to the estate of Alistair Te Ariki Campbell for permission to reproduce lines from his poems 'Looking at Kapiti' and 'Sanctuary of Spirits' (as published in *Kapiti: Selected Poems*, Pegasus Press, 1972).

We are also grateful for the assistance of Creative New Zealand.

Opposite Hauraki Gulf

Following Titi Islands

GODWIT

First published by Penguin Random House New Zealand, 2016

Text © Bruce Ansley, 2016
Photography © Jane Ussher, 2016

Design by Carla Sy © Penguin Random House New Zealand
Cover photographs: Rakino Island (front); Dog Island (back)
Maps on pages 380–1 by Janet Hunt
Printed and bound in China by Leo Paper Products Ltd

A catalogue record for this book is available from the National Library of New Zealand.

ISBN 978-1-77553-846-2

penguin.co.nz